Abandoned Women and Boudoir Resentment

Women and Gender in China Studies

VOLUME 13

The titles published in this series are listed at *brill.com/wgcs*

Abandoned Women and Boudoir Resentment

The Construction of the Feminine Voice in Early Medieval Chinese Literature

By

Qiulei Hu

BRILL

LEIDEN | BOSTON

Cover illustration: Gu Kaizhi (*c.*345–*c.*406), attr., "palace ladies," (left side) and attr. "the Instructress" (right side). Details from the Admonitions of the Instructress to the Court Ladies (女史箴圖), British Museum collection.

Library of Congress Cataloging-in-Publication Data

Names: Hu, Qiulei, author.
Title: Abandoned women and boudoir resentment : the construction of the feminine voice in early medieval Chinese literature / by Qiulei Hu.
Other titles: Abandoned women and boudoir resentment
Description: Leiden ; Boston : Brill, [2023] | Series: Women and gender in China studies, 1877-5772 ; volume 13 | Includes bibliographical references and index. | Summary: "This book studies the formation of the male-constructed conventional voice of women in Chinese literature from the 3rd to 6th century. It highlights specific moments during which the feminine voice became recognized, accepted, and stabilized, including the shift of focus from the performative to the textual in female representations; the formation of a male literary community; the popularity of romanticized historical narratives; and the emerging sense of literary history. This study emphasizes the historicity of the feminine voice and strives to question and challenge established notions about textual stability, authorship, the literary canon, and literary history"— Provided by publisher.
Identifiers: LCCN 2023006442 | ISBN 9789004541009 (hardback ; acid-free paper) | ISBN 9789004546455 (ebook)
Subjects: LCSH: Chinese literature—221 B.C.-960 A.D.—History and criticism. | Women in literature. | LCGFT: Literary criticism.
Classification: LCC PL2283 .H8 2023 | DDC 895.109/0024—dc23/eng/20230501
LC record available at https://lccn.loc.gov/2023006442

Typeface for the Latin, Greek, and Cyrillic scripts: "Brill". See and download: brill.com/brill-typeface.

ISSN 1877-5772
ISBN 978-90-04-54100-9 (hardback)
ISBN 978-90-04-54645-5 (e-book)

For my family

Contents

Acknowledgments

In the many years of researching for and writing this book, I have accumulated numerous "debts of personal favors" (*renqing zhai* 人情債) from mentors, colleagues, friends, and family members. I thank Qian Zhixi 錢志熙 for introducing me to the wonderful world of early medieval Chinese literary texts. My greatest intellectual debt is to Stephen Owen, who taught me to approach familiar texts with an open mind and critical eyes, and to never take any received knowledge for granted: this book grew out of these precepts. Stephen Owen, Xiaofei Tian, Wai-yee Li, Sarah Allen, Anna M. Shields, David R. Knechtges, and Hong Yue read chapters of this study at various stages of their completion and provided invaluable feedback that helped improve the volume in many ways. Michael Puett has been a mentor and a friend for many years, whose never-failing belief in this project and boundless optimism kept me going at times when I was in doubt.

I have presented ideas from this book at academic conferences, workshops, and invited lectures, including the Association for Asian Studies annual conferences and its regional conferences; the American Oriental Society annual conferences and its Western Branch conferences; the Modern Language Association annual convention; the Association of Chinese and Comparative Literature annual conference; the Early Medieval China group workshop; the Center for East Asian Studies at University of California, Berkeley; and Jackson School of International Studies at University of Washington. I am grateful to the organizers of these events, especially Madeleine Yue Dong, Paula Varsano, Jen-der Lee, Antje Richter, and Keith Knapp. The comments and suggestions I received from participants on these occasions—notably those from Paul W. Kroll, Robert Joe Cutter, David R. Knechtges, Meow Hui Goh, Nanxiu Qian, and Paul R. Katz (Kang Bao 康豹)—helped me to revise and refine my arguments.

Writing an academic book is often a lonely experience, but mine was made easier and more enjoyable by many friends and colleagues who have been around to offer emotional support, thoughtful feedback, professional advice, and joyful companionship: they include Hong Yue, Wangling Jinghua, Sun Chengjuan, Ling Xiaoqiao, Maria Sibau, Weijen Teng, Suh-Jen Yang, Yukiko Shigeto, Brian Dott, Chas McKhann, Wencui Zhao, Sharon Alker, Bokyung Kim, Zhang Yue, He Jianye, Cheng Zhangcan 程章燦, Kyunghee Pyun, and Paul Almonte.

This book has received generous support from several research grants. A one-year dissertation completion fellowship from the Graduate Society at Harvard University funded the conceptual stage. Two semesters of sabbatical leave at Whitman College made it possible for me to rethink the structure of the book and write two new chapters. I was able to present parts of the manuscript at various academic events and get professional copyediting help thanks to the professional development fund for adjunct faculty provided by the Professional Staff Congress of the City University of New York.

Parts of this book have been published in previous forms in academic journals including *Nan Nü: Men, Women and Gender in China*, published by Brill, and *Early Medieval China*, published by Taylor & Francis Ltd, on behalf of Early Medieval China Group. Detailed publication information can be found in the footnote and bibliography sections. I am grateful to the editors of these two journals, Harriet T. Zurndorfer and J. Michael Farmer, and to the publishers for giving permission to include the material in this book.

I thank the Women and Gender in China Studies series editor Grace S. Fong and members of the editorial board—Louise Edwards, Nicola Spakowski, Robin D.S. Yates, and Harriet T. Zurndorfer—for publishing the volume in this series. My gratitude also goes to the excellent editorial team at Brill, especially Patricia Radder, who was generous in providing her time and expertise in the editing process. The two anonymous reviewers of my manuscript gave insightful comments and helpful suggestions that greatly helped to improve the text. The remaining mistakes, of course, are entirely my own.

I owe my deepest gratitude to my family. I thank my parents, Zhang Hua 張華 and Hu Shizhu 胡仕株, for their unconditional love and support. Deprived of opportunities for higher education during the Cultural Revolution, they firmly believe in the power of knowledge and always encourage me to pursue my passions in study. Together with my in-laws, Wu Liuxia 吳柳霞 and Liu Qingsong 劉青松, they took care of both my daughters when they were young so that I could work on this book. My daughters, Veronica Wenxin Liu 劉文心 and Valentina Yutian Liu 劉雨田, are sources of endless joy and love. I want to thank them for tolerating mom's occasional neglects and for offering much needed distractions from work. Finally, this book could not have been completed without the loving support of my husband, Shixin Liu, who always believes in me and is always there for me. It is to my family that I dedicate this book.

Introduction

Male writing in the feminine voice, often known as *daiyan* 代言,[1] is a prominent literary trend in pre-modern China. Although the literary culture was always dominated by elite men, a large number of works were written by men in the voices of women. In their literary cross-dressing as women, male writers created conventions about the feminine voice that not only guided their own composition but also exerted considerable influence on the way women wrote when they entered the literary arena. At the very center of these conventions is the expression of loneliness and melancholy by a lady in her private chamber longing for her absent lover, traditionally encapsulated in terms of "boudoir resentment" (*guiyuan* 閨怨) and "abandoned women" (*qifu* 棄婦). In the past few decades, studies on women's writing in late imperial China (1368–1911) have flourished with the emergence of new materials and the rediscovery of previously overlooked documents. The rich corpus of women's writings and secondary sources makes it possible to examine women's literary products and activities in a thorough and comprehensive manner. Scholars have explored how late imperial women writers expressed their agency and defined their own voices in literature.[2] Many discuss women's reactions to the culturally sanctioned voices of women in literary writing: from adjusting their own style, resistance to conforming to cultural norms, to clever manipulation of them. An equally important issue is the established conventions about the feminine voice against which late imperial women writers defined their own voices and subjectivity. How exactly did these established conventions come into being?

1 The phrase "*daiyan*" literally means "to speak on behalf [of another person]" and could refer to persona composition with or without gender crossing. *Daiyan* is often used for male writers assuming a woman's voice because it has become one of, if not the, most common forms of persona writing. Exceptions exist, of course, such as the 3rd-century poet Lu Ji's 陸機 (261–303) two "Poems Presented to the Wife on Behalf of Gu Yanxian" (Wei Gu Yanxian zengfu shi 為顧彥先贈婦詩). Lu Qinli 逯欽立 (1910–1973), *XianQin Han WeiJin Nanbeichao shi* 先秦漢魏晉南北朝詩 (Beijing: Zhonghua shuju, 1983) 1.682.

2 Notable examples of scholarship on this topic include Maureen Robertson, "Voicing the Feminine: Constructions of the Gendered Subject in Lyric Poetry by Women of Medieval and Late Imperial China," *Late Imperial China* 13, no. 1 (June 1992): 63–110; Susan Mann, *Precious Records: Women in China's Long Eighteenth Century* (Stanford, CA: Stanford University Press, 1997); Grace Fong, *Herself an Author: Gender, Agency, and Writing in Late Imperial China* (Honolulu: University of Hawai'i Press, 2008); and Xiaorong Li, *Women's Poetry of Late Imperial China: Transforming the Inner Chambers* (Seattle: University of Washington Press, 2012).

 | DOI:10.1163/9789004546455_002

This book studies the formation of the conventional, male-constructed voice of women in literature. It argues that it emerged as a major literary trope in the 3rd century and became stabilized during the early medieval period. This time period often refers to the four centuries between the two great dynasties, the Han 漢 (206 BCE–220 CE) and the Tang 唐 (618–907), but it is defined in this study as roughly from the beginning of the 3rd century to the second half of the 6th century. I include the final two decades of the Han dynasty, known as the Jian'an 建安 period (196–220), because, as I will show, it marks the beginning of many new cultural and literary trends that had significant impacts on the formation of gender conventions. By the 6th century, conventions about the feminine voice in literature had taken hold and had been canonized in the literary composition and literary scholarship of the Liang 梁 dynasty (502–557).

Previous scholarship on the conventional feminine voice has explored a number of different themes. Despite its focus on the late imperial period and on women's poetry, Maureen Robertson's "Voicing the Feminine" is a pioneering study of the male-constructed feminine voice, or "literati-feminine voice" in Robertson's wording, in medieval poetry and its impact on women's writing in the Ming 明 (1368–1644) and Qing 清 (1644–1911) dynasties. Building on Robertson's study, Xiaofei Tian's dissertation "Configuring the Feminine: Gender and Transvestitism in the Southern Dynasties Poetry" demonstrates how Southern-dynasties poets created a new ideal of femininity to express the marginal, unconventional, or subversive.[3] Paul Rouzer's *Articulated Ladies: Gender and the Male Community in Early Chinese Texts* reveals the innate connection between the discourses of gender and politics and delineates how male literati employed female images and voices to express their thoughts, emotions, and desires in a politicized community.[4] The allegorical comparison between the husband–wife relationship and the ruler–minister one constitutes the basic framework of Rouzer's analysis of literary works. With attention to larger cultural and historical contexts, his study sheds much new light on familiar texts in women's voices. While its main subject is the genre of *ci* 詞 (song lyrics), Maija Bell Samei's *Gendered Persona and Poetic Voice: The Abandoned Woman in Early Chinese Song Lyrics* also examines the formulation of the abandoned woman topos in the tradition of *shi* 詩 (poetry) in the first chapter, as the background for the development of the female persona in *ci*.[5]

3 Xiaofei Tian, "Configuring the Feminine: Gender and Literary Transvestitism in Southern Dynasties Poetry" (PhD diss., Harvard University, 1998).

4 Paul Rouzer, *Articulated Ladies: Gender and the Male Community in Early Chinese Texts* (Cambridge, MA: Harvard University Asia Center, 2001).

5 Maija Bell Samei, *Gendered Persona and Poetic Voice: The Abandoned Woman in Early Chinese Song Lyrics* (Lanham, MD: Lexington Books, 2004).

Samei traces the image in works from the *Shijing* 詩經 (The book of songs) and Tang dynasty poems and divides its connotations into two categories, allegorical and erotic, each evoking a set of conventional motifs and expressions. Chia-Ling Mei 梅家玲 observes a gradual loss of diversity in the literary image of the longing woman from the Han to the Jin 晉 dynasty (266–420) and attributes it to the influence of Confucian ideas about gender roles and the literati's adherence to the allegorical tradition.[6] All five studies employ methodologies and approaches from Western gender studies and feminist criticism while emphasizing the distinct cultural contexts of pre-modern China. Gender in pre-modern Chinese society was rarely viewed on its own, as an independent attribute of an individual person, but was considered in relation to one's familial, social, and political roles, such as husband/wife, father/mother, son/daughter, ruler/minister, and so forth. This correlative view of gender was also the basis for the political interpretation of the abandoned woman as a veiled allegory of the frustrated but loyal minister. Although this interpretation is not applicable to all individual works, the unique position of gender in a broader social network in pre-modern China dictates that we always situate the literary expression of gender in its historical and social contexts.

When it comes to poetic voice and persona writing, another study that must be acknowledged is Joseph Allen's *In the Voice of Others: Chinese Music Bureau Poetry*.[7] Allen's work has made immense contributions to the study of *yuefu* 樂府 poetry, or Music Bureau poetry, including the shift of focus from musicality to intertextuality in the study of the *yuefu* genre and his insightful assertion of the determinate role of literati imitations in the configuration of the *yuefu* tradition and its generic conventions. The "voice" in its title, however, (mostly) does not concern specific types of persona or voice such as that of the abandoned woman. Allen's interest resides in literati imitations of existing *yuefu* titles that integrate the voice of others (i.e. earlier poets writing under the same title) with their own voices. Nevertheless, Allen's study provides much inspiration and information for my discussion of gendered voices in early poetry, especially in *yuefu* poetry.

While it has become a widely accepted view that the conventional female image and voice in Chinese literature were largely male constructs, my study

6 Chia-Ling Mei, "Han Jin shige zhong 'sifu wenben' de xingcheng jiqi xiangguan wenti" 漢晉詩歌中「思婦文本」的形成及其相關問題, in *Han Wei Liuchao wenxue xinlun: Nidai yu zengda pian* 漢魏六朝文學新論：擬代與贈答篇 (Taipei: Liren shuju, 1997), pp. 63–100.

7 Joseph Roe Allen, *In the Voice of Others: Chinese Music Bureau Poetry* (Ann Arbor: University of Michigan Press, 1992).

intends to reveal the *historicity* of the construction. In their tracing of the conventions about the feminine voice in literature, both Rouzer and Samei note the indeterminacy and fluidity in gendered voices in the *Shijing* and *Chuci* 楚辭 (The lyric of Chu). Mei also points out diverse representations of women's images and voices in writings before the Jian'an period. Yet these fascinating issues are not pursued in much depth due to the different focuses of their studies. My study begins with the questions when and why such indeterminacy and fluidity gave way to a more clearly defined and marked gendered voice, as well as what happened to the diversity in female images and voices in the process. Like other long-lasting and influential phenomena in literature, the construction of the feminine voice was not caused by a single factor but was a complex process that occurred under specific cultural and historical circumstances of the early medieval period. For example, the shift in focus from the performative to the textual in female representations brought attention to women's inner world in the 3rd century; the formation of a male literary community in the Jian'an period gave rise to a different type of female image and voice in literary writing; romanticized historical narratives popular in the 4th and 5th centuries made an association between famous historical women and five-syllable poems about resentment and abandonment; and the emerging sense of literary history over the course of the early medieval period led to a re-evaluation of gender roles and gendered voices in early poetry.[8] Instead of creating a linear and teleological narrative about the rise of the feminine voice in Chinese literature, my study highlights specific moments in early medieval literary history during which the conventional feminine voice became recognized, accepted, and stabilized. It addresses many relevant literary phenomena such as the changing concept of authorship, the development of five-syllable poetry, and the role of literary criticism and literary anthology. With a heightened attention to details and specifics, this study strives to question and challenge many established notions about textual stability, authorship, interpretation, the literary canon, and literary history.

It is also important to state at the outset what this book is not. First, it is not my intention to tell a story about the development of gendered voices from fluidity to fixation. Certain dominant trends in the changing perception and expression of gender can be revealed through critical examination of available sources. But the extensive loss of literary works and other textual materials makes it impossible to construct a neat and linear history. Moreover, the

8 When this study uses the adjective "early" in the (usually rough) dating of works (i.e. early period, early poetry, early literature, etc.), it generally refers to the period before the 3rd century, unless otherwise noted.

conventional feminine voice that took shape in the early medieval period never completely eclipsed other voices of women in literature. As my study shows, traces of unconventional voices and images of women from this period have survived to give us a glimpse at what existed outside the culturally sanctioned expressions of gender. In the first chapter of her book, Samei tries to "consider the trajectory of the development of the abandoned woman convention from its folk roots through its allegorical and erotic adaptations by literati poets."[9] Aside from the problematic distinction between "the folk" and "literati poets,"[10] most attributions of authorship and compositional contexts this trajectory is built upon cannot be accepted without critical examination.[11] By focusing on practical details rather than an overarching narrative, my goal is to break down such narratives about a linear trajectory and reveal the complexity, inconsistency, and fragmentation in the actual history.

Second, this book does not attempt to search for "female subjectivity/agency" or the lack thereof in literary works. This is partly a practical measure, because, unlike for the late imperial period, the scarcity of reliable works by pre-Tang women writers makes any claim of female agency questionable. Even the very limited number of women-authored works were passed down to the present through collecting, editing, and transmission by (mostly) male literati. It is problematic to detect "female subjectivity" based on a heavily filtered corpus. Moreover, the male-constructed gender conventions were so dominant that they were accepted by many women as they took on the role of the writer. When a woman author speaks in a masculine voice in a poem to project "heterosexual desire" on another woman, do we see it as an expression of subversive female subjectivity or an affirmation of the tradition? In the

---

9 Samei, *Gendered Persona and Poetic Voice*, p. 43.

10 All literary works she associates with the folk tradition, including poems from the "Airs" (*feng* 風) section of the *Shijing* and the *Wusheng* 吳聲 (Wu Songs) and *Xiqu* 西曲 (Western Tunes) corpus of the Southern dynasties, were collected, edited, partially composed, and transmitted by elite literati. For a critical discussion of the "folk/literati" division in early literature, see Charles H. Egan, "Reconsidering the Role of Folk Songs in Pre-T'ang 'Yüeh-Fu' Development," *T'oung Pao* 86 (2000): 47–99, esp. p. 97.

11 For example, Samei treats songs in women's voices in some *Wusheng* pieces as composed by (folk) women writers: Samei, *Gendered Persona and Poetic Voice*, pp. 65–68. Her discussion of Cao Zhi's "Song of Planting Hemp" (Zhongge pian 種葛篇) applies the allegorical interpretation despite the fact that (1) no extratextual evidence about the compositional background is available, and (2) the poem is apparently a *yuefu* poem and its speaking voice a persona that does not necessarily have to do with the author: Samei, *Gendered Persona and Poetic Voice*, pp. 58–60. Due to space limitations (her main subject being the much later genre *ci*), there is also much that is left undiscussed in this long "trajectory" that covers over 1000 years.

absence of authorial intents or compositional contexts, we may never know. In sum, it is not only impossible, but also fruitless, to assert a clear demarcation between "female subjectivity" and "male subjectivity" in reality as well as in literary writing.

Given the long-lasting significance and influence of the gender conventions formed in the early medieval period, one would expect a study of this subject to have existed long ago. Why is this not the case? One reason lies precisely in their profound influence on later literary tradition. As a result, these gender conventions have often been taken for granted as a major part of the literary tradition from its very beginning, and thus many scholars see no need to trace their construction and formation. The image of the "abandoned woman," because of its prevalence in literature, is often taken to reflect the historical reality of women being passive and submissive victims of a male-dominated society.[12] Recent scholarship on women's status in pre-modern Chinese society, however, has largely dismissed the overly generalizing view about the victimization of women, one that had been advocated since the May Fourth movement. Instead, scholars have demonstrated more nuance and complexity in women's access to and relationship with power.[13] Even though there is little information available regarding women's social lives in the period under examination in this study, sources suggest a much more diverse picture of

12 This line of reasoning has much to do with the pseudo-Marxist literary criticism that dominated pre-modern Chinese literary research in mainland China for a few decades after 1949. Having now been mostly abandoned, its influence can still be seen in many recent studies that treat literary representations as truthful and unmediated reflections of social and historical reality. See, for example, Hu Ming 胡明, "Guanyu zhongguo gudai de funü wenxue" 關於中國古代的婦女文學, *Wenxue pinglun* 3 (1995): 95–108; Yuan Guangxue 袁廣雪 and Zhang Shichang 張士昌, "Cong wenxue zuopin kan zhongguo gudai nüxing diwei de bianhua" 從文學作品看中國古代女性地位的變化, *Jinzhong xueyuan xuebao* 29, no. 4 (2012): 70–74; and Zheng Shanshan 鄭珊珊, "Zhongguo gudai nüxing wenxue yu nüxing yishi" 中國古代女性文學與女性意識, *Fujian luntan* 2 (2016): 117–22.

13 See, for example, Patricia Ebrey, *The Inner Quarters: Marriage and the Lives of Chinese Women in the Sung Period* (Berkeley: University of California Press, 1993); Dorothy Ko, *Teachers of the Inner Chambers: Women and Culture in Seventeenth-Century China* (Stanford, CA: Stanford University Press, 1994); Lisa Raphals, *Sharing the Light: Representations of Women and Virtue in Early China* (Albany: State University of New York Press, 1998); Rebecca Doran, *Transgressive Typologies: Constructions of Gender and Power in Early Tang China* (Cambridge, MA: Harvard University Asia Center, 2017); and Jinhua Jia, *Gender, Power and Talent: The Journey of Daoist Priestesses in Tang China* (New York: Columbia University Press, 2018).

women's life experiences than has been represented by the conventional feminine image and voice in literature.[14]

The lack of primary and secondary sources on women's writing is another obstacle. In particular, the significant loss of pre-Tang women-authored literary works makes it difficult to study gender in literature. After all, how do we talk about the "construction" of gender conventions by early medieval male literati if there are only a few surviving works by women authors? How do we explore the motives and rationales behind the construction when there is seldom any mention or discussion of authorial intentions? Instead of speculating on or circumventing the missing voices of women, this study takes their lack as an important point of its examination. By closely reading and comparing works by women authors that survived through primary sources of different natures, it explores the reasons why certain voices of women were preserved and transmitted whereas others were neglected and marginalized. This approach also reveals the crucial role literary criticism and anthologies of the early medieval period played in shaping the concept of women's authorship. In this regard, the lacunae in literary materials become informative and telling. At the same time, the lack or scarcity of materials should not prevent us from making reasonable and well-grounded conclusions, inferences, and hypotheses, so long as they are based on close and critical examinations of available sources.

1 Keywords

In my discussions of the formation of gender conventions in early medieval literature, a few keywords occur with high frequency, including "gender," "literary voice," "literary persona," and "female" and "feminine" voice. Because they are not new or unique to this study and appear in numerous other studies on gender in literature (of China and other cultures), it is imperative to define my usage of them in comparison with existing scholarship.

Judith Butler has pointed out that gender should be taken not as a biological fact or innate state of being, but as an enacted performance of ideas about gender.[15] The socially constructed dichotomy of male/female conceals much complexity and fluidity in the rich reality of human interaction and psychology.

14 Chapter 5 of this book has an extensive discussion of this topic.

15 According to Butler, "there is no gender identity behind the expressions of gender; that identity is performatively constituted by the very 'expressions' that are said to be its results": Judith Butler, *Gender Trouble: Feminism and the Subversion of Identity* (London: Routledge, 1990), p. 25.

Although with a quite different focus, Butler's emphasis on the power of linguistic performativity, rather than any innate biological quality, in creating and enforcing gender identity has inspired me to bypass the issue of the female/male subjectivity of the authors. Instead, I investigate how certain emotions, expressions, and tropes became associated with a specific gender identity in literature. The concept of gender in pre-modern China, as many scholars have stressed, was not an isolated and independent social category but was subsumed within the larger *yin–yang* cosmology.[16] The emphasis on correlation rather than segregation of genders allows for a much more fluid boundary between the male and the female, which forms an interesting parallel to Butler's views on gender fluidity. The conventional feminine voice in Chinese literature is formed in a similar way as gender identity is constructed, according to Butler, through repetition and performance "within a highly rigid regulatory frame."[17] The exploration of the process of formation of the feminine voice in Chinese literature, therefore, offers a unique perspective in a multicultural and multidisciplinary conversation about the discursive construction of gender.

"Literary voice" is another term that deserves some explanation. Literary writing in China has long been associated with the expression of thoughts and emotions. This is especially true for the genre of *shi* 詩 poetry (hereafter poetry unless there is a need to specify), the literary genre that enjoyed the highest esteem and popularity in pre-modern China and is the main focus of this study. Following the premise of "speaking one's intent" (*yanzhi* 言志),[18] poems often take the form of first-person monologue in a fragmented moment of the speaker's life. Literary voice is the key medium to convey the "intent." At the same time, it is common for a poem to leave out information about the speaking voice, such as explicit markers of its gender. Moreover, there is a wide spectrum of relationships between the literary voice in the text and the writer's own voice. On one end is the poet faithfully articulating what is on his or her

16 See, for example, Raphals, *Sharing the Light*, pp. 139–93; Ping Yao, "Changing Views on Sexuality in Early and Medieval China," *Journal of Daoist Studies* 8 (2015): 52–68, esp. pp. 53–57; and Tani E. Barlow, "Theorizing Women: *Funü, guojia, jiating*," in *Body, Subject, and Power in China*, ed. Angela Zito and Tani E. Barlow (Oxford: Oxford University Press, 1994), pp. 253–89. Samei also takes the *yin–yang* binary as the reason behind male poets' adaptation of a female persona: Samei, *Gendered Persona and Poetic Voice*, p. 9.

17 Butler, *Gender Trouble*, p. 33.

18 The "Great Preface" (Da xu 大序) to the *Shijing* that set the foundation of traditional Chinese poetics defines poetry as the place "where the intent goes" (*zhi zhi suo zhi* 志之所之) and the vocal manifestation of "what exists in the heart" (*Zai xin wei zhi, fa yan wei shi* 在心為志，發言為詩). Kong Yingda 孔穎達 (574–648), ed., *Maoshi zhengyi* 毛詩正義, *Shisanjing zhushu zhengyi* edition (Beijing: Beijing daxue chubanshe, 1999), 1.7.

mind at the moment of composition. On the other end is the persona composition, in which the poet adopts the identity and voice of someone else to convey sentiments on their behalf. One of the most common forms of persona composition in pre-modern China is male writers taking on a woman's voice and expressing her feelings. The multiple layers of relationship between the male author of *ci* and his female persona is the subject of Samei's book.[19] Samei's analysis of the gendered persona in *ci* is based on a set of highly stylized conventions that had become widely accepted by the end of the Tang dynasty. Although there are similarities in the way she and I use "literary voice and persona," I am less interested in probing the relationship between the persona and the author in individual works than I am in how certain kinds of literary voices came to be associated with a particular gender.

I largely follow Robertson's definition of the term "feminine" and the "feminine voice":

> I use the words "feminine" and "masculine" here to refer not to the biological reality of sex, but to the binary patterns of socially constructed gender, behavioral and attitudinal differences which are culturally given at the individual's birth and which become integral to both social personhood and existential selfhood. These specific patterns of difference are ideologically founded and are actualized and sustained in social behavior, including speaking, writing, and reading. Thus, no matter who speaks or writes, the voice one hears, or "hears," from the speaking subject in a poem is in some sense an acquired voice. I shall use the word "voice" to refer to discursivity, with discursive difference consisting of differences in the "position" of speaking subjects in texts vis-à-vis the use of representational codes, address, interest, or relationship to a dominant political or gender ideology.[20]

In contrast, I use the term "female voice" or "women's voices" to denote literary voices of biological women authors. This distinction can be helpful, for example in the discussion in Chapter 5 about women's voices that were left out or neglected in popular literary anthologies and works of literary criticism from the 6th century. The reason, I argue, is that they did not fit the established

---

19 In Samei's view, the operation of the conventions about gendered voice in *shi* poetry is influential yet distinct from early *ci*, due to the latter's close association with popular and performance culture: Samei, *Gendered Persona and Poetic Voice*, pp. 4–5. As I will show in this book, the early history of *shi* poetry, especially the five-syllable genre, had a no less close association with performance and anonymity than *ci*.

20 Robertson, "Voicing the Feminine," pp. 67–68.

conventions about the feminine voice. In early poetry with less certainty about authorship, however, it is often difficult to distinguish between the (biological) "female" and the (epistemological and discursive) "feminine." My discussions therefore generally focus on the gendered voice as represented in the texts and treat it as a related but separate issue from the author's gender. For example, although the feminine voice is first and foremost a male construct, it is entirely possible, and often the case, for female writers to willingly take on the conventional feminine voice in their writings.

"Performance" is another recurrent concept, especially in the discussion about the gradual loss of gender indeterminacy and fluidity in poetic expression in Chapters 3 and 4. Used in the context of gender, this concept inevitably recalls Butler's theory about gender and performance. Yet the idea of performance in my study is very different from Butler's. Butler's "performance" refers primarily to the stylized repetition of social acts and social behavior. The performance nature of early Chinese poetry, however, is rooted in the peculiar modes of literary production and circulation at the time. As Stephen Owen shows, extant "old poems" (*gushi* 古詩) and *yuefu* poems traditionally with a Han dynasty dating are in fact "one poetry," with a shared repertoire of materials that were chosen and arranged in individual works for specific occasions.[21] The composition of a work was not necessarily seen as a creative act controlled by the original mind of an individual author, but instead was viewed as the performance of familiar themes, sentiments, and expressions on stage, in oral or written rendition. The concept of performativity in this sense has as much to do with (textual and oral) applicability and role-playing as with theatrical presentation.[22] In Butler's theoretic frame, it is the performance of certain rigid and normative ideas about gender that created and stabilized the clear-cut categories of "the male" and "the female."[23] Yet my study shows that the performative context in early poetry constitutes the main reason for the gender

21 Stephen Owen, *The Making of Early Chinese Classical Poetry* (Cambridge, MA: Harvard University Asia Center, 2006), p. 73.

22 Xiaofei Tian uses the notion of "performativity" in her discussions of the "Nineteen Old Poems" (Gushi shijiu shou 古詩十九首): "By performativity I not only refer to the possible performance of the 'old poems' or of segments of the 'old poems' by singers of both sexes in front of an audience, but also to the act of meaning-production by members of the audience and eventually, in a textual tradition, by readers. In other words, singers, members of an audience, and readers help realize this poetry's narrative fullness": Tian, "Woman in the Tower: 'Nineteen Old Poems' and the Poetics of Un/concealment," *Early Medieval China* 15 (2009): 3–21, esp. 19.

23 Butler, *Gender Trouble*, pp. 16–25. Butler also points out that the key role of performance in the making of gender identity leaves room for potentially subversive gender performance such as cross-dressing. See Butler, *Gender Trouble*, pp. 128–41.

indeterminacy and fluidity in received texts. The shift from this performative context to a textual one over the course of the early medieval period created the need for more definitive and coherent gender in literary expression.

2 Primary Sources

Owen emphasizes the idea of "two centers" of the creation of the early Chinese classical poetry: the time when they were supposed to have been composed, that is, the Han and Wei dynasties; and that of the Southern dynasties, when they were systematically collected, edited, and canonized as part of a common literary legacy. The second center arguably played a more crucial role in literary history because it created the corpus of a tradition and shaped later understandings of it through its interpretation.[24] A similar argument can be made about the making of gender conventions. The two extant anthologies from the 6th century—the *Wen xuan* 文選 (The selection of refined literature) and *Yutai xinyong* 玉臺新詠 (New songs from the jade terrace)—not only serve as the primary sources of many literary works discussed in this study, but also are themselves fascinating objects of critical examination. They both represent the keen interest among 6th-century literati in organizing and presenting the literary past. Their selection of literary texts is guided by the editors' views of literature as well as popular literary tastes of the time, the relationships between which could vary from total agreement to utter opposition. In his preface to the anthology, Xiao Tong 蕭統 (501–531), the editor of the *Wen xuan*, compares the making of the anthology to gardening, in which one takes the necessary steps of weeding, culling, and trimming to create a beautiful and wholesome vista. With its compilation, he was committed to organizing numerous and miscellaneous texts from the literary past into an orderly and representative selection to demonstrate its glory.[25] Xiao Tong's contemporary Xu Ling 徐陵 (507–583)

---

24 Owen, *The Making of Early Chinese Classical Poetry*, pp. 23–72.

25 Xiao Tong, ed., *Wen xuan* (Shanghai: Shanghai guji chubanshe, 1980), p. 2. David Knechtges discusses and compares the criteria of selection in *Wen xuan* and *Yutai xinyong* in "Culling the Weeds and Selecting Prime Blossoms: The Anthology of Early Medieval China," in *Culture and Power in the Reconstitution of the Chinese Realm, 200–600*, ed. Scott Pearce, Audrey Shapiro, and Patricia Ebrey (Cambridge, MA: Harvard University Asia Center, 2001), pp. 200–44. He believes the two anthologies represent two opposite views of literature, namely, the conservative and Confucian-oriented style in the *Wen xuan* and the sentiment-oriented and literary style preferred by the *Yutai xinyong*. For a comprehensive study of Xiao Tong's literary views in the context of contemporary discussions and debates on the nature, value, and function of literary writing, see Wang Ping, *The Age of Courtly Writing: Wen xuan Compiler Xiao Tong (501–531)* (Leiden: Brill, 2012),

claims in the preface to the *Yutai xinyong* that the anthology is compiled for palace ladies to enjoy during their leisure time. His selection of poems seems to reflect an interest in poems about women or in women's voices.[26] Literary anthologies are biased in their representations of literary works, both those of the past and contemporary works. But they are also good indicators of the changing views and tastes in literature. Their decisions to include certain literary works in women's voices while leaving out others shed light on how gendered voice was perceived in literary writing at the time.

Whether aimed at being their guide, follower, or reformer, the *Wen xuan* and *Yutai xinyong* were compiled with contemporary literary tastes in mind. This sets them apart from another type of primary source on which this study relies: literary encyclopedias (*leishu* 類書), such as the *Yiwen leiju* 藝文類聚 (Collection of literature arranged by categories), which collates quotations, excerpts, and phrases on a topic from literary works of different genres. The goal is often to provide reference and aid for literary composition. Instead of catering to the reading pleasure of a contemporary audience, encyclopedias organize and transmit knowledge of the world to provide handy "toolboxes" of raw materials for contemporary and future writers to utilize.[27] The preface to the *Yiwen Leiju*, written by its editor Ouyang Xun 歐陽詢 (557–641), explains the editorial principles:

---

pp. 51–104. Wang believes that Xiao Tong's literary views have to be understood in relation to his status as Crown Prince. While acknowledging the nature of literature as a human response to nature's stimuli and its expressive function, he also stresses its moral and didactic function.

26 Xu Ling 徐陵 (507–583), ed., *Yutai xinyong jianzhu* 玉臺新詠箋注 (Beijing: Zhonghua shuju, 1985), pp. 11–13. The purpose of the compilation of the *Yutai xinyong* has long been a topic of scholarly debate. A Tang source associates it with the "palace-style poetry" (*gongti shi* 宮體詩) popular in the court of Xiao Gang 蕭綱 (503–551), Xu Ling's patron and later Emperor Jianwen 簡文 of the Liang dynasty. Xiaofei Tian examines various views about the agenda of the anthology and argues that the anthology was indeed made for female readership and with little interest in making political or moral statements: Xiaofei Tian, *Beacon Fire and Shooting Star: The Literary Culture of the Liang (502–557)* (Cambridge, MA: Harvard University Asia Center, 2007), pp. 190–91. The preface is examined in detail in Chapter 5 of the current book.

27 For a brief introduction to the *Yiwen leiju*, see Jessey J. C. Choo, "*Yiwen leiju*," in *Early Medieval Chinese Texts*, edited by Cynthia L. Chennault, Keith N. Knapp, Alan J. Berkowitz, and Albert E. Dien (Berkeley: Institute of East Asian Studies, University of California Press, 2015), pp. 454–64. For a general introduction to the genre of encyclopedias, see Xiaofei Tian, "Literary Learning: Encyclopedias and Epitomes," in *The Oxford Handbook of Classical Chinese Literature*, edited by Wiebke Denecke, Wai-yee Li, and Xiaofei Tian (Cambridge: Oxford University Press, 2017), pp. 132–146.

> 撰其事且文，棄其浮雜，刪其冗長。... 其有事出於文者，便不破之為事，故事居其前，文列於後，俾夫覽者易為功，作者資其用。可以折衷今古，憲章墳典云爾。
>
> We compiled both facts [in various categories] and literary texts, removed the superficial and messy, delete the superfluous and tedious ... If there is a fact mentioned in a literary text, we would not break apart the literary text for the sake of keeping the fact. Therefore we will list the fact first, followed by the literary text as its source. In so doing, readers can easily accomplish their goals [to find information about the fact] and writers can make their own use of it (i.e. the literary text). This arrangement makes it possible [for its users] to keep a good balance on the knowledge from the present and the past, and to model on the classics.[28]

The *Yiwen leiju* regularly shortens texts and removes sections deemed insignificant or irrelevant for readers (*lan zhe* 覽者) and writers (*zuozhe* 作者).[29] At the same time, it takes great pride in collecting all available textual knowledge and representations of the world. Primary sources of this type are essential for the current study, for they provide information and texts missing from the mainstream account of early medieval literature. They also balance and supplement the picture of pre-Tang literature portrayed in popular literary anthologies and works of literary criticism.

Another major source of literary texts in this study is the "Treatise on Music" (Yue zhi 樂志) of the *Song shu* 宋書 (History of the [Liu-]Song dynasty), compiled by Shen Yue 沈約 (441–513). As part of a historical project, the treatise preserves musical/performative texts used in court rituals and banquets. Owen summarizes its importance:

> The "Treatise on Music" of the *Song shu* did not "select" poems for readers; it conserved. It conserved material of an imperial musical repertoire that included both ritual and secular texts. The "Treatise on Music" is a precious survivor because it preserves texts from a performance tradition, with all the extraneous lines and textual problems, without making those texts fit the shape of "poetry" as it appeared in the sixth century.[30]

28 Ouyang Xun, *Yiwen leiju* (Shanghai: Shanghai guji chubanshe, 1965), p. 27.

29 For a discussion of *Yiwen leiju*'s approach to literary texts and its impact on later reception of literature of the Six dynasties, see Lin Xiaoguang 林曉光, "Lun *Yiwen leiju* cunlu fangshi zaocheng de Liuchao wenxue bianmao" 論《藝文類聚》存錄方式造成的六朝文學變貌, *Wenxue yichan* 3 (2014): 34–44.

30 Owen, *The Making of Early Chinese Classical Poetry*, pp. 63–64.

Thanks to the conservative nature of the treatise, it retained, rather than "fixed," the "textual problems" in early performance texts. As this study will show, these perceived problems often contain fascinating information regarding changes and transformations in literary tastes and practice, particularly in relation to gender. Guo Maoqian's 郭茂倩 (fl. 1084) *Yuefu shiji* 樂府詩集 (Collection of music bureau poetry) is another important primary source of early musical texts. The collection represents a cumulation of the scholarship on *yuefu* poetry since the 6th century. Textual problems exist, and the categorization and presentation of early *yuefu* works in the collection may reflect much later developments. With all its flaws, the *Yuefu shiji* is indispensable in the study of pre-Tang poetry because it preserves, often as citation, a large number of early medieval texts about *yuefu* poetry that otherwise would have been lost.[31] Instead of dismissing it altogether as an unreliable source of early *yuefu* tradition, the more fruitful approach is to treat it with critical caution and avoid relying solely or even primarily on it when it comes to early musical texts.

The construction of conventions about the feminine voice occurred across a wide spectrum of literary texts, including four-syllable and five-syllable poetry, *fu* 賦 (rhapsody), literary criticism, and prose narratives. Yet this study places special emphasis on five-syllable poetry, a genre that gained much popularity and prominence among the literati during the early medieval period. A large proportion of literary texts surviving from this period were written in this genre. The majority of the literary works preserved in the aforementioned primary sources, especially the two anthologies *Wen xuan* and *Yutai xinyong*, are five-syllable poems. This genre is also the focus of Zhong Rong's 鍾嶸 (*c.*469–518) *Shi pin* 詩品 (Gradation of poetry), a work of literary criticism. In addition to literary works in different genres, this study also investigates conceptual and discursive changes in gender in different modes of literary writing, including imitation, impersonation, group and individual composition.

Works of literary criticism from the early medieval period, such as Zhong Rong's *Shi pin* and Liu Xie's 劉勰 (fl. late 5th to early 6th century) *Wenxin diaolong* 文心雕龍 (The literary mind and the carving of dragons), are valuable sources for this study. Their accounts of the literary past and comments on individual authors and works provide a rare chance to learn about contemporary views on gender, women writers, and women's writing. Moreover, their silence on certain writers or works is worth investigating.

31 For examinations of this collection and its organizing principles, see Hans Frankel, "Yüeh-fu Poetry," in *Studies in Chinese Literary Genres*, ed. Cyril Birch (Berkeley: University of California Press, 1977), pp. 69–107; and Allen, *In the Voice of Others*, pp. 37–68.

Lu Qinli's three-volume *XianQin Han Wei Jin Nanbeichao shi* collects poems from pre-Qin 先秦 through the Sui 隋 dynasty (581–618) from some 300 different sources and arranges them in chronological order. For each individual poem, Lu meticulously includes available information about its sources, contexts, textual variants, and contending authorship. It is an indispensable and handy tool for the current study as well as for all studies on pre-Tang literature and culture.

3 A Case Study

Many of the issues concerning gender conventions in poetic voice discussed previously manifest themselves in the textual history of a poem titled "Ballad on a Pond" (Tangshang xing 塘上行). The poem is included in most modern anthologies of Chinese women's literature as written by Empress Zhen 甄皇后 (182–221), the principal wife of Cao Pi 曹丕 (187–226), Emperor Wen of the Wei dynasty. Although the empress is known in official history for her flawless virtue and extraordinary talents, it is her legendary beauty and alleged romantic liaison with her brother-in-law, Cao Zhi 曹植 (192–232), that caught the fancy of later readers and made her one of a handful of renowned women in early medieval China. Later accounts of her life are often mixtures of historical facts, fiction, and anecdotes.[32] The "Ballad on a Pond," as the only literary work attached to her name, constitutes an indispensable element of her story.

But there is a complicated textual history behind the poem. Its first appearance in textual history is as Cao Cao's 曹操 (155–220) work in the "Treatise on Music" of the *Song shu*.[33] A slightly different version of the same poem is found in the *Yutai xinyong*, attributed to Empress Zhen.[34] The 11th-century *Yuefu shiji* has Cao as the author of the poem but cites a short preface suggesting the poem was written by Empress Zhen.[35] Besides Empress Zhen and Cao Cao,

32 Robert Joe Cutter has done a thorough study of the historical development of her stories. See Robert Joe Cutter, "The Death of Empress Zhen: Fiction and Historiography in Early Medieval China," *Journal of the American Oriental Society* 112, no. 4 (1992): 577–83.

33 *Song Shu* 21.612–13; *XianQian Han Wei Jin Nanbeichao shi* 1.406–07.

34 *Yutai xinyong jianzhu* 2.56–57.

35 Guo Maoqian, *Yuefu shiji* (Beijing: Zhonghua shuju, 1979) 35.521–22. As a general rule, the collection groups poems with the same or derived titles in chronological order, usually from "old lyrics" (*guci* 古辭) to literati compositions. This arrangement evokes a sense of a continuous musical tradition. However, musicality and performativity are largely absent from most poems in the collection, especially those composed by named literati. Guo's grouping of individual poems also needs to be treated with caution. On the one hand, we cannot uncritically accept that all poems within a group belong to the same

Cao Pi is also mentioned as a possible author in Li Shan's 李善 (d. 689) commentary to the *Wen xuan*.[36] So who exactly is the author of this poem? Why are there many competing ascriptions of authorship? Why did the attribution to Empress Zhen, despite its much later occurrence in textual history, become the most widely accepted one?

Below I translate the earliest version of the poem in the *Song shu*:

蒲生我池中	Rushes grow in our pond;
蒲生我池中	rushes grow in our pond,
其葉何離離	how lush their leaves are!
傍能行儀儀	Others can carry out ceremonies;
莫能縷自知	nobody can know that thoroughly on their own.
衆口鑠黃金	The words of many can melt gold,
使君生別離	and made you separate from me in life.
（一解）	(the first stanza)
念君去我時	I think of the time when you left me;
念君去我時	I think of the time when you left me.
獨愁常苦悲	Lonely and sorrowful, I am always bitter and grievous.
想見君顏色	I bring your appearance to mind;
感結傷心脾	my feelings tangle and harm my heart.
今悉夜夜愁不寐	Now night after night I cannot sleep because of sorrow.
（二解）	(the second stanza)
莫用豪賢故	Do not, for the sake of the powerful and the worthy;
莫用豪賢故	do not, for the sake of the powerful and the worthy,
弃捐素所愛	discard the one you have always loved.
莫用魚肉貴	Do not, for fish and meat are valuable,
弃捐葱與薤	discard the onions and the leeks.
莫以麻枲賤	Do not, for hemp and silk are cheap,
弃捐菅與蒯	discard the rushes and the reeds.
（三解）	(the third stanza)
倍恩者苦枯	The one who betrays favor worries about withering;
倍恩者苦枯	The one who betrays favor worries about withering.
蹶船長苦沒	A broken boat is always in danger of sinking.
教君安息定	Please, my lord, be peaceful and

tradition; on the other hand, since Guo had at his disposal many sources that are no longer available, we have to take his grouping seriously.

36 *Wen xuan* 28.1315.

慎莫致倉卒	be careful not to act in haste.
念與君一共離別	I think of once being parted from you—
亦當何時共坐復相對	when again can we sit together to face each other?
（四解）	(the fourth stanza)
出亦復苦愁	Going out, I am still bitter and sad;
入亦復苦愁	coming inside, I am still bitter and sad.
邊地多悲風	At the borderland the sorrowful wind often blows,
樹木何蕭蕭	how swaying and rustling it moves the trees!
今日樂相樂	Today we enjoy ourselves together;
延年壽千秋	may you prolong your life and live a thousand years!
(五解)	(the fifth stanza)[37]

The "Treatise on Music" gives the following information preceding the poem: "Ballad on Growing Rushes on the Pond (or: Growing Rushes, Ballad on a Pond), Emperor Wu's lyric, five stanzas" (蒲生塘上行， 武帝詞， 五解). The poem contains too many repetitive and puzzling/unintelligible expressions to be aesthetically appealing. There is virtually no consistency in style, meaning, or rhyme. The five stanzas (*jie* 解) are linked for no apparent reason other than a general concern with separation. Although each stanza contains confusing and conflicting elements that defy easy interpretation, the fourth one is especially so. It is difficult to determine the gender and poetic role of the speaker within each individual stanza and even more so throughout the entire poem.

Over the next few centuries, this poem came to be associated with Cao Cao's daughter-in-law, Empress Zhen. The *Yuefu shiji* quotes the following account from the *Yedu gushi* 鄴都故事 (Stories of the capital Ye):

> 魏文帝甄皇后，中山無極人。袁紹據鄴，與中子熙娶后為妻。後太祖破紹，文帝時為太子，遂以后為夫人。后為郭皇后所譖，文帝賜死後宮。臨終為詩曰:“蒲生我池中，綠葉何離離。豈無兼葭艾，與君生別離。莫以賢豪故，棄捐素所愛。莫以麻枲賤，棄捐菅與蒯。莫以魚肉賤，棄捐蔥與薤。”

> Empress Zhen of Emperor Wen of Wei was a native of Wuji of Zhongshan. When Yuan Shao occupied Ye, he married the empress to his middle son, Yuan Xi. Later Taizu [i.e. Cao Cao] defeated Yuan Shao. Emperor Wen was the Crown Prince at that time and thereafter took the empress as the principal wife. Later, the empress was slandered by Empress Guo and

37 *Song Shu* 21.612–13.

> Emperor Wen ordered her to die in the rear palace. Before her death she composed the following poem: "Rushes grow in our pond; / how lush the green leaves are! / How do I not have the reeds or the rushes; / With you, my lord, I am separated in life. / Do not, for the sake of the worthy and the powerful; / discard the one you have always loved. / Do not, for hemp and silk are cheap;/discard the rushes and the reeds. / Do not, for fish and meat are cheap; / discard the onions and the leeks."[38]

The *Yedu gushi* no longer exists, but it is listed in the "Letters and Records" (Shu zhi 書志) chapter of the *Shi tong* 史通 (All about historiography) as a geographic work from the North, along with the *Luoyang qielan ji* 洛陽伽藍記 (Records about the monasteries of Luoyang) written around 547.[39] Based on the title and a few extant fragments, it is most likely a collection of romanticized accounts of historical events taking place in the city of Ye. The contextualization of the poem is problematic. The poem speaks of a "separation in life" (*sheng bieli* 生別离), while the story places the empress at the end of her life. Imageries such as the reeds, the rushes, fish, meat, the onions, and the leeks are ill fitting for a royal romance. The poem's imperative and admonishing tone ("Do not ...") sounds odd and inappropriate as the empress's words to the emperor. Notwithstanding these troubling details and its late occurrence, this became the most popular background story of the poem's composition and Empress Zhen its most widely accepted author.

The *Yutai xinyong* version of the "Ballad on a Pond," attributed to Empress Zhen, contains some notable variants to the *Song shu* version:

蒲生我池中	Rushes grow in our pond;
其葉何離離	How lush their leaves are!
傍能行仁義	Others can carry out humanity and justice;
莫若妾自知	nobody understands that better than *your concubine*.
衆口鑠黃金	The words of many can melt gold,
使君生別離	and made you separate from me in life.
念君去我時	I think of the time when you left me.
獨愁常苦悲	Lonely and sorrowful, I am always bitter and grievous.
想見君顏色	I bring your appearance to mind;
慼結傷心脾	my feelings tangle and harm my heart.

38 *Yuefu shiji* 35.521–22.

39 Liu Zhiji 劉知幾 (661–721), *Shi tong* (*Sibucongkan* edition) 8.11b.

念君常苦悲	Thinking of you, I am always bitter and grievous.
夜夜不能寐	Night after night I cannot sleep.
莫以豪賢故	Do not, for the sake of the powerful and the worthy,
弃捐素所愛	discard the one you have always loved.
莫以魚肉賤	Do not, for fish and meat are valuable,
弃捐葱與薤	discard the onions and the leeks.
莫以麻枲賤	Do not, for hemp and silk are cheap,
弃捐菅與蒯	discard the rushes and the reeds.
出亦復苦愁	Going out, I am still bitter and sad;
入亦復苦愁	coming inside, I am still bitter and sad.
邊地多悲風	At the borderland the sorrowful wind often blows;
樹木何修修	how swaying and rustling it moves the trees!
從軍致獨樂	Joining the army, you have reached your own happiness;
延年壽千秋	may you prolong your life and live a thousand years![40]

This poem tells a story far more coherent and comprehensible than the *Song shu* version. The puzzling fourth stanza is gone. Irregular lines with more than five characters are either replaced by standard five-syllable lines or eliminated. The seven-syllable line 13 of the *Song shu* version (今悉夜夜愁不寐) becomes a couplet (念君長苦悲/夜夜不能寐).[41] The unusual expression *jinxi* 今悉 is dropped. A gender-specific pronoun, "your concubine" (*qie* 妾), takes the place of the awkward *lü* 縷 in line 4 and offers the first-person female perspective. The last stanza of the *Song shu* version introduces a bleak frontier scene with little connection with the rest of the poem. In contrast, the phrase "join the army" (*congjun* 從軍) in the *Yutai xinyong* version puts the addressee in the army and explains the earlier description of the frontier. The *Song shu* version has the conventional ending template in performance texts: "we enjoy ourselves together" (*le xiang le* 樂相樂), in contrast with "reaching your own happiness" (*zhi dule* 致獨樂) in the *Yutai xinyong* version. The latter better

40 *Yutai xinyong jianzhu* 2.56–57; *XianQin Han Wei Jin Nanbeichao shi* 1.406–07.

41 This kind of "rewriting" of irregular lines to fit the overall rhythm of a poem or song is quite common in later versions of musical texts preserved in the "Treatise on Music." See Owen, *The Making of Early Chinese Classical Poetry*, pp. 319–26.

matches the sentiment of abandonment conveyed in the rest of the poem as well as the story about the empress.

The previous analysis gives us reason to believe that the *Yutai xionyong* version of "Ballad on a Pond" was developed from the *Song shu* version to present a consistent voice of a virtuous and obedient wife, as well as a relatively coherent story about abandonment and betrayal. In its portrayal, the woman's husband has left her, due to malicious slanders, to join a military campaign. While feeling deeply sorrowful and resentful, she still cares about him and sends him her best wishes. Besides making sense of a rather confusing poem and fixing its rhyme and style, the *Yutai xinyong* version also makes the poetic voice a better fit for the ascribed author Empress Zhen, one of the most famous "abandoned women" in pre-Tang China.

Multiple cultural and historical factors contributed to the attribution of the poem to the empress. The beautiful and talented Empress Zhen and her connection to Cao Pi, Cao Cao, and Cao Zhi have appealed to the popular imagination since as early as the early 5th century.[42] An entry in the *Shishuo xinyu* 世說新語 (New accounts of tales of the world), a 5th-century collection of anecdotes, quotes Cao Cao's words that he attacked the city of Ye for the sake of the empress, but that his son Cao Pi got her first.[43] Her alleged affair with Cao Zhi is first mentioned in an otherwise unknown text named "Ji" 記 (Records) quoted in Li Shan's commentary to the *Wen xuan*, as the story behind Cao Zhi's famous "*Fu* on the Luo Goddess" (Luoshen fu 洛神賦). It says that after the wrongful death of the empress, Cao Pi gave Cao Zhi a pillow that had belonged to her. When Cao Zhi crossed the Luo river on the way back to the fief, the empress's spirit visited him in a dream and claimed that she had become the river goddess. Cao Zhi wrote the *fu* to commemorate her after the encounter.[44]

Contesting accounts exist about the cause of her death. The *Wei shu* 魏書 (History of the Wei dynasty) records that the empress died of natural causes. But all other historical or quasi-historical records, including the *Sanguo zhi* 三國志 (Records of the Three Kingdoms), the *Yedu gushi*, and the "Ji," attribute her death to the loss of imperial favor to and evil slanders by Empress Guo.[45] Along with the growing body of legends about the empress, literary works such

42 Cutter, "The Death of Empress Zhen," pp. 580–81.

43 Liu Yiqing 劉義慶 (403–44), *Shishuo xinyu jianshu* 世說新語箋疏, annotated by Yu Jiaxi 余嘉錫 (Shanghai: Shanghai guji chubanshe, 1993) 35.1.917.

44 *Wen xuan* 19.895–96. The text is translated in Cutter, "The Death of Empress Zhen," pp. 577–78.

45 Cutter suggested that the overall pro-Wei sentiment in the *Wei shu* was the reason for its silence regarding the more sinister interpretation of the cause of Empress Zhen's death: Cutter, "The Death of Empress Zhen," pp. 582–83.

as the "Ballad on a Pond" have been attached to her or her story. The process continued well beyond the early medieval period. Cao Zhi's collected works include a "Song of Floating Duckweeds" (Fuping pian 浮萍篇), which speaks of sorrow and resentment in the voice of an abandoned wife.[46] The same poem appears in the *Yiwen leiju* with a different title, "Ballad on Growing Rushes" (Pusheng xing 蒲生行).[47] This title has little to do with the poem itself—which is about floating duckweeds—but takes the first two words from the "Ballad on a Pond." It should also be noted that the "Treatise on Music" of the *Song shu* gives "Growing Rushes" as an alternative title, or as part of the title to the "Ballad on a Pond." Later readers inevitably made the connection, including the Qing dynasty scholar Song Changbai 宋長白:

> 甄逸女將終，作《塘上行》曰："蒲生我池中，其葉何離離。旁能行仁義，莫若妾自知。"子建傷之，作《蒲生行・浮萍篇》曰："浮萍寄清水，隨風東西流。恪勤在朝夕，無端獲罪尤。"即用其語以命題，不待遺枕之賚，而始賦洛神也。
>
> When Zhen Yi's daughter [i.e. Empress Zhen] was about to die, she composed the "Ballad on a Pond," saying, "Rushes grow in our pond; / how lush their leaves are! / Others can carry out humanity and justice; / nobody understands that better than your concubine." Zijian [Cao Zhi's courtesy name] mourned her death and composed "Ballad on Growing Rushes: Song of Floating Duckweeds." It reads, "The floating duckweed attaches itself to clear water; / along with the wind, it flows east and west. / I am respectful and diligent day and night; / for no reason I receive blame and punishment." This is to name his own poem with her words ["rushes grow in our pond"]. Cao Zhi had already written about the Luo Goddess (Empress Zhen) before he was bestowed the pillow that she left behind.[48]

The attribution of the "Ballad on a Pond" to Empress Zhen offered the absent voice of the female protagonist in this legendary romance and provided a cultural significance that would not have been possible with the authorship of Cao Cao. Moreover, the link between the "Ballad on a Pond" and "Song of Floating Duckweeds" made it easy to apply the allegorical reading of the feminine voice to both poems. If the abandoned woman in the "Ballad" is usually

46 *XianQin Han Wei Jin Nanbeichao shi* 1.424.

47 *Yiwen leiju* 41.742.

48 *San Cao zhiliao huibian* 三曹資料彙編 (Beijing: Zhonghua shuju, 1980), p. 173.

read as the empress's self-reference, the similar articulator in Cao Zhi's poem is often taken as a metaphor for the frustrated poet who felt his talent was not recognized by the ruler, his brother Cao Pi.[49] Such an allegorical reading does not contradict Song Changbai's interpretation of the poem as Cao Zhi speaking in the empress's voice. On the contrary, it is the basis of the allegory: the frustrated minister finds his voice in the abandoned woman, who, in this case, happens to be his lover. These intertwined narrative and poetic elements made the empress's authorship of the "Ballad on the Pond" almost irresistible. Even Lu Qinli, an erudite scholar who is always cautious about questionable attributions, chose to list the poem under Empress Zhen's name despite acknowledging the alternative authorship of Cao Cao, for "all anthologies and records say its lyric was written by Empress Zhen" 諸集錄皆云其詞甄后所作.[50]

It is hard to know exactly when Empress Zhen became a possible "author" of the ballad, but it is very likely that the late 3rd-century poet Lu Ji had her story in mind when writing his "Ballad on a Pond."

江蘺生幽渚	The river grass grows on the secluded islet;
微芳不足宣	its slight fragrance is hard to notice.
被蒙風雨會	Coming upon the meeting of wind and rain,[51]
移居華池邊	it is moved to live by the Splendid Pond.[52]
發藻玉臺下	It sprouts under the Jade Palace;[53]
垂影滄浪淵	and casts shadows in the deep pool of dark green water.
沾潤既已渥	It has already received abundant moisture;
結根奧且堅	and planted its roots deep and strong.
四節逝不處	Four seasons have passed without cease;
繁華難久鮮	it is difficult to keep the glory fresh.
淑氣與時殞	Gentle vitality disappears with time;
餘芳隨風捐	the remaining fragrance wastes away in the wind.
天道有遷易	The Way of Heaven involves change and alteration;
人理無常全	human principles lack eternal perfection.

49 This tendency to read Cao Zhi's poems in the feminine voice as political allegory will be further discussed in Chapter 2.

50 *XianQin Han Wei Jin Nanbeichao shi* 1.407.

51 "The meeting of wind and rain" is a reference to a chance emergence into prominence, often related to an able minister being recognized by a ruler.

52 "The Splendid Pond" refers to a heavenly pond on Mount Kunlun where immortals dwell. It is a common metaphor for the imperial palace.

53 "The Jade Palace" is the legendary residence of the Heavenly Emperor and is often used in poetry to refer to the imperial palace.

男歡智傾愚 When a man is in love, his intelligence collapses;
女愛衰避妍 when a woman loses favor, she avoids other beauties.
不惜微軀退 I do not grudge the withdrawal of my humble body,
但懼蒼蠅前 but only fear the advance of flies.[54]
願君廣末光 I wish the lingering light of you would extend,[55]
照妾薄暮年 to shine on your concubine's twilight years.[56]

Although it is not labeled as an imitation, Lu Ji's poem is placed in the lineage of the earlier "Ballad on a Pond" by Li Shan's commentary to the *Wen xuan* and the *Yuefu shiji*.[57] This poem uses the growing river grass to introduce a sad story about betrayal, slander, and abandonment, which bears an unmistakable resemblance to both versions of the earlier poem.[58] Like the *Yutai xinyong* version, Lu Ji's poem marks the speaker's gender explicitly with the first-person pronoun "*qie*" and makes the addressee her husband, the "*jun*" 君. Differently from both versions of the earlier poem, however, Lu's poem contains many explicit references to the imperial family, including the "Splendid Pond" (*huachi* 華池) in line 4, the "Jade Palace" (*yutai* 玉臺) in line 5, and "The lingering light" (*moguang* 末光) in the last couplet. In particular, the relocation of the river grass from a secluded islet to an extravagant imperial environment fits the empress's life experience. She was first married to the son of Yuan Shao 袁紹 (d. 202) and then taken by Cao Pi to be his principal wife after Yuan's defeat. The passage of the woman's prime and her fear of slander in lines 9–18 speak to the empress's loss of favor and her death by evil slander. Lu Ji's poem is written in an elevated linguistic register without "improper" metaphors and

54 "Flies" is a common reference to slanders and villains.

55 The *Wen xuan* commentary quotes Sima Xiangru's 司馬相如 (179–117 BCE) "Essay on the *Feng* and *Shan* Sacrifices" (Feng shan shu 封禪書) to explain the meaning of "*moguang*": "make me receive the lingering light of the sun and the moon" (*Shi huo riyue zhi moguang* 使獲日月之末光): *Wen xuan* 28.1316. The same expression is also found in the *Shi ji* 史記 (Records of the Grand Historian) biography of Xiao He 蕭何 (d. 193 BCE), where Xiao's personal accomplishments are said to depend on the "lingering light" of the rising Han dynasty (*Ji Han xing, yi riyue zhi moguang* 及漢興，依日月之末光): *Shi ji* (Zhonghua shuju, 1959) 53.2020.

56 *Wen xuan* 28.1315–16.

57 It comes right after the *Song shu* and *Yutai xionyong* versions of "Ballad on a Pond" in the *Yuefu shiji*: *Yuefu shiji* 35.523.

58 Lu Ji's poem is certainly later than the *Song shu* version of the "Ballad on a Pond," but it is hard to tell whether Lu Ji's poem precedes the *Yutai xinyong* version or vice versa, although I believe Lu's poem is later than both versions and likely is modeled on the *Yutai xinyong* version.

expressions such as fish and meat, the onions and the leeks, and so forth.[59] In sum, the tone, plot, sentiment, and expressions in Lu Ji's poem match the voice of Empress Zhen much better than the earlier poem.

Li Shan's commentary cites the following lines from the *Ge lu* 歌錄 (Register of songs):

> 塘上行，古辭。或云甄皇后造，或云魏文帝，或云武帝。歌曰：蒲生我池中，葉何一離離。

> "Ballad on a Pond" is an old lyric. Some say it was created by Empress Zhen, some say Emperor Wen, and some say Emperor Wu. The song goes: "Rushes grow in our pond; / how lush the leaves are!"[60]

This account brings up another candidate for authorship—Cao Pi—and places Cao Cao, the "original" author, at the end of the list. This may indicate that Cao Cao is the least likely choice among the three. As the "Ballad on a Pond" came to be read in the voice of an abandoned woman, and specifically of the empress, and new texts emerged to support this reading, Cao Cao's authorship gradually faded from discussions about the poem. It re-entered the conversation in the Ming dynasty,[61] but was often taken as a target of dispute due to a perceived gender difference in poetic expression. The typical argument is found in the following statements by the Ming critic Xu Xueyi 許學夷 (1563–1633) and the Qing critic Zhu Qian 朱乾, respectively:

> 甄后樂府《塘上行》，情思纏綿，從肺腑中流出，與文君《白頭吟》媲美。或以爲孟德作，何耶？

> The emotion in Empress Zhen's *yuefu* poem, "Ballad on a Pond," is touching and lingering. It flows from the bottom of her heart. It is comparable

---

59 The elevation of register is a common feature in Lu Ji's imitation of earlier five-syllable poems, such as his imitations of the "Nineteen Old Poems" (Gushi shijiu shou 古詩十九首). Owen argues that it is one of the defining characteristics of "imitation" (*ni* 擬) at the time: Owen, *The Making of Early Classical Chinese Poetry*, pp. 261–85.

60 *Wen xuan* 28.1315. The *Ge lu* has long been lost, but it is likely a collection of music-related texts from the early medieval period.

61 It is not clear why Cao Cao's name was largely ignored before the Ming, but one explanation could be that Cao Cao was not seriously considered as a poet until the Ming dynasty. The renewed interest in his poetry is largely a result of his image in the popular storytelling tradition that later accumulated in the full-length novel *Sanguo zhi yanyi* 三國志演義 (Romance of the Three Kingdoms).

> to Zhuo Wenjun's "Chant of White Hair."[62] Some people believe it was written by Cao Cao. How could that be?[63]

> 凡魏武樂府諸詩皆借題寓意，於己必有所為，而《蒲生篇》則但為棄婦之詞，與魏武無當也，知其非魏武作也。

> All *yuefu* poems by Emperor Wu of the Wei use old titles to convey his own ideas and definitely have to do with himself. But the "Song of Growing Rushes" is merely the words of an abandoned woman. It does not suit Emperor Wu. Therefore, we know it was not written by Emperor Wu.[64]

These verdicts on authorship are based on a two-step inference. First, the experience of abandonment and the resultant melancholic sentiment belong exclusively to women. Second, a tough-minded warrior and politician such as Cao Cao would never express such feminine feelings in his poems. But the second step apparently does not take into consideration the performative nature of the earliest version of the poem in the *Song shu*. Cao Cao was known for his fondness of music and often composed poems for musical performance. Pei Songzhi's 裴松之 (372–451) commentary to the *Sanguo zhi* quotes the Wei dynasty historian Wang Chen 王沈 (d. 266): "Whenever [Cao Cao] composed a new poem, he would set it to the strings and pipes and turn it into a musical movement" (及造新詩，被之管弦，皆成樂章).[65] All his extant poems are preserved in the "Treatise on Music" as part of the court performance tradition, including the "Ballad on a Pond." It could have been intended to be performed by an entertainer of any gender without necessarily conveying any personal sentiments. Therefore the judgement of authorship based on emotion is fundamentally flawed.

More pertinent to this study, however, is the association of abandonment and emotional attachment with women's literary voice. This explains why the persona in the *Song shu* version of the poem tends to be taken as a woman despite the inconsistency in the poetic voice and absence of an explicit gender marker. Once this voice found a named historical person—Empress Zhen—this association completely overshadowed the possible authorship of Cao Cao (as well as Cao Pi) and became an integrated part of the poem's meaning.

62 Zhuo Wenjun is the wife of Sima Xiangru. Legend has it that she wrote the "Chant of White Hair" to convey her resentment after learning of Sima Xiangru's plan to take a concubine. The poem and the attached narrative are discussed in Chapter 3.

63 *San Cao ziliao huibian*, p. 19.

64 Ibid., p. 36.

65 *Sanguo zhi* 三國志 (Beijing: Zhonghua shuju, 1959) 1.53.

The case of the authorship of the "Ballad on a Pond" illustrates some very interesting issues regarding gender and gendered voice in Chinese literature. There is considerable inconsistency and indeterminacy in the gendered voice in the *Song shu* version of the "Ballad on a Pond." This inconsistency and indeterminacy are reduced to a great extent, if not completely, in the *Yutai xinyong* version. Lu Ji's imitation reworks the material in the same direction as the *Yutai xinyong* version and makes it even better suited for the voice of the empress. In later versions or imitations of the "Ballad on a Pond," the resentment of an abandoned woman became the central and dominant sentiment.

This case study also demonstrates the significant and often determinant roles primary sources of different natures played in the textual and interpretative history of the "Ballad on a Pond."[66] As mentioned earlier, the *Song shu*, with its purpose to preserve the court music tradition, records the lyric in its original, performative form. This performative nature holds the key to the ambiguity and inconsistency in its gendered voice—it makes it possible to adapt the voice to specific occasions of performance where the performer could be male or female. In contrast, the *Yutai xinyong* was compiled for a reading audience (as explicitly stated in its preface) whose prior reading experience has given them certain expectations regarding the gendered voice. In the absence of a performative setting, gender indeterminacy became an obstacle to understanding the poem. We may reasonably speculate that the *Yutai xinyong* version of the "Ballad on a Pond" was one of the written renditions of the *Song shu* version that chose the feminine voice for the speaker. There may have been other renditions with a different gendered voice (i.e. a masculine voice such as Cao Cao's). They did not survive, probably because the masculine voice was not seen as suitable for the poem. This choice of gendered voice is also echoed (or predicted) by Lu Ji's imitation of "Ballad on a Pond." Lu's poem marks the voice with *qie*, a common first-person female pronoun in poetry, and makes the poem her direct speech to a heartless lover. The fading of the performative context and the emergence of a textual or written context had a

66 In a recent article, Tian calls attention to the importance of the primary source, or "textual carrier" (*wenben zaiti* 文本載體), in the studies of texts from a manuscript culture. She analyzes the "Ballad on a Pond" as an example of how later interpretation (or misinterpretation) of the poetic texts and choices of textual variants affected the attribution of authorship. She argues that Cao Cao's possible authorship should not be disregarded since certain elements in the poem resonate with emotions expressed in poems that are traditionally accepted as Cao Cao's works. See Xiaofei Tian, "*Yutai xinyong* yu zhonggu wenxue de lishizhuyi jiedu" 玉臺新詠與中古文學的歷史主義解讀, *Huadong shifan daxue xuebao* 48 (2016): 10–17, esp. pp. 15–17.

great impact on literature, including the need for a more definitive and coherent gendered voice.

The "assignment" of gendered voice and authorship during the early medieval period was not an isolated or accidental phenomenon. It was closely connected to other cultural factors. From the attribution to Cao Cao to the attribution to Empress Zhen, the concept of "authorship" was perceived to be more individual and the sentiment of abandonment was increasingly associated with the feminine voice. The legends about the empress and her romance with Cao Zhi served as a magnet that attracted texts to be attached to both characters, including the "Ballad on a Pond" and "*Fu* on the Luo Goddess." By joining the cultural narrative, these literary works gained new meaning and significance and were better remembered, transmitted, and represented in later sources. Moreover, the allegorical associations of the feminine voice added political and moral significance to poems about romantic love and longing, which made it easy to read the author's own life and thoughts into the poem under the principle of "*yanzhi*," speaking one's intent.

4 Structure and Content

This book contains five main chapters. The first three chapters explore the reasons and motivations for male literati to assume a woman's voice in writing in the changing literary, cultural, sociopolitical, and moral contexts of early medieval China. These persona compositions by male literati configurated and consolidated the conventions surrounding the feminine voice. Building on the first three chapters, Chapters 4 and 5 examine the complex roles these conventions played in the early medieval literati's reception and interpretation of both early and contemporaneous literary works, which have had a profound influence on our understanding of pre-Tang literature.

Chapter 1 traces changes in the representation of women in literary works from the Han dynasty to the 3rd century. Through a comparison between male literati's persona compositions in women's voices and their portrayals of women from a third-person perspective, it investigates reasons for the popularity of persona composition in the 3rd century. The analysis of different representations of women from the court *fu* in the Han dynasty to poems by 3rd-century literati such as Cao Zhi, Fu Xuan 傅玄 (217–278), and Lu Ji shows increasing moral anxiety among literati writers regarding the depiction of female beauty. The main source of this anxiety is the presence of the sensualizing male gaze and the woman's direct, and sometimes intentional, exposure to it. Some 3rd-century poets shifted the focus of representation from the woman's external appearance to her inner world to reduce the anxiety. This shift toward interiority made it both natural and necessary for male writers to assume the feminine voice. The loss of the imperial, performative setting of literary composition in the Han court *fu* also had considerable moral, political, and literary effects on the transformations in the portrayal of women.

Chapter 2 discusses Jian'an writings about women and their social and political functions. The inward shift in the representation of women discussed in Chapter 1 first became a notable literary phenomenon in literary writings in the Cao–Wei courts during the Jian'an period. Writers such as Wang Can 王粲 (177–217) and Cao Zhi transformed the image of the beautiful woman from a symbol of imperial power to that of an ideal personality and companionship, and from a mysterious and threatening "other" to one of "us." The portrayal of an ideal woman became a means to construct a literary and political community with shared ambitions and values. The woman's longing for a worthy match was used to express the yearning for friendship in this context. Affected by Jian'an writers' pessimistic views of human emotions (*qing* 情), the feminine image and voice are characterized with melancholy and laments over inevitable conflict and loss. It is through the Jian'an literati's persona compositions that the lament of an abandoned and lonely woman became a major trait of the feminine voice in literature.

Chapter 3 elucidates the major literary and cultural associations of the feminine voice, including the five-syllable poetic genre, the trope of the abandoned woman, and the sentiment of boudoir resentment. Jian'an writing in the feminine voice established a connection between the feminine voice and the five-syllable genre. The association of the five-syllable poetry with performance and impersonation makes it a perfect literary medium for gender crossing in persona composition. The characterization of the feminine voice with abandonment and resentment, first seen in Jian'an persona writings, was reinforced in poems attributed to abandoned women in romanticized historical stories popular in the 4th and 5th centuries. Many of these attributions were taken in the tradition as authentic voices of women, which led to the view that five-syllable poetry originated in women's writings. This chapter also reveals the changing perceptions of the nature, function, and social status of five-syllable poetry over the course of the early medieval period.

Chapter 4 examines the indeterminacy and fluidity of gender in the five-syllable "old poems" and *yuefu* dated before the 3rd century. In their imitations, rewritings, and interpretations of earlier works, early medieval literati assigned definitive gendered voices to them and considerably reduced the indeterminacy and fluidity. Relatively indeterminate gender expressions in earlier works were gradually forced into a neat "map" of more determinate ones, as certain literary topics, styles, and sentiments became closely tied to the feminine voice. This mapping process also pushed out of the picture images and voices of women that do not fit the established conventions, such as the elusive and manipulative woman.

Chapter 5 studies the reception and transmission of women's writings in the early medieval period. It shows a consensus regarding women's poetic voices in popular literary discourse of the 6th century, reflected in extant literary anthologies and works of literary criticism. Voices of women writers that differ from the conventional feminine voice, including expressions of philosophical transcendence, sensual desire, and authority, were excluded or downplayed and only left traces in encyclopedic, anecdotal, and historical sources. The selective reception and preservation of women's writings in popular literary discourse concealed the rich diversity in women's actual voices and contributed to the canonization of the conventional feminine voice.

The Epilogue of the book explores a constructed cultural other to the established image and voice of women in literati's writings: the voices of southern local girls in the corpus of Wu songs (*wuge* 吳歌). With bold expressions of desire, theatrical displays of sensual beauty, and emotional independence, these voices of the "local" were the antithesis of the conventional feminine voice. The elite literati's interest in them reflects a fascination with something completely different from what they perceived as commonplace for women's voices in their own literary world.

CHAPTER 1

A New Type of Gaze and the Rise of the Feminine Voice

The potential harm that female beauty or appearance (*se* 色) could bring to one's cultivation of virtue (*de* 德) is a major concern in early Confucian texts. Confucius (Kongzi 孔子) (*c.*551–479 BCE) famously declares, twice in the *Analects* (Lun yu 論語), that he has never seen anyone who is fond of virtue in the same way as he is of beauty.[1] King Xuan of Qi 齊宣王 bluntly admitted to Mencius (Mengzi 孟子) (*c.*372–289 BCE) that his weakness (*ji* 疾) in the fondness for female beauty (*haose* 好色) might get in the way of his governance of the state. Even though Mencius validated the king's desire for beauty as long as the king would satisfy the same desire of his people, the conversation makes it clear that the fondness for beauty requires explanation and justification, which Mencius provided by turning it into a political analogy.[2] Historical accounts such as the *Zuo zhuan* 左傳 (Zuo tradition) and *Lienü zhuan* 列女傳 (Biographies of exemplary women) have no shortage of cautionary tales about the dire consequences brought upon a state and its people by the ruler's indulgence in female beauty.[3]

The literary display of female beauty has induced similar unease and anxiety. The authoritative interpretative traditions since the Eastern Han, including the Mao commentary to the *Shijing* and Wang Yi's 王逸 (*c.*89–158) commentary to the *Chuci*, often justify the representation of women as allegories for political discourse. For example, Mao views the depictions of charming and sensuous girls in the "Air from the State of Zheng" (*Zheng feng* 鄭風) as a critique of the moral degradation and political unrest in the state caused by the king's negligence of his duties; Wang Yi explains Qu Yuan's 屈原 (*c.*343–277 BCE) pursuit of an elusive goddess as a metaphor for his search for a worthy lord. This interpretative scheme legitimizes writing about women and desire by imbuing it with political and moral significance, and it contributed to the official

1 Cheng Shude 程樹德, *Lun yu ji shi* 論語集釋 (Beijing: Zhonghua shuju, 1990) 18.611; 32.1094. Here the word 色 has a broader connotation about sensual pleasure or visual beauty than just female appearance, but female beauty is certainly a main component or manifestation of it.

2 Yang Bojun 楊伯峻 (1909–1992), *Mengzi yizhu* 孟子譯註 (Beijing: Zhonghua shuju, 1960) 2.5.37.

3 See Raphals, *Sharing the Light*, pp. 61–70.

 | DOI:10.1163/9789004546455_003

recognition of the status of the two collections as Confucian classics (*jing* 經) in the Eastern Han. Much scholarly work has been done on the interpretative traditions of these two works and their treatments of female images and romantic topics.[4] Yet outside this classic tradition, there were writings on the topic of women and sensual desire that were not read as part of a greater political or moral discourse. How, then, were they received by contemporary and later readers? Was there a similar moral unease in the portrayal of female beauty? If so, what caused the unease and how, if ever, was it resolved? These are questions that this chapter is going to address.

This chapter examines writings about women in literary works from the Han up to the 3rd century. With a close analysis of different types of female representations, I argue that the moral anxiety primarily lies in the theatrical display of the female body and the presence of the sensualizing male gaze in the represented scene. I borrow the concept of the "male gaze" from writings in feminist film theory. As Laura Mulvey puts it, "the determining male gaze projects its fantasy onto the female figure, which is styled accordingly."[5] The omnipotence and omnipresence of the male gaze, both literally and figuratively, and its objectification of women in traditional narrative films, reveal the patriarchal structure of society. Mulvey distinguishes the pleasure of scopophilia, or seeing the image on screen as an object of sexual stimulation, and the pleasure of the narcissistic construction of the ego, or identifying with the image that is seen. In the context of Chinese poetry, Robertson has discussed the creation of an eroticized object as the projection of male fantasies and desire by the presence of the male gaze in poems written by male authors in the feminine voice.[6] My study differentiates between two different types of the male gaze, namely, the sensualizing gaze that treats the woman as pure object of desire, and the sympathetic gaze that seeks identification with the woman. As an effort to annihilate the moral anxiety associated with the portrayal of women, there was a visible tendency in 3rd-century literary works to downplay or remove the beholder and his sensualizing gaze from the scene and to turn the focus away from the woman's body to her inner world. In addition to reducing eroticism, this shift of focus also leaves room for the allegorical

4 See, for example, David Hawkes, "The Quest of the Goddess," in *Studies in Chinese Literary Genres*, ed. Cyril Birch (Berkeley: University of California Press, 1974), pp. 42–68; and Donald Holzman, "Immortality-Seeking in Early Chinese Poetry," in *The Power and Culture: Studies in Chinese Culture History*, ed. Willard. J. Peterson, Andrew H. Plaks, and Ying-Shih Yu (Hong Kong: Chinese University Press, 1994), pp. 103–18.

5 Laura Mulvey, "Visual Pleasure and Narrative Cinema," in *Visual and Other Pleasures* (London: Palgrave, 1989), pp. 14–26, esp. p. 19.

6 Robertson, "Voicing the Feminine," pp. 68–72.

interpretation that projects the author's (and readers') empathy, rather than sensual desire, toward the woman portrayed. The emergence of the sympathetic gaze was the main reason behind the rise of the feminine voice in literary expression.

1 Women as Objects of the Sensualizing Gaze in Early Court *Fu*

The literary theme of the quest for a goddess has an especially close association with the genre of *fu* in the Western Han (206 BCE–9 CE). Extant works of *fu* are products of the princely and imperial courts. The court setting of Western Han *fu* affected their portrayal of women in profound ways. The representation of women is often mediated, with a speaker describing a woman to his audience: the ruler. The most well-known examples are the "*Fu* on Gaotang" (Gaotang fu 高唐賦) and its sequel "*Fu* on the Goddess" (Shennü fu 神女賦), both attributed to Song Yu 宋玉 (fl. 3rd century BCE).[7] Despite his exhaustive use of lexicon and rhetoric to describe a woman's physical beauty, the *fu* speaker's real interest did not lie in the woman he is describing, but in the representation's influence on his royal audience. In the imperial context, the portrayal of women in Western Han court *fu* stressed the exclusiveness of the ruler's experience by denying other people's access to the woman—including that of the speaker. In both "*Fu* on Gaotang" and "*Fu* on the Goddess," the king commands the composition, which serves to ensure him either a future meeting or a re-enactment of (*fuxian* 復見) a previous meeting with the goddess. The speaker Song Yu, despite being the active seeker of the goddess in the *fu*, pursues her only for the king's pleasure and only in words. He leaves all hope of actual interaction and consummation to the king.

The beginning section of the "*Fu* on the Goddess" describes a dream encounter with the enigmatic goddess as the reason for the *fu*'s composition. The two protagonists—Song Yu (*yu* 玉) and the king (*wang* 王)—are mentioned repeatedly. The similarity between the two words raised suspicions among later readers about possible textual variants or copying errors, primarily regarding

7 *Wen xuan* 19.875–95. Many scholars accept that these *fu* originate in the Han. Their topics, structure, and linguistic features strongly resemble the epideictic *fu* in the Western Han courts. See "Song Yu," in *Ancient and Early Medieval Chinese Literature: A Reference Guide, Part Two*, ed. David Knechtges and Taiping Chang (Leiden: Brill, 2013), pp. 1007–10. For overviews of debates about Song Yu's authorship, see Wai-yee Li, *Enchantment and Disenchantment: Love and Illusion in Chinese Literature* (Princeton, NJ: Princeton University Press, 1993), p. 25, note 46; and Rouzer, *Articulated Ladies*, pp. 369–70, note 21.

the identity of the dreamer. The earliest source of this text is the 6th-century anthology *Wen xuan*, which names the king as the dreamer. The revisions on the following translation by David Knechtges are made based on the texts in *Wen xuan*:

> 其夜王寢，果夢與神女遇，其狀甚麗。王異之，明日以白玉。玉曰："其夢若何？"王曰："晡夕之後，精神怳忽，若有所喜。紛紛擾擾，未知何意。目色髣髴，乍若有記。見一婦人，狀甚奇異。寐而夢之，寤不自識。罔兮不樂，悵然失志。於是撫心定氣，復見所夢。"
>
> That night, while the king was asleep, he indeed dreamed of having an encounter with a goddess whose appearance was extremely beautiful. The king wondered about this, and the next day he told Song Yu about it. Song Yu said, "What was your dream like?" The king replied, "After the twilight, my spirit felt befuddled and confused, as if something propitious had occurred. But I was perplexed and puzzled, and did not know what it meant. My eyes could only vaguely discern her, but I can recall my momentary impression. I saw a woman unusual in appearance. Asleep, I dreamed of her; Awake, I cannot remember her form. And thus I felt depressed and unhappy, sad and frustrated. And then, stroking my breast, I calmed my spirit, and again visualized what I had seen in my dream."[8]

Unable to clearly recall or relate his erotic dream, the king asked Song Yu to elaborate upon it: "Try to compose a *fu* on her on my behalf" 試為寡人賦之！Since the 11th century, scholars have argued that the two characters *wang* and *yu* should be switched, and that Song Yu, rather than the king, met the goddess in a dream.[9] The debate is largely due to a seeming "paradox" in the text: why would the king, as the dreamer himself, need another person to

8 *Wen xuan* 19.886–87. David R. Knechtges, trans., *Wen xuan or Selections of Refined Literature*, Vol. 3: *Rhapsodies on Natural Phenomena, Birds and Animals, Aspirations and Feelings, Sorrowful Laments, Literature, Music, and Passions* (Princeton, NJ: Princeton University Press, 1996), pp. 340–41, with modifications. Knechtges explains his acceptance of Shen Gua's change based on the logic of the dialogue in a note on page 411.

9 Owen also takes Song Yu as the dreamer. See Stephen Owen, ed. and trans., *An Anthology of Chinese Literature: Beginning to 1911* (New York: W. W. Norton, 1996), pp. 190–93. Although Rouzer gives reasons for reading the text both ways, he is more inclined to read Song Yu as the dreamer as well; see Rouzer, *Articulated Ladies*, pp. 60–61. For an overview on the debates, see Li, *Enchantment and Disenchantment*, p. 28, note 50; and Yang Ming 杨明, "Shishui mengjian le wushan shennü—guanyu Song Yu 'Shennü fu' de yiwen" 是誰夢見了巫山神女——關於宋玉《神女賦》的異文, *Zhangzhou shifan xueyuan xuebao* 20 (2006):

recount his own experience? There are four reasons to follow the *Wen xuan*. To begin with, the debate only began more than a thousand years after the alleged composition of the *fu*, and almost five hundred years after its earliest extant textual edition. No questions were raised regarding the two characters until Shen Gua 沈括 (1031–1095).[10] Second, the character *guo* 果 at the beginning of the passage, meaning "indeed" or "as a result," strongly suggests the realization of an earlier expectation or promise, the most logical possibility of which is Song Yu's promise of *the king's* meeting with the goddess in its prequel, "*Fu* on Gaotang."[11] Third, it is not completely absurd that the king would need Song Yu to describe the king's own dream given the mediated nature of court *fu*, where it is common for a ruler to need someone else to describe his own experience. The above passage also makes it clear that the dreamer was not able to recollect his own memory of the goddess when he woke up and was in a state of confusion even within the dream. In contrast, Song Yu's ability to describe someone else's (i.e. the former king's) dream is well tested in the "*Fu* on Gaotang." Lastly, any confusion between the two characters hinges on treating the *fu* as reading/visual text and would be meaningless in its original form as oral performance at court.[12]

This beginning passage of the "*Fu* on the Goddess" demonstrates the division of power between the speaker and his royal audience in early court *fu* on women. The speaker possesses the power of rhetoric and imagination, whereas the ruler holds the real power of experiencing and consummating the pleasure promised by the *fu*. The ruler's exclusive ownership of the experience is accentuated even by the physical description of the goddess in the "*Fu* on the Goddess":

骨法多奇	The pattern of her bones is of unusual form,
應君之相	a physiognomy fitting for you, my lord.
……	

48–53. Li concludes that "it seems more plausible that Sung Yü should be the dreamer" whereas Yang holds the opposite opinion.

10 Shen Gua, *Mengxi bitan quanyi* 夢溪筆談全譯, trans. Hu Daojing 胡道靜, Jin Liangnian 金良年, and Hu Xiaojing 胡小静 (Guiyang: Guizhou renmin chubanshe, 1998), pp. 896–98.

11 At the end of the "*Fu* on Gaotang," Song Yu suggests that the king employ worthy ministers and cultivate moral governance, by which means, according to him, the king's meeting with the goddess can be accomplished. *Wen xuan* 19.881–82.

12 The epideictic *fu* of the Western Han, as Martin Kern points out, were meant in their own times for oral performance, not as reading texts. See Martin Kern, "Western Han Aesthetics and the Genesis of the *Fu*," *Harvard Journal of Asiatic Studies* 63 (2003): 383–437, esp. pp. 407–19.

他人莫覩	No one else could see her;
王覽其狀	only the king saw her form.[13]

Rouzer argues that the speaker's relationship with the goddess can never be consummated and must be kept purely at the verbal level in order to maintain the king's ultimate authority.[14] Similarly, Cheng Yu-yu points out the king's "demasculinization" (*fengjian yange* 封建閹割) of Song Yu in the "*Fu* on Gaotang" and "*Fu* on the Goddess." Female beauty, Cheng argues, is displayed only for the king and serves to fulfill his desire.[15] The actual consummation, therefore, is always promised to attract and sustain the king's interest but delayed for the king's sole enjoyment. The ruler may be, as Rouzer puts it, "impotent" in rhetoric,[16] but there is no need for him to possess rhetorical skills. With actual political power he can order the literati at his court to create entertainments or fantasy catered to his desires. This further accounts for the king's need for Song Yu to relate his own dream.

The ruler's exclusive ownership in early court literature even extends beyond the experience of female beauty. In another *fu* attributed to Song Yu but most likely composed in the Western Han, "*Fu* on the Wind" (Feng fu 風賦), the enjoyment of the wind itself is said to be the ruler's privilege:

此獨大王之風耳	This is uniquely the wind of your majesty;
庶人安得而共之	how could common people get to share it?[17]

In the same vein, Sima Xiangru's 司馬相如 (179–117 BCE) "*Fu* on the Imperial Park" (Shanglin fu 上林賦) draws a definitive line between the property of the "Son of Heaven" (*tianzi* 天子) and that of the feudal lords (*zhuhou* 諸侯).[18] The final message warns the feudal lords against the danger of bragging about their own trivial possessions, which would "degrade the lord and bring harm to themselves" (*bianjun zisun* 貶君自損). The Son of Heaven's exclusive right to unbounded wealth is the reflection of his absolute authority, so for the feudal lords to enjoy similar luxury would amount to a challenge to imperial power.[19]

13 *Wen xuan* 19.888. I use Knechtges's translation in *Wen xuan or Selections of Refined Literature*, Vol. 3, p. 345, with modifications.

14 Rouzer, *Articulated Ladies*, pp. 66–67.

15 Cheng Yu-yu, "Meili de zhouxuan—Shennü lunshu yu xingbie yanyi" 美麗的周旋——神女論述與性別演義, in *Xingbie yu jia guo: Han Jin cifu de Chu sao lunshu* 性別與家國：漢晉辭賦的楚騷論述 (Shanghai: Sanlian shudian, 2006), pp. 1–53, esp. pp. 16–19.

16 Rouzer, *Articulated Ladies*, p. 64.

17 *Wen xuan* 13.581–82.

18 Ibid. 8.361–86.

19 "Now that you, as minor feudal lords, enjoy the extravagance that is fit only for an emperor, I am afraid your people will suffer its ill consequences." 夫以諸侯之細，而樂萬乘之奓，僕恐百姓被其尤也. Ibid. 8.378.

In a unified empire, the emperor enjoyed supreme power and unchallenged possession of "all under heaven" (*tianxia* 天下), as stated by Dong Zhongshu 董仲舒 (179–104 BCE):

> 唯天子受命於天，天下受命於天子，一國則受命於君。
>
> Only the Son of Heaven receives the mandate from Heaven. All under heaven receive their mandate from the Son of Heaven. A state receives its mandate from its ruler.[20]

As the receiver of heaven's mandate, the emperor stood at the center of the cosmos and was the only intermediary between the human world and heaven. He was entitled to unquestioned sovereignty on all matters. The unique mediated structure of early court *fu*, with the speaker describing a dazzling object—such as a woman—to the ruler, was a literary reflection of the political concept of empire.[21] In its imperial context, the portrayal of women, whether divine or mortal, was never the ultimate goal but served to confirm and reinforce the ruler's sovereignty.[22] The woman could be arrogant, powerful, and unpredictable—in many ways the mirror image of a willful sovereign. Her unfathomability perfectly analogizes his inscrutable, fickle mind.

The sense of security and certainty under the unified empire gave rise to a confidence about the ability to control desire and bring it to a proper cause in early court *fu*. Beautiful women are paraded as part of the imperial glory in Sima Xiangru's "*Fu* on the Imperial Park" and Mei Sheng's 枚乘 (d. 140 BCE) "Seven Stimuli" (Qi fa 七發).[23] Their depictions of women are closely tied to the genre's alleged persuasive function to lead the ruler to the righteous path. In both works, beautiful women constitute part of a long list of sensual

20 Dong Zhongshu, *Chunqiu fanlu* 春秋繁露 (*Sibu beiyao* edition) 41.11a.

21 In his discussion of the function of epideictic *fu* of the Han, Knechtges makes the following observation: "The impression the poet may wish to convey … is that the park and its emperor occupy the center of the cosmos, and that everything radiates from the seat of imperial power": David R. Knechtges, "To Praise the Han: The Eastern Capital Fu of Pan Ku and His Contemporaries," in *Thought and Law in Qin and Han China*, ed. W. L. Idema and E. Zürcher (Leiden: Brill, 1990), pp. 118–39, esp. pp. 119–21.

22 Robert Joe Cutter discusses what he calls the "blazon" tradition in the description of women in *fu*, which is to itemize and name various body parts and decorations in exhaustive detail. This important rhetorical device, Cutter believes, is meant to affirm and exalt imperial power by engaging in a kind of "rhetoric of property," in which listing equals the claim of possession. See Robert Joe Cutter, "To Make Her Mine: Women and the Rhetoric of Property in Early and Early Medieval *Fu*," *Early Medieval China* 19 (2013): 39–57, p. 54.

23 *Wen xuan* 8.361–86 and 34.1559–75.

pleasures along with music, food, palaces, hunting, excursions, and the like. Female beauty is presented as a powerful tool to warn the ruler of the danger of indulging materialist pleasure and awaken him to the importance of moral governance. In the "*Fu* on the Imperial Park," for example, the speaker's remonstrance against the ruler falls on deaf ears until he gives an extensive description of beautiful women:

> 於是酒中樂酣，天子芒然而思，似若有亡，曰：“嗟乎！此大奢侈！朕以覽聽餘閒，無事棄日。順天道以殺伐，時休息於此。恐後葉靡麗，遂往而不返，非所以為繼嗣創業垂統也。”
>
> And then, in the midst of drinking, during the rapture of music, the Son of Heaven becomes disconsolate, as if He had lost something. He says, "Alas! This is too extravagant! During Our leisure moments from attending to state affairs, with nothing to do We cast away the days; following the celestial cycle, We kill and slaughter, and from time to time rest and repose here in this park. But We fear the dissolute dissipation of later generations, that once they have embarked on this course they will be unable to turn back. This is not the way to create achievements and pass down a tradition for one's heirs."[24]

The transition from sensual indulgence to moral realization is so smooth that no explanation or inference is needed. In an article on Western Han views of *fu*, Kern points out that the structure of early court *fu*, namely an exhaustive display of pleasant objects followed by moral instruction, does not indicate a conflict or paradox in the writer's intent but reflects an agenda to "use sex to illustrate ritual" (*yi se yu yu li* 以色喻於禮), as stated in the newly excavated *Kongzi shilun* 孔子詩論 (Confucius' discourse on the *Shi*).[25] This agenda holds the key to turning the theatrical display of female beauty into an effective moral tool. The triangular structure (the woman—the speaker—the ruler) in early court *fu* ensures no direct interaction between the woman and the intended target of her charm—the ruler. The speaker controls the ruler's experience of and desire for female beauty and channels the woman's seductive power to convey the intended moral messages. This mediated representation

---

24 *Wen xuan* 8.376. I use Knechtges's translation in David R. Knechtges, trans., *Wen Xuan or Selections of Refined Literature*, Vol. 2: *Rhapsodies on Sacrifices, Hunting, Travels, Sightseeing, Palaces and Halls, Rivers and Seas* (Princeton, NJ: Princeton University Press, 1987), p. 109.

25 Kern, "Western Han Aesthetics and the Genesis of the *Fu*," p. 425.

of women made it possible for *fu* writers in the imperial Han court to exert influence over their powerful audience.

Although it is always brought into control by the rhetorical power of the genre, the potential danger of female beauty is still a central concern of early court *fu*, perhaps because the *fu*'s rhetorical power in evoking sensual desire often, quite ironically, eclipses its power in delivering moral suasion. Nothing more clearly demonstrates the moral anxiety associated with female beauty and sensuality than a group of *fu* on the topic of "pacifying the passions" (*dingqing* 定情), in which the speaker, a courtier, relates to the ruler his encounters with a seductive beauty and his successful control of his desire. Examples include the "*Fu* on Master Dengtu the Lecher" (Dengtu zi haose fu 登徒子好色賦), "*Fu* on Indirect Remonstrance" (Feng fu 諷賦) attributed to Song Yu, and "*Fu* on a Beauty" (Meiren fu 美人賦) attributed to Sima Xiangru. All depict femmes fatales intending to distract the speaker from the moral path of serving a worthy ruler, who is the audience in the *fu* as well as its (potential) audience in the real world. The woman's direct and willing exposure to the male gaze poses a threat to existing moral and political orders. But in the end the speaker brings the situation under control and declares his moral integrity and loyalty to his audience.

All three *fu* on pacifying the passions follow a common plot scheme: the speaker is accused of being lustful and disloyal to the ruler on the basis that his handsome appearance and flowery words would cause trouble in the ruler's harem. "Being lecherous," or literally "being fond of female beauty" (*haose* 好色), is equivalent to disloyalty (*buzhong* 不忠) to the ruler and a threat to imperial authority; therefore, vulnerability to sensual desire represents the most severe flaw of a subject. The challenge faced by the speaker is both moral and political. In a move to clear himself, the speaker describes to the ruler, in the main section of the *fu*, a previous confrontation with an extremely attractive woman and his firm rejection of her attempt at seduction (note the same mediated structure in the representation). In so doing, the speaker demonstrates not only his ability to resist the irresistible, but also his incorruptible loyalty to his audience. He could now claim to be more trustworthy and virtuous than those who have never been put under serious test, such as his accuser. This logic is eloquently stated in the "*Fu* on a Beauty":

> 古之避色，孔墨之徒，聞齊饋女而遐逝，望朝歌而回車。譬於防火水中，避溺山隅，此乃未見其可欲。何以明不好色乎？
>
> In the ancient times there were those who avoided female beauty like Confucius and Mozi. Learning that the state of Qi was going to bestow

> beautiful women [to the ruler of Lu], Confucius left Lu to a remote place. Seeing the city of Zhaoge from afar, Mozi turned his carriage around.[26] Their behaviors can be compared to staying in the water to avoid fire or hiding in the mountains to avoid drowning. They have never seen what is desirable. How can we be sure that they are not lecherous?[27]

Confucius and Mozi kept their virtue intact only because they never confronted "what is desirable." The real challenge lies in the direct exposure of female beauty to the sensualizing male gaze. In the "*Fu* on Master Dengtu the Lecher," the most extensive account of a dangerous encounter with a seductress comes from one Qin Minister of Zhanghua 秦章華大夫:

> 吾少曾遠遊，周覽九土，足歷五都。出咸陽，熙邯鄲，從容鄭衛溱洧之間。

> When I was young I went on a distant journey. I viewed the nine regions of the realm, and passed through the cities of the five directions. I left Xiangyang to enjoy myself in Handan. I lingered about the Zhen and Wei rivers in Zheng and Wei.

是時向春之末	At this time, at the end of spring,
迎夏之陽	Just as we greeted the first sun of summer,
鴒鶊喈喈	Orioles were chirping,
群女出桑	And a group of girls went out to pick mulberry leaves.
此郊之姝	The young lasses of this country town
華色含光	Glow with resplendent color and allure.
體美容冶	Their figures are pretty, their faces ravishing,
不待飾裝	And require no makeup or adornment.[28]

The political context of this romantic encounter should not be taken lightly. Placed in the Warring States setting of the *fu*, the distant journey (*yuanyou* 遠遊) through different states of the minister-to-be is not merely a pleasant excursion but serves the purpose of seeking employment under a worthy ruler.

---

26 The city's name "Zhaoge," "singing in the morning," goes against Mozi's condemnation of music.

27 *Yiwen leiju* 18.331.

28 *Wen xuan* 19.893–94. I use Knechtges's translation in *Wen Xuan or Selections of Refined Literature*, Vol. 3, p. 353.

The area of Zheng and Wei is traditionally associated with sensual pleasure and a lack of moral restraint, a fitting location for the beguiling mulberry-picking girls to distract the speaker from his political pursuit. Not surprisingly, the sensualizing gaze (*guan* 觀) at the most beautiful girl among them gives rise to illicit desire and improper behavior. The speaker addresses her with charming words and, at least for that moment, seems to have forgotten his goal of becoming a loyal subject. The girl responds to the man in an elusive yet provocative way:

於是處子	And then, the young maid
恍若有望而不來	seemed to be gazing expectantly, but she would not approach;
忽若有來而不見	suddenly she seemed about to approach, then disappeared.
意密而體疏	Her air seemed cordial, but her person remained distant;
俯抑異觀	with each movement, up or down, was a different view.
含喜微笑	with happy heart, smiling faintly,
竊視流眄	her rolling eyes cast furtive glances at me.[29]

Her attitude is rather ambiguous, rejecting and encouraging the speaker's desire at the same time. Unlike the beautiful women in the "*Fu* on the Imperial Park" and "*Fu* on the Goddess" who are being controlled by the speaker's rhetoric, the woman takes control of the game and manipulates his desire. But just as further transgression is expected, both the speaker and the girl decide to comply with ritual propriety (*shouli* 守禮), and the encounter comes to a sudden halt with a positive reflection on the speaker's moral integrity:

目欲其顏	My eyes took pleasure in her appearance,
心顧其義	but in my heart I saw her virtue.
揚詩守禮	In declaiming poems and upholding the rites,
終不過差	we never transgressed the bounds of propriety.[30]

The problem caused by "eyes" (*mu* 目), that is, the beholding of a beautiful woman, has found solution in the "heart"/mind (*xin* 心), which keenly observes

29 *Wen xuan* 19.894; *Wen Xuan or Selections of Refined Literature*, Vol. 3, p. 354.

30 *Wen xuan* 19.894; *Wen Xuan or Selections of Refined Literature*, Vol. 3, pp. 354–55.

ritual propriety. The speaker's reputation as a loyal subject has been rectified, hence he is now known as the "Qin *Minister* of Zhanghua."

Unlike the mulberry-picking girl, the seductress in the other two *fu* on pacifying the passions does not restrict herself and has her mind set on seducing the speaker. Just like the Qin minister, the speaker Sima Xiangru is on his way to serve Prince Liang at the beginning of the "*Fu* on a Beauty" out of admiration for the prince's "sublime virtue" (*dawang zhi gaoyi* 大王之高義). When passing the area of Zheng and Wei, he is greeted by a beautiful lady in a scented chamber:

女乃歌曰	The woman then sang:
獨處室兮廓無依	I am in the chamber by myself, alas, lonely and with no one to rely on,
思佳人兮情傷悲	thinking of the fair person, alas, I feel distressed and sad.
有美人兮來何遲	There is a beautiful person, alas, how late he came!
日既暮兮華色衰	The sun is already set, alas, my flowery appearance has withered;
敢託身兮長自思	Dare I entrust myself [to you]? alas, for a long time I ponder alone.[31]

The song speaks directly to the speaker and invites him not only to listen but also to behold. Noticing his hesitation, the woman exposes herself more:

女乃弛其上服	The woman then removed her upper garment,
表其褻衣	and revealed her under clothes.
皓體呈露	her dazzling body was exposed,
弱骨豐肌	with tender frame and fine appearance.
時來親臣	At that time she got intimate with me, your subject,
柔滑如脂	[her skin] soft and smooth as congealed ointment.[32]

The threat to corrupt the speaker's virtue comes not only from the woman's exposed body, but also from her willingness and readiness to seduce. Like the Qin minister, the speaker (Sima Xiangru) controls himself with a righteous heart and steadfast intent:

31 *Yiwen leiju* 18.331.

32 Ibid.

臣乃脈定於内	I, your subject, stabilized my pulse within,
心正於懷	rectified my heart in my bosom,
信誓旦旦	I made a solemn vow,
秉志不回	preserved my intent, and never turned back.
翻然高舉	All of a sudden, I rose up and left,
與彼長辭	and bid fare well with her forever.[33]

The *fu* ends here, but we know what happened next: he left the woman for Prince Liang, the audience of his self-defense. The "intent" he claims to have preserved is the one to serve the worthy prince. His rejection of the seductress offers a most convincing pledge of loyalty as a subject (*chen* 臣) and gives the final layer of satisfaction to his royal audience.[34]

Two conclusions can be drawn from the previous analysis of the portrayal of women in early court *fu*. First, subjecting female beauty to the sensualizing male gaze is a source of moral anxiety due to its potential to lead people astray, including both the subject and the ruler. For the ruler, the indulgence in female beauty and sensual desire represents the utmost temptation, capable of shaking the foundation of moral governance. For the subject, it could corrupt his loyalty to the ruler. Second, the solution to this anxiety is in the *fu*'s imperial setting. The mediated nature of the representation, with a speaker describing the woman to his ruler, dictates that the danger of female beauty is always contained and never leads to sinister consequences. The seductress is tamed by the *fu* rhetoric and, even better, rechanneled to persuade the ruler to exercise moral governance or to prove the speaker's loyalty to the ruler.

Without this setting of a unified empire that imposes moral and political authority, what would the representation of women entail? To what different consequences would it lead? As the imperial context faded with the decline of the centralized empire, so did the confidence about bringing female beauty under control. The claim to illuminate a moral lesson with extravagant descriptions of sensual pleasure, including beautiful women, received much

33 Ibid.

34 Rouzer discusses "*Fu* on Master Dengtu the Lecher" and "*Fu* on a Beauty" in *Articulated Ladies*, pp. 48–58. He argues that the two works treat the *fu* rhetoric as their very subject and represent a more "playful consideration of the imperial poet and his position." Rouzer believes that they "parody the poet's power to manipulate and move the ruler" by showing that the "subtle phrases" (*weici* 微辭, i.e. the rhetoric of the *fu*) present no real threat to imperial power and authority (p. 48). Although his analysis of the *fu* rhetoric in these works is sound, these *fu* are not merely playful parodies but convey serious political messages as well, including the demonstration of moral propriety and loyalty as the essential qualities for a minister.

criticism at the end of the Western Han for giving "a hundred encouragements followed by a single remonstrance" (*quanbai fengyi* 勸百諷一).[35] Without a powerful moral center or political authority, theatrical displays of the female body in front of the sensualizing gaze could easily result in disorder. Since the 3rd century, there has been a tendency in literati representations of women to avoid theatrical displays of female beauty and to downplay or eliminate the object–beholder structure in poetic expression. The focus of the presentation is shifted from the theatrical/public display and gendered gaze to the woman's inner thoughts, and the perspective of the description makes an inward turn. Instead of the projection of male desire, the woman is represented as an object of sympathy.[36] These changes are most evident in two female images prevalent in early and early medieval poetry: the mulberry-picking girl and the woman in a tower.[37]

2 Mulberry-Picking Girls: Theatricalizing and De-theatricalizing the Female Body

The *yuefu* poem "Mulberries by the Path," preserved in the "Treatise on Music" of the *Song shu*, depicts an encounter with a beautiful lady that resembles that of the Qin minister of Zhanghua in many ways, sans the imperial setting. Due to the performative nature of *yuefu* poems, their representation of women focuses on the theatrical display of external beauty, not unlike the mediated

35 From Yang Xiong's 揚雄 (53 BCE–18 CE) famous critique of the epideictic *fu* of the Western Han. See *Fa Yan yishu* 法言義疏, annotated by Wang Rongbao 汪榮寶 (Taipei: Yiwen yinshuguan, 1968) 3.81.

36 It is not always easy to draw a clear line between sympathy and desire, especially in the literary description of a beautiful woman. But there is keener attention to her inner world as opposed to her external beauty and charm.

37 Since the transformation in the representation of women was largely the result of the absence of a higher authority and the court setting, the literary works discussed below are mostly poetry rather than *fu*, which is characterized by its mediated structure. These two influential images are the subjects of two previous studies: Joseph Allen, "From Saint to Singing Girl: The Rewriting of the Lo-fu Narrative in Chinese Literati Poetry," *Harvard Journal of Asiatic Studies* 48, no. 2 (1988): 321–61; and Tian, "Configuring the Feminine," pp. 93–168. Allen traces the transformations of the Luofu narrative from the *yuefu* poem to late imperial dramatic genres. Tian demonstrates how palace-style poems in the Southern dynasties created a new, subversive aesthetics of femininity by rewriting the images of Luofu and the "wanderer's wife" with a focus on female sexuality and desire and a resistance to allegorical associations. Many of the poems examined here are discussed and translated in these two studies, albeit with different focuses. I will make specific references in the following discussion.

depiction of women in early court *fu*. Yet the absence of the imperial setting in which a higher authority presides over the representation makes a great difference in its outcome.

At the beginning of "Mulberries by the Path," a narrator's voice introduces its protagonist, Luofu 羅敷. She is depicted with a detailed inventory of clothing items and accessories on her body:

日出東南隅	The sun rises from the southeast
照我秦氏樓	And shines on the halls of our house of Qin.
秦氏有好女	And the house of Qin has a lovely girl
自名爲羅敷	Who calls herself by the name Luofu.
羅敷善蠶桑	Luofu is skilled with silkworms
採桑城南隅	She picks mulberry leaves south of the city wall.
青絲爲籠係	The straps of her basket are of blue silk,
桂枝爲籠鈎	Its handle, a branch of cinnamon;
頭上倭墮髻	Her hair has a trailing ponytail,
耳中明月珠	in her ears are bright moon pearls.
緗綺爲下裙	Her skirt below is saffron damask,
紫綺爲上襦	Of purple damask, her vest above.[38]

In his comparative study of "Mulberries by the Path" and European pastoral poems, Jean-Pierre Diény points out that the sericultural activity in both cultures brought women to a public place, exposed them to the sensualizing gaze of passing aristocrats, and made them vulnerable to their sexual advances.[39] If the gaze is only implied in the previous lines, the next section brings it to the fore:

行者見羅敷	When passers-by see Luofu, they
下擔捋髭鬚	drop their loads and stroke their beards.
少年見羅敷	When young men see Luofu,
脫帽著帩頭	Their hats fall off and their headbands show.
耕者忘其犁	Men at the plow forget the share;
鋤者忘其鋤	men with the hoe forget the hoe,

38 *XianQin Han WeiJin Nanbeichao shi* 1.259–60. I use Owen's translation in *An Anthology of Chinese Literature*, p. 234, with modifications.

39 Jean-Pierre Diény, *Pastourelles et magnanarelles: Essai sur un thème littéraire chinois* (Geneva and Paris: Droz, 1977). It is translated into Chinese in Qian Linsen 錢林森 trans., *Munü yu canniang* 牧女與蠶娘 (Shanghai: Shanghai guji chubanshe, 1990), pp. 154–206.

來歸相怨怒 When they go home there are always complaints and anger,
但坐觀羅敷 all because of gazing at Luofu.[40]

The characters *jian* 見 and *guan* 觀, both meaning "to see," "to gaze at," are used repeatedly in these lines. The gaze gives rise to illicit desire and stops men from fulfilling their duties. The condition of "forgetting" (*wang* 忘), which literally means the loss (*wang* 亡) of the heart/mind (*xin* 心), forms a striking contrast with the mind's ability to subjugate desire caused by the sight of beautiful women in the *fu* on pacifying the passions.

Like the mulberry-picking girl in the "*Fu* on Master Dengtu the Lecher," Luofu's subjection to the sensualizing male gaze gives rise to illicit desire and diverts the men from their proper duties. But unlike the Qin minister, Luofu's beholders do not feel the need to restrict their actions in the absence of a higher authority. The result is disastrous. The next section singles out one individual beholder, a lord governor, who attempts to make Luofu the object of his desire exclusively:

使君從南來 A lord governor came from the south,
五馬立踟躕 and he halted his five-horse team;
使君遣吏往 the lord governor sent a clerk,
問此誰家姝 to ask who that maiden is.
秦氏有好女 The house of Qin has a lovely girl,
自名爲羅敷 who calls herself by the name Luofu.
羅敷年幾何 And just how old is Luofu?
二十尚不足 Not yet up to twenty,
十五頗有餘 and just beyond fifteen.
使君謝羅敷 The lord governor invites Luofu:
寧可共載不 Would you like to ride with me?
羅敷前致辭 Luofu stepped forward and said,
使君一何愚 Lord governor, you are a foolish man:
使君自有婦 you have a wife of your own,
羅敷自有夫 I, Luofu, have a husband who is mine.[41]

40 *XianQin Han Wei Jin Nanbeichao shi* 1.260; Owen, *An Anthology of Chinese Literature*, pp. 234–35, with modifications.

41 *XianQin Han Wei Jin Nanbeichao shi* 1.260; Owen, *An Anthology of Chinese Literature*, p. 235, with modifications.

The governor's aggressive move is the consequence of the exposure of Luofu's beauty to the male gaze and a threat to the existing order in the poem. Subjected to an intense sensualizing gaze by her audience within and outside the text, the unavailability of Luofu's beauty for any individual's exclusive ownership allows her to fulfill the collective fantasy of her beholders.[42] Had the governor succeeded, the game of seduction and desire at the center of the poem would have ended forever. One may counter that Luofu identifies herself as someone's wife at the end of the poem, yet the final monologue, with a detailed description of her "husband," deserves a closer look:

東方千餘騎	In the east are a thousand riders and more,
夫婿居上頭	and my husband is head of them all.
何用識夫婿	How can you tell who my husband is?—
白馬從驪駒	He rides a white horse, a black colt behind.
青絲繫馬尾	the horse's tail is wound in blue silk,
黃金絡馬頭	and gold is the halter on its head,
腰中鹿盧劍	At his waist is a wound-pommel sword,
可值千萬餘	worth more than a million.
十五府小吏	At fifteen he was a minor county clerk,
二十朝大夫	by twenty, a great lord at court.
三十侍中郎	by thirty, in the Emperor's entourage,
四十專城居	by forty, the master of a city.
為人潔白皙	His skin is smooth, his skin is white,
鬑鬑頗有鬚	his beard is wispy and long,
盈盈公府步	He walks with slow pace through the courts,
冉冉府中趨	with stately steps he goes through the hall.
坐中數千人	Several thousand men in the seat
皆言夫婿殊	all say that my husband is extraordinary.[43]

This dashing image of the husband has puzzled many readers. Some have found incredible the apparent elite status of the husband, since Luofu's sericultural activities by the roadside indicate that she is of commoner status or at the most a member of the lower-gentry class. The husband should be read as a male counterpart to Luofu herself. Luofu's response does not deliver a convincing

42 As Owen puts it, the woman "is magically protected within a frame created by the distance of collective admiration." See Stephen Owen, *Mi-lou: Poetry and the Labyrinth of Desire* (Cambridge, MA: Harvard University Press, 1989), p. 68.

43 *XianQin Han Wei Jin Nanbeichao shi* 1.260; Owen, *An Anthology of Chinese Literature*, p. 235, with modifications.

or even believable reason for her rejection but instead reinforces theatricality and the sensualizing gaze with another round of display of male beauty. Just as the third-person narrator introduces her to a group of male beholders at the beginning of the poem, the dazzling appearance of her counterpart draws the attention of the beholding eyes of "several thousand men." With this new object of the sensualizing gaze, the *yuefu* poem manages to sustain its audience's desire from beginning to end while ostensibly averting it from overlong viewing of the female body. Allen takes Luofu to be a virtuous wife under the influence of "conservative Han Confucian tradition," based on her rejection of the lord governor's advance with a pledge of faith to her husband.[44] Yet her "rejection" is not meant to end the game of seduction and desire, but rather to sustain it. More importantly, the assumption of Luofu's voice in this part of the poem does not result in the adoption of her viewpoint or access to her inner world. The poem ends here, with the woman taking full control of the seductive game. The loss of moral order (the illicit advance of the governor) and social order (the governor being ridiculed by a mulberry-picking girl) remains unresolved.

Building on observations by the 18th-century art critic Diderot (1713–1784), Michael Fried suggests an important transformation in the depiction of female figures in French paintings from the mid-1750s to 1781. Painters such as Chardin, Greuze, and Carle Van Loo began to depict beautiful women in a state of complete absorption and total oblivion to the presence of a beholder to avoid any erotic overtone and to convey a genuinely empathic feeling toward the painted object. The practice was a direct response to the earlier Rococo tradition, in which human figures, especially seductive women, were exhibited as if they were on stage and fully aware of being the object of beholding eyes. Fried argues:

> In Diderot's writings on painting and drama the object–beholder relationship as such, the very condition of spectatordom, stands indicated as theatrical, a medium of dislocation and estrangement rather than of absorption, sympathy, self-transcendence; and the success of both arts, in fact their continued functioning as major expressions of the human spirit, are held to depend upon whether or not painter and dramatist are able to undo that state of affairs, to *de-theatricalize beholding* and so make it once again a mode of access to truth and conviction, albeit a truth and a conviction that cannot be entirely equated with any known or experienced before. What is called for, in other words, is at one and

44 Allen, "From Saint to Singing Girl," p. 327.

> the same time the creation of a new sort of object—the fully realized *tableau*—and the constitution of a new sort of beholder—a new "subject"—whose innermost nature would consist precisely in the conviction of his absence from the scene of representation.[45]

By depicting characters in an absorbed state, the artist could convince the audience that they are oblivious to beholders and thus authentic and sincere in their actions. The dialectics between theatricality and sincerity, and spectatordom and sympathy, in an object–beholder relationship lend helpful insights to the present study. The portrayal of Luofu in "Mulberries by the Path" shows much theatricality and leaves little or no room for sympathy or reflection. The governor is the opposite of the ideal beholder in Fried's view who must be absent from the scene of representation. His abrupt intrusion into the world of Luofu accentuates its theatricality and causes disturbance. To avoid theatricality and eroticism, there has been a tendency since the 3rd century in literati representations of women to create a "new sort of object" as well as a "new sort of beholder." Like what Fried observes in 18th-century French paintings, these writers shifted the focus from the theatrical display of women's external appearance to their inner thoughts, weakened the sensualizing gaze, and created more sympathetic and invisible beholders. They represent women as objects of sympathy and sometimes give them a voice and "subjectivity." In her study of transformations in the goddess image in *fu* on the goddess, Wai-yee Li shows an inward turn in Cao Zhi's "*Fu* on the Luo Goddess" that provides the goddess with psychological complexity and lyrical subjectivity that are absent in previous *fu*. To avoid the presence and gaze of a higher authority, Cao Zhi's *fu* makes the audience of the *fu* the coachman, rather than a ruler.[46] The same tendency is present in his portrayal of women in poetry. His "Song on a Beauty" (Meinü pian 美女篇) is traditionally viewed as being inspired by, if not an imitation of, "Mulberries by the Path":[47]

美女妖且閑	A beautiful girl, charming and refined,
採桑歧路間	picks mulberry leaves in the fork of the road.
柔條紛冉冉	Tender branches are bountiful and drooping,
落葉何翩翩	How elegant their leaves fall down!

45 Michael Fried, *Absorption and Theatricality: Painting and Beholder in the Age of Diderot* (Chicago, IL: University of Chicago Press, 1980), p. 104, italic in the original.

46 Li, *Enchantment and Disenchantment*, pp. 33–40.

47 Both Diény and Allen treat this poem as a literati's imitation of the earlier *yuefu* ballad. See Diény, *Pastourelles et magnanarelles*, p. 111; and Allen, "From Saint to Singing Girl," pp. 333–34.

攘袖見素手	She folds up her sleeves and reveals her fair hands,
皓腕約金環	Gold bracelets bind her gleaming wrists.
頭上金爵釵	In her hair is a golden bird hairpin,
腰佩翠琅玕	Around her waist a green pendant made of *langgan* jade.
明珠交玉體	Bright pearls are on her jade body,
珊瑚間木難	Coral mixes with the *mu'nan* pearls.
羅衣何飄颻	How her gauze garment flaps!
輕裾隨風還	her light skirt moves along with the wind.
顧盼遺光彩	Her glance leaves a gleam;
長嘯氣若蘭	making a long whistle, her breath is like the orchid.
行徒用息駕	Those who are traveling, for her, stop their carriages;
休者以忘餐	those who are resting, for her, forget their meals.
借問女安居	May I ask where the girl lives?
乃在城南端	Right at the south end of the city wall.
青樓臨大路	The painted halls overlook a great road,
高門結重關	its tall gate held with double hinges.
容華耀朝日	Her handsome look is brighter than the dawn sunlight,
誰不希令顏	Who would not value her fine appearance!
媒氏何所營	Who has the matchmaker sought for her?
玉帛不時安	Jade and silk are not arranged on time.[48]
佳人慕高義	The fair lady admires high virtue,
求賢良獨難	finding a worthy companion is truly hard.
衆人徒嗷嗷	The crowd makes much noise to no avail,
安知彼所觀	How could they understand what she sees?
盛年處房室	In her prime she stays inside her chamber,
中夜起長嘆	In midnight, she rises and heaves a long sigh.[49]

In comparison with "Mulberries by the Path," Cao Zhi's poem keeps the extensive depiction of the woman's appearance but significantly downplays the sensualizing gaze and theatricality. For one thing, it reduces the prominent presence of the watching crowd. Although the same word "*jian*" 見 appears in the fifth line, it does not have an active subject to indicate the presence of

48 Jade and silk are betrothal gifts.

49 *XianQin Han Wei Jin Nanbeichao shi* 1.431–32.

the male gaze within the poem. It could be read as an intransitive verb (pronounced *xian*) meaning "revealing" or "appearing" rather than "seeing." The only active gaze in the poem occurs in lines 13–14: "Her glance leaves a gleam; / making a long whistle, her breath is like the orchid" 顧盼遺光彩/長嘯氣若蘭. And its direction is purposefully reversed, with the woman as the agent.[50] Unlike the listing of beholders' reactions to Luofu's beauty in the *yuefu* ballad, the description here is kept to a minimum: "Those who are traveling, for her, stop their carriages; / those who are resting, for her, forget their meals" 行徒用息駕/休者以忘餐. The lines read more figuratively than realistically, especially compared with the vivid description of the effects Luofu's beauty has on her viewers. The withdrawal of the male gaze from the represented world is further ensured in lines 17–20, which locates the woman in a secluded mansion behind "double hinges." The removal of the lord governor also guarantees the absence of the male gaze in the representation.

Yet the greatest departure from previous portrayals of the mulberry-picking girl occurs toward the end of the poem in the woman's self-expression. The perspective turns inward and Cao Zhi assumes the voice of the "fair lady" (*jiaren* 佳人) to lament people's failure to understand her views (*suoguan* 所觀, lit. what *she* sees) and her failure to find a worthy companion (*qiuxian* 求賢). The woman shows no interest in playing the game of desire with her beholders like her literary predecessors. She is so deeply absorbed in her melancholic thoughts as to be oblivious to her surroundings. The sensualizing gaze transforms into a sympathetic one when the poetic voice gains full access to the woman's inner world and turns her into the object of sympathy, or, as Diény puts it, the "object of contemplation."[51] The represented world resembles what Fried calls "the fully-realized *tableau*," that is, a self-sufficient and perspicuous unity of meaning that does not depend on beholders' reactions. Beholders of the woman's beauty, now completely excluded from the represented scene to take the role of the reader, are invited to identify with the woman and her thoughts.

Fu Xuan's 傅玄 (217–278) "Ballad: The Prelude" (Yange xing 艷歌行) transforms the image of Luofu in a similar way to Cao Zhi's "Song on a Beauty":

50 This could be an allusion to the "Song on a Fair Lady" (Jiaren ge 佳人歌) that Li Yannian 李延年, a musician in the court of Emperor Wu of the Han, sang about his sister, Lady Li. The song has the line "With one glance she could topple a city; / with another she could topple a state" 一顧傾人城/再顧傾人國. *Han shu* 97a.3951.

51 Diény, *Pastourelles et magnanarelles*, p. 111.

日出東南隅	The sun rises from the southeast
照我秦氏樓	and shines on the halls of our house of Qin.
秦氏有好女	And the house of Qin has a lovely girl
自字為羅敷	who calls herself by the name of Luofu.
首戴金翠飾	Her hair is fastened with gold and feathered ornaments,
耳綴明月珠	Her ears decorated with bright moon pearls.
白素為下裾	Of pure-white silk is her skirt,
丹霞為上襦	Of crimson embroidery is her vest.
一顧傾朝市	With one look she topples both court and market
再顧國為虛	with a second the state becomes a wasteland.
問女居安在	Ask where the girl lives;
堂在城南居	Its halls stand south of the city wall.
青樓臨大巷	The painted halls overlook a great lane.
幽門結重樞	Its secluded gate held with double hinges.
使君自南來	A lord governor comes from the south.
駟馬立踟躕	and he halted his four-horse team.
遣吏謝賢女	He sends a clerk to ask this worthy girl,
豈可同行車	could she share his carriage with him?
斯女長跪對	The girl kneels in respect to answer,
使君言何殊	"Lord governor, how extraordinary are your words.
使君自有婦	The lord governor has a wife of your own,
賤妾有鄙夫	And I, your humble servant, have a lowly husband.
天地正厥位	Heaven and earth give each their proper place.
願君改其圖	I hope you will, my lord, change your plans."[52]

Allen points out that an important difference in Fu Xuan's poem is the omission of the lines about Luofu's mulberry picking at the beginning of the poem.

52 *XianQin Han Wei Jin Nanbeichao shi* 1.554–55. I use Allen's translation in "From Saint to Signing Girl," pp. 327–28, with modifications. Allen treats "The Prelude" as a literati's imitation of an early *yuefu* poem with changes on both textual and moral levels. Owen, however, suggests that Fu Xuan's is not an "imitation" of the *Song shu* version, but a different rendition of the Luofu narrative that bears traces of elite aesthetics and morality. See Allen, "From Saint to Singing Girl," pp. 324–33; and Owen, *The Making of Early Chinese Classical Poetry*, pp. 336–41. Either way, Fu Xuan's poem, like Cao Zhi's "Song on a Beauty," represents an attempt to correct moral problems in the Han ballad created by the presence of the male gaze.

He views it as a deliberate revision on Fu Xuan's part to make her a "chaste aristocratic lady."[53] This omission serves another purpose, which is to avoid her exposure to the crowd and their gaze and to reduce the theatricality in her portrayal. Allen also notes that Fu Xuan describes Luofu's beauty in a more abstract way by alluding to the "Song on a Fair Lady" in lines 9–10. There is the same shift in the direction of the gaze as in Cao Zhi's "Song on a Beauty." Fu Xuan's version shows an even more conscious weakening of the sensualizing gaze. The narrative element about eager beholders of Luofu's beauty is still there, but their presence is rendered figurative by the following lines that place Luofu behind a hinged gate (lines 11–14). It almost seems abrupt when a governor enters the scene and invites her for a ride. This disparity may be explained by the strong force of tradition: Luofu's interaction with the governor is too essential a component in the plot—it is arguably the central element—to be discarded altogether. Yet Fu Xuan still avoids the sensualizing gaze in this section by confining the communication to that between Luofu and a messenger/clerk (*li* 吏). In "Mulberries by the Path," the clerk comes on stage only to ask about Luofu's identity. In Fu Xuan's poem he has a conversation with Luofu on behalf of/instead of the governor. In the earlier poem, Luofu is not afraid to confront the governor and even "steps forward" (*qian* 前) when she speaks up. Here she acts with modesty and restraint, with "respectful kneeling" (*chang gui* 長跪), while responding to the unsolicited invitation.[54] The poem also ends with Luofu's monologue:

使君自有婦	The lord governor has a wife of your own,
賤妾有鄙夫	And I, your humble servant, have a lowly husband.
天地正厥位	Heaven and earth give each their proper place.
願君改其圖	I hope you will, my lord, change your plans.

Luofu rejects the governor with modesty (referring to herself humbly with "*jian*" 賤 and "*bi*" 鄙) and Confucian ritual propriety (comparing the relationship of husband–wife with that of heaven–earth) and leaves out all the elaborate bragging about her husband's appearance and demeanor. Despite its terseness, her rejection is much firmer and more convincing than it is in "Mulberries by the Path." In sum, the Luofu of "Mulberries by the Path" is constantly "stepping forward": she steps forward into a public space; she steps

53 Allen, "From Saint to Singing Girl," p. 329.

54 Although the character "*gui*" 跪 refers to a sitting position and does not necessarily indicate the person's subservient status as in later times, it is nonetheless a gesture of respect and submission.

forward toward the sensualizing male gaze; and she steps forward again to face and talk to the governor. In contrast, Fu Xuan's Luofu keeps "stepping back" to avoid exposure and confrontation: she steps back from the public space into a locked chamber; she steps back from the clerk bearing the governor's invitation; and eventually she steps back from illicit desire and the male gaze. All the "stepping back" constitutes the poet's attempt to gain "access to truth and conviction" as Fried describes. Yet it must be noted here that it is not "truth and conviction" about the woman herself, but only as they are perceived by the male literati author, Fu Xuan. While gaining a voice and the "subjectivity" of a proper and loyal wife, Luofu loses her power to manipulate her beholders and to control the game of seduction.

The following story about the composition of "Mulberries by the Path" is from Cui Bao's 崔豹 (fl. 290–306) *Gujin zhu* 古今註 (Commentary on the past and present):

> 《陌上桑》者，出秦氏女子。秦氏，邯鄲人，有女名羅敷，為邑人千乘王仁妻。仁後為趙王家令。羅敷出采桑於陌上，趙王登臺見而悅之，因置酒欲奪焉。羅敷巧彈箏，乃作《陌上桑》之歌以自明，趙王乃止。

> "Mulberries by the Path" was written by a woman from the house of Qin. The house of Qin originated in Handan and had a daughter named Luofu, who was married to Wang Ren, her fellow townsman from Qiancheng. Wang Ren later served Prince Zhao as his Household Provisioner. When Luofu went out to pick mulberry leaves by the path, Prince Zhao saw her from a terrace and took delight in her. Thereupon he prepared a banquet and wanted to take her by force. Luofu was skillful at playing the zither, therefore she composed the song "Mulberries by the Path" to elucidate herself. Prince Zhao then stopped.[55]

This account provides many details that are not found anywhere else that locate Luofu within a social and familial structure and justify her exposure to male beholders. She has a husband with a name and an official position.

55 *XianQin Han Wei Jin Nanbeichao shi* 1.259. Allen follows the Tang scholar Wu Jing 吳競 (670–749) to believe that this passage "clearly is not a reference to the poem ('Mulberries by the Path') at all," in "From Saints to Singing Girls," p. 326, note 7. But the story has too many common elements from the ballad to be considered irrelevant. There is also no (mention of) other "Mulberries by the Path" in received texts that better matches Cui Bao's account. I am inclined to read this account as a new interpretation of "Mulberries by the Path" rather than about a completely different poem.

The husband's position as Prince Zhao's household provisioner conveniently explains her encounter with the prince. There is no viewing crowd in the "path" (*moshang* 陌上) where she picks mulberry leaves. Luofu does not intend to attract the attention of beholders but is accidentally spotted by the prince from a high terrace. This setup also indicates that Luofu, absorbed with her sericultural duties, could not have noticed the presence of the sensualizing gaze. This contextual story fixed the problem of Luofu's *self-conscious and theatrical* display of her beauty, at the expense of deviating from the source poem in certain details. More importantly, the account describes the poem as Luofu's self-elucidation (*ziming* 自明), turning the focus of representation from Luofu's external beauty to her subjectivity. Compared with the mulberry-picking girls in Han *fu* and the *yuefu* ballad, these 3rd-century reconstructions portray a woman who is seen, as opposed to a woman who intentionally exhibits herself. Readers are encouraged to identify with the woman and to sympathize with her thoughts, rather than to identify with her male beholder(s) in the poem and to sexualize her body.

3 The Woman in a Tower: The Emergence of the Sympathetic Gaze

In addition to the genre of *yuefu*, the theatrical display of female beauty under the male gaze is common among the so-called old poems (*gushi*), five-syllable poems traditionally dated to the Eastern Han.[56] One example is the second of the "Nineteen Old Poems" (Gushi shijiushou 古詩十九首) (hereafter Poem II), a series of anonymous poems preserved in the *Wen xuan*:

青青河畔草	Green, green is the grass by the riverside,
鬱鬱園中柳	Lush are willows in the garden.
盈盈樓上女	Lovely is the woman in a tower,
皎皎當窗牖	Shining and bright, she sits in front of the window.

56 The distinction between *yuefu* and "old poems" is not definitive. There are considerable overlaps between the two categories and scholars have argued that at least part of the "Nineteen Old Poems" are performative texts and belong to the *yuefu* tradition. Allen believes they should be considered as part of the *yuefu* genre in terms of intratextuality; see Allen, *In the Voice of Others*, p. 98. Daniel Hsieh, "The Origin and Nature of the 'Nineteen Old Poems'," *Sino-Platonic Papers* 77 (1998): 1–49, holds a similar view. Owen believes that "old poems" and *yuefu* poems are "one poetry": Owen, *The Making of Early Chinese Classical Poetry*, p. 73. Tian, in "Woman in the Tower," shows that performativity is the key attribute of the "Nineteen Old Poems."

娥娥紅粉妝	Putting on beautiful makeup with red rouge,
纖纖出素手	She shows her fair and slender hands.
昔為倡家女	In the past she was a girl of a singer's family;
今為蕩子婦	Now she is the wife of a wandering man.
蕩子行不歸	The wandering man left and did not return;
空床難獨守	It is hard for her to keep the bed empty.[57]

The poem describes a game of seduction between the woman in a tower and the speaker gazing at her from below. Like Luofu in "Mulberries by the Path," the woman deliberately exhibits her charm to her beholder through the open window. Their interaction is loaded with strong erotic tension. Interestingly, the fifth poem from the same series (hereafter Poem V) features another woman in a tower and someone standing underneath:

西北有高樓	To the northwest stands a tall tower,
上與浮雲齊	its top is level with drifting clouds.
交疏結綺窗	Its windows are meshed and latticework,
阿閣三重階	with eaves all around, three flights of stairs.
上有弦歌聲	From above came song and the sound of a zither,
音響一何悲	how sad the echoes are!
誰能爲此曲	Who could make this song?
無乃杞梁妻	It must be Qiliang's wife![58]
清商隨風發	The clear *shang* spread with the wind,
中曲正徘徊	and then they faltered, mid-melody;
一彈再三歎	each strumming is followed by three sighs,
慷慨有餘哀	impassioned and filled with lingering melancholy.
不惜歌者苦	I do not care that the singer feels pain,
但傷知音稀	What hurts is that few understand the tune.[59]

57 *Wen xuan* 29.1344; *XianQin Han WeiJin Nanbeichao shi* 1.329.

58 The story of Qiliang's wife is first told in the *Zuo zhuan*, which only mentions the death of her husband on the battlefield. More details of the story appear in *Shuo yuan* 說苑 (Garden of talks) and *Lienü zhuan*, both compiled by Liu Xiang 劉向 (*c.*77–6 BCE), including that she cried so hard over Qiliang's death that the city wall collapsed and that she threw herself in a river afterward. See Yang Bojun, *Chunqiu Zuo zhuan zhu* 春秋左傳註 (Beijing Zhonghua shuju, 1981), pp. 1084–85.

59 "*Zhiyin*" alludes to the celebrated friendship between Yu Boya 俞伯牙 and Zhong Ziqi 鐘子期. Boya was an extraordinary zither player and only Ziqi could understand the subtle meaning in his music. When Ziqi passed away, Boya broke his zither and vowed never to play again, for no one could truly appreciate his music anymore. See Lü Buwei 呂不韋 (d. 253 BCE), *Lüshi chuqiu* 呂氏春秋 (Beijing: Zhonghua shuju, 1954) 14.740.

願爲雙鴻鵠	I wish we could become two swans,
奮翅起高飛	to fly with great wingbeats high and away.[60]

Poems II and V are received very differently in the tradition. Poem II has been read as a satire (*ci* 刺) against morally corrupt people, whereas Poem V has been seen as an allegory of a loyal minister's lament over his ruler's failure to recognize his talents. Chen Zuoming 陳祚明 (1623–1674) commented on the woman's behavior in Poem II: "facing the window and showing her hands, wherein the satire is obvious" 當窗出手，諷刺顯然.[61] Li Shan took the "northwest" (*xibei* 西北) in the beginning of the poem as a reference to the ruler and stated that Poem V "illustrates that people with great talents do not get illustrious positions in office. Those who know their men are rare" 此篇明高才之人，仕宦未達，知人者稀也.[62] The reason for these polarized responses lies in the treatment of the object–beholder dynamic in each poem.

In his *Gushi shijiushou dinglun* 古詩十九首定論(Definitive discussions on the "Nineteen Old Poems"), the late 17th-century literary critic Wu Qi 吳淇 gives a detailed analysis of Poem II starting from the first two couplets, which "introduce the woman in the tower by what the poet sees" 以所見興起樓上女.[63] The order in which various objects are described in the poem mirrors how they appear to the beholder. His eyes are first drawn by the view of green grasses on the riverbank; as the thick green spreads onto the willows, his vision is directed into a private garden. Gazing upwards beyond the tops of the willow branches, the beholder notices a lovely woman standing by a window in a tower. Behind this sequence of depiction is the male gaze seeking its object. The green and lush scenery of spring adds strong sexual connotations. Wu Qi notes that the woman is clearly aware of herself being the object of the male gaze:

> 其興趣全在起手"青青"二句，振起一篇精神，分明從作者眼中拈出，卻又似於女之眼中拈出，分明從作者眼中虛擬女之意中，卻又似女之意中眼中之感，恰有符於作者之眼中意中，真有草蛇灰線之妙也。
>
> The [poem's] flavor lies entirely in the beginning couplet, which initiates the spirit of the whole piece. It obviously depicts what is in the author's

60 *Wen xuan* 29.1345; *XianQin Han Wei Jin Nanbeichao shi* 1.330. I use Owen's translation in *An Anthology of Chinese Literature*, pp. 259–60, with modifications.

61 Sui Shusen 隋樹森 (1906–1989), *Gushi shijiushou jishi* 古詩十九首集釋 (Beijing: Zhonghua shuju, 1955) 2.4.

62 *Wen xuan* 29.1345.

63 *Gushi shijiushou jishi* 3.10.

> eyes, yet also seems to depict what is in the woman's eyes. The poet is clearly speculating on what the woman thinks, but what the woman feels and sees seems to match the poet's observation and thoughts. This couplet indeed achieves the marvelous effect of "a snake in the grass [leaving] a trace of ash."[64]

A snake leaves a faint but visible trace after crawling through the grass. The expression *caoshe huixian* 草蛇灰線 is used in traditional literary criticism to praise a writer's supreme literary skill in conveying deeper meaning through subtle hints. According to Wu Qi, the woman is not simply sharing the alluring spring view with her beholder but is also expressing highly sensual intent (*yi* 意) to him through seductive glances. The woman's activities by the window in lines 3–6—applying makeup and exposing her hands—are self-consciously theatrical displays of the female body. The window (*chuangyou* 窗牖) assumes the function of the "stage" for her performance. Next, Wu Qi gives a rather humorous summary of the erotic tension between the two, using the keyword "*jian*" (to see 見) multiple times:

> 樓下之人，既見河畔有草，園中有柳；從樓牕之中，見有弄妝之女；彼樓上女豈不由窗牖中見草之青青於河畔，柳之鬱鬱於園中乎？故此青青鬱鬱者，在作者之見界中，亦在此女之見界中，一片艷陽景物，撩撩逗逗，在旁人猶自難堪，況空床蕩子之婦，自幼出身於倡家者乎？此不必更寫入此女眼中，而即可懸擬其意中矣。

> The person under the tower has already seen the grass at the riverbank and willows in the garden. He has, through a window in the tower, also seen a woman applying makeup. How, then, could the girl in the tower not have seen, also through the window, the green grass by the river and lush willows in the garden? Therefore the greenness and lushness are in the eyes of both the poet and the woman. Such an alluring and provocative view on a bright spring day is hard to bear even for bystanders, not to mention a wandering man's wife born to a singer's family who sleeps in an empty bed! The poet does not need to write what the woman sees, and [*we*] can already speculate what is going on in her mind.[65]

Wu attributes the strong erotic undertone to the "seeing" or "gazing" on both sides of the window. The speaker sustains his own viewpoint throughout the

64 Ibid.
65 Ibid. 3.11.

poem and feels no urge to explore the woman's thoughts or emotions. The poem's last two couplets could be read in multiple ways. I translated it as the speaker's speculation of the woman's identity, but they could also be her own words. In fact, the 8th-century encyclopedia *Chuxue ji* 初學記 (A primer for beginners) cites a version of the poem with the line "she says she was a girl of a singer's family, / now she is married to a wandering man" 自云倡家女，嫁為蕩子婦.[66] Either way, the woman's exposure to a beholder gives rise to illicit desire. The last line leaves open the question of her chastity and gives room for erotic expectation. As in "Mulberries by the Path," the woman is represented as a pure object of male sensual desire. Readers are invited to take the perspective of the beholder and project their fantasy on the woman. The subject of Wu Qi's final sentence ("we") includes the speaker in the poem as well as the poem's audience. Even if the last four lines of Poem II are taken as the woman's own articulation, her speech defines her as a former performer and the wife of a wanderer (note that the speaker may well be a wanderer himself) who longs for someone to share her bed and fill in for her absent husband. Like Luofu's final monologue in "Mulberries by the Path," this speech provokes, rather than stops, the sensualizing gaze and desire.

Wu Qi compares the poem with Wang Changling's 王昌齡 (*c.*698–757) quatrain "Boudoir Resentment" (Guiyuan 閨怨):

閨中少婦不曾愁	In her boudoir a young wife has never felt sorrow,
春日凝妝上翠樓	On a spring day, she puts on elaborate makeup and climbs the emerald tower.
忽見陌頭楊柳色	Suddenly she catches sight of the color of willows by the path,
悔教夫婿覓封侯	and regrets letting her husband seek fame and office.[67]

The poem is reminiscent of Poem II in many ways, but there are a few notable differences. In Wang's poem, a lonely wife's observation of a spring scene triggers a very proper sentiment—longing for her absent husband—rather than a desire and welcome for a temporary companion. Most importantly, the woman is completely occupied with the longing and unaware of the presence of another person, as Wu Qi duly observes: "the color of willows is written from the viewpoint of the young wife and not from that of the poet" 此柳色寫入少

66 Xu Jian 徐堅 (659–729), ed., *Chuxue ji* (Beijing: Zhonghua shuju, 1962) 19.457.

67 *Quan Tang shi* 全唐詩 (Beijing: Zhonghua shuju, 1960) 143.1446.

婦眼中，不從作者眼中寫也.[68] The poet erases all traces of a beholder in the world of presentation and makes it self-contained and closed to the outside world. Like Cao Zhi's "Song on a Beauty," the poem also turns reflective toward the end by assuming the woman's viewpoint.

Wu Qi's discussion of Poem v also takes up the issue of beholding and perspective:

> 此亦不得於君之詩。自托於歌者，然不於歌者口中寫之，卻於聽者口中寫之，且於遙聽未面之人口中寫之。
>
> This is also a poem about not being recognized by the ruler. The poet entrusts his feelings to the singer. But he writes in the voice of the listener, not the singer. Furthermore, he writes in the voice of someone listening from afar and never seeing the singer's face.[69]

The keyword is "someone listening from afar and never seeing the singer's face" 遙聽未面之人. The first two couplets of Poem II establish an active beholder by tracing the movement of his gaze. In contrast, the first two couplets of Poem v hide the woman in a soaring tower behind closed windows. The speaker, without seeing her, sympathizes with the sorrow in the music she plays. The woman, absorbed in grief, is also ignorant of the presence of the speaker due in part to the complete obstruction of the view. With no hint of sensuality or transgression, Poem v almost reads like a conscious moral "correction" to Poem II: there is no theatrical portrayal of female beauty; the woman is completely engrossed in her own thoughts; and the speaker identifies emotionally, not erotically, with the woman.

The coexistence of two distinct representations of the woman in a tower confirms Zhong Rong's remark about the "Nineteen Old Poems" being "mixed and heterogeneous" (*zongza* 總雜).[70] Poem v removes the active beholder and his sensualizing gaze from the scene and portrays the woman as completely absorbed in her activities (zither-playing and singing) and thoughts (grief over the death of her husband). The poetic speaker is also presented as engrossed in his emphatic feeling toward the woman. This tactic is taken up by many 3rd-century literati rewritings of the woman in a tower, including a poem by Cao Zhi. Two slightly different versions of this poem are preserved in the *Song shu* as "Poem on Resentment" (Yuan shi 怨詩) and in the

68 *Gushi shijiushou jishi* 3.12.

69 Ibid., 3.14.

70 Cao Xu 曹旭, ed., *Shi pin jizhu* 詩品集註 (Shanghai: Shanghai guji chubanshe, 2011), p. 91.

Wen xuan as "Poem on Seven Sorrows" (Qi ai shi 七哀詩), respectively. Below I translate the *Wen xuan* version:

明月照高樓	The bright moon shines on a high tower,
流光正徘徊	the lingering radiance is still hanging about.
上有愁思婦	Up in the tower there is a woman with grievous thoughts;
悲歎有餘哀	her sad sigh contains endless sorrow.
借問歎者誰	May I ask who is the person sighing?
云是宕子妻	[She] says that she is the wife of a wandering man.
君行踰十年	You, my lord, have left for over ten years,
孤妾常獨棲	and I, your lonely concubine, always stay alone.
君若清路塵	You are like dust on a clean road;
妾若濁水泥	I am like mud in a turbid river.
浮沉各異勢	Rising and sinking, we are each in a different situation;
會合何時諧	when could a meeting be possible?
願爲西南風	I wish to turn into the southwest wind,
長逝入君懷	flying a long way to your bosom.
君懷良不開	Your bosom surely is not open;
賤妾當何依	on whom should I, your humble concubine, depend?[71]

This poem does not explicitly establish a connection to Poem 11 but apparently treats the same subject: a lonely woman in a tower whose husband—also a "wandering man" (*dangzi* 蕩/宕子)—has gone away. The opening lines in Poem 11 describe natural objects in a way that suggests the presence and movement of a beholder's view. In contrast, Cao Zhi's opening couplet uses an impersonal perspective—that of the moonlight—to enter the woman's chamber. The third couplet introduces an interlocutor, whose only role is to bring out the woman's voice for the rest of the poem. If Poem 11 tells us nothing about the woman's inner world, Cao Zhi's poem delves deep and reveals it in her own words. Her deep absorption in thoughts about her husband results in a sudden shift to a direct conversation with him, probably in her imagination, in lines 7–16. The *Song shu* version has an extra final stanza (*jie* 解) at the end:

71 *Wen xuan* 23.1086; *XianQin Han Wei Jin Nanbeichao shi* 1.458–59.

我欲竟此曲	I wish to conclude this song;
此曲悲且長	this song is sad and long.
今日樂相樂	Today we enjoy ourselves together;
別後莫相忘	when we part, please do not forget each other.[72]

Like the blessing for longevity in the *Song shu* version of the "Ballad on a Pond" (they share the line "今日樂相樂"), the final couplet is a typical ending template in *yuefu* poems. Normally they do not have a thematic connection to the rest of the poem, but in this poem they continue the flow of emotion and accentuate the speaker's empathy with the woman. The urging of his friends at the gathering not to forget each other plays on the woman's lament since she was indeed "forgotten" by her husband after they parted ways. In this ending stanza, the voices of the poetic speaker and the woman become one and the same, both yearning for a good match and lasting affection.

Lu Ji's imitation of Poem 11 shows an explicit attempt to correct the original's moral problem:

靡靡江離草	Thick and flourishing are the deerweeds,
熠熠生河側	brilliant and luminous, they grow by the river.
皎皎彼姝女	Bright and pure is the beautiful girl,
阿那當軒織	Graceful and elegant, she weaves in front of the window.
粲粲妖容姿	Splendid are her charming face and demeanor,
灼灼華美色	Dazzling is her lovely complexion.
良人游不歸	My good man has gone traveling and not returned,[73]
偏棲獨隻翼	I dwell in a remote place all by myself.
空房來悲風	Into the empty chamber comes the gloomy wind,
中夜起嘆息	In the middle of the night, I rise and heave a deep sigh.[74]

The first three couplets describe the spring scenery and the woman from an omniscient rather than a personal viewpoint. As Xiaofei Tian points out, the two changes Lu Ji made to the portrayal of the woman, namely, the addition of the weaving activity and removal of her makeup, are morally significant and transform her into a faithful wife.[75] The woman still faces the window,

72 *Song shu* 21.623.

73 "*Liangren*" is a common way to address the husband in poetry.

74 *XianQin Han Wei Jin Nanbeichao shi* 1.687.

75 Tian, "Configuring the Feminine," pp. 108–10.

but instead of exposing her hands to put on makeup—an action indicating her inviting attitude—she occupies them with a wifely duty, weaving, which keeps her eyes concentrated downward. In comparison with her counterpart in Poem 11, she pays no attention to the outside world. The window, the crucial prop for the moral transgression in Poem 11, is still open but has lost its theatrical function. The only link between the inner chamber and the garden or outside world is the impersonal "gloomy wind" blowing into the empty chamber at midnight. No questions are left unanswered about the woman's nightlife. I translate the last two couplets in the voice of the woman, but they could also be the revelation of the woman's thoughts and emotions from a third person viewpoint. Either way, the poetic perspective is turned inward, and empathic understanding takes the place of the sensualizing gaze. Lu Ji's imitation replaces the melodrama between a seductress and a beholder with a lonely wife's lyric self-expression. The woman is given a subjectivity if not yet a voice.

4 Conclusion

In 3rd-century rewritings of earlier female images, the elimination of the theatrical display and sensualizing gaze helps transform women from objects of sensual desire to those of sympathy, and the speaker from the desiring beholder to her empathizer and *zhiyin*. The creation of this new kind of gaze and new kind of object makes the representation of women a moment for lyric reflection and contemplation and justifies it morally. It should be noted that the subjectivity and voice of women were constructed by male writers to reflect their ideas and ideals. Even though it is no longer her body and appearance, the focus of representation is still not her authentic voice or interiority, but something or someone else that she is made to symbolize. An allegorical connection is established between the image of the abandoned woman and that of a loyal and frustrated minister (often the male poet himself), as in Liu Lü's 劉履 (1317–1379) interpretation of Cao Zhi's "Poem on Seven Sorrows":

> 子建與文帝同母骨肉，今乃浮沉異勢，不相親與，故特以孤妾自喻，而切切哀慮也。

> Zijian [Cao Zhi] and Emperor Wen [Cao Pi] were born to the same mother. Now they are in distinctive situations—one is rising and the

> other sinking—and are no longer close. So Cao Zhi deliberately compares himself to a lonely concubine to express his earnest sorrow and worries.[76]

Regardless of its validity, this allegorical reading takes the attention away from the woman and turns her into a metaphoric reference to the poet's life experience and concerns. Her voice does not belong to her but is an echo of the poetic speaker's voice. Ironically, by providing the woman with a literary voice and subjectivity, 3rd-century writers reshaped the dangerous woman in early literature with their own ideas about proper womanly behavior and emotion and made her easily available to project their own thoughts and sentiments in an allegorical way.[77]

---

76 *San Cao ziliao huibian*, p. 121.

77 Mulvey asserts that the scopophilic and narcissistic male gaze are not mutually exclusive and often work simultaneously in cinematic works: Mulvey, "Visual Pleasure and Narrative Cinema," pp. 16–19. In the same vein, the sensualizing and sympathetic male gaze cannot be neatly separated in literary representations of women. What I have shown in this chapter is a general tendency toward a shift of focus from one to the other, rather than a complete replacement. For example, the sensualizing male gaze stands in the center of the portrayal of beautiful women in many poems from the 6th-century southern courts anthologized in the *Yutai xinyong*, as amply demonstrated by Robertson. See Robertson, "Voicing the Feminine," pp. 68–72.

CHAPTER 2

Longing for a Worthy Match: Jian'an Writing about Women and the Beginning of a Poetic Tradition

The inward shift in the representation of women first became a notable phenomenon in the writing of Jian'an literati.[1] Jian'an refers to the reign of the last Han emperor—Emperor Xian 漢獻帝 (r. 189–220)—and is a watershed moment in the history of China. The Han empire, weakened by the combined forces of famines, peasant rebellions, and warlords, was in rapid decline and on the edge of total collapse. Emperor Xian had become the puppet of his minister Cao Cao, who gave orders on his behalf and obtained the title "King of Wei" (Wei wang 魏王) in 216. The once unified Han empire was divided among a few powerful warlords who fought each other for supremacy. Yet this period of war, chaos, and destruction gave rise to one of the most vibrant periods in Chinese literature. An unprecedented flourishing of literary activity brought elevated attention to literary writing (*wen* 文). It was also during the Jian'an period that the genre of five-syllable poetry first became popular among the literati. The success of Jian'an literature had much to do with the patronage of three members of the Cao family: Cao Cao and his sons Cao Pi and Cao Zhi. During the Jian'an period, the Cao courts, which were originally located the city of Xu 許 (in modern-day Xuchang, Henan province) and moved to the city of Ye 鄴 (in modern-day Handan, Hebei province) after 208, became a center of literary activity.[2]

A crucial element of Jian'an literary writing is its court context. Recent scholarship has shed much light on aspects of community building during this period, such as food and feasts, letter writing, and poetry exchanges.[3] It has

---

1 An earlier version of this chapter, which includes a section from Chapter 1, "Women as Objects of the Sensualizing Gaze in Early Court *Fu*," is published as "In Search of a Perfect Match: Jian'an (196–220) Writing about Women and the Formation of a Literati Community," *Nan Nü: Men, Women and Gender in China* 21 (2019): 194–223.

2 For an overview of this period and its cultural and literary significance in Chinese history, see Xiaofei Tian, *The Halberd at Red Cliff: Jian'an and the Three Kingdoms* (Cambridge, MA: Harvard University Asia Center, 2018).

3 Robert Joe Cutter's study of Cao Zhi's symposium (*gongyan* 公宴) poems is among the earliest scholarly attempts to read Jian'an writings in their court group composition context. See Robert Joe Cutter, "Cao Zhi's Symposium Poems," *Chinese Literature: Essays, Articles, Reviews* 6 (1984): 1–32. In a more recent article, Cutter makes the following observation regarding the

 | DOI:10.1163/9789004546455_004

proven fruitful to consider Jian'an literature within the larger network of contemporary intellectual and political environments. This chapter examines how Jian'an writings about women helped build a literary community in a time of chaos and at the same time shaped conventions about the feminine voice in poetry. The collapse of the centralized empire created a new environment for literary composition at the Cao courts, with profound changes in the dynamics between the ruler and the literati as well as in the nature and function of court writing. Jian'an literati reduced the entertaining and performative elements in their writing and turned the imagined beautiful woman from the embodiment of imperial power and privilege into a symbol of their ideal personality and shared values.[4] In Jian'an writing about women, the discourses of male friendship and romantic love are often intertwined and hard to distinguish from each other. Anna Shields argues that friendship crosses the boundary between public and private realms to create a space for equal relations based on shared interest.[5] Friendship resembles romantic love in that it is based on voluntary choice instead of social or moral obligation or unequal power dynamics. It is

---

literary activities in the city of Ye: "Common titles and themes, prefaces to poems and rhapsodies, and letters and other documents regarding circumstances of composition all testify to the existence of a salon-like environment in which Jian'an literati frequently wrote": Cutter, "To Make Her Mine," especially p. 43. Cutter has also discussed the role of food and feasts in creating group identity and cultural memory for the Jian'an poets. See Robert Joe Cutter, "Gastropoetics in the Jian'an Period: Food and Memory in Early Medieval China," *Early Medieval China* 24 (2018): 1–23. In *The Halberd at Red Cliff*, Tian discusses Jian'an writing and community building in its social and historical contexts. The second chapter examines community building in the aspects of food and feast, as well as letters and exchange: Tian, *The Halberd at Red Cliff*, pp. 79–158. Other studies that examine Jian'an writing in its court context include Hsiang-Lin Shih, "Jian'an Literature Revisited: Poetic Dialogues in the Last Three Decades of the Han Dynasty" (PhD diss., University of Washington, 2013); and Christopher Connery, *The Empire of the Text: Writing and Authority in Early Imperial China* (Lanham, MD: Rowman & Littlefield, 1998), pp. 141–72.

4 Borrowing Eve Sedgwick's concept of "male homosocial desire," Rouzer analyses poetry about women written in the 5th- and 6th-century southern courts (later known as the "palace style [*gongti*]," which will be discussed further in Chapter 5) to show how the portrayal of women, either from a spectator's viewpoint or by assuming their own voices, became tools for self-expression and competition in the male political community. See Rouzer, *Articulated Ladies*, pp. 117–56. Competition, rather than community, is at the center of these poems, which forms an interesting contrast to the Jian'an writings examined in this chapter.

5 Anna M. Shields, *One Who Knows Me: Friendship and Literary Culture in Mid-Tang China* (Cambridge, MA: Harvard University Asia Center, 2015), pp. 52–53. Shields also observes that "friendship often assumed greater prominence as a form of social interaction in eras when the dominant political structures were under stress or undergoing significant change" (p. 56). She gives the end of the Eastern Han as an example of such a time.

not uncommon for Jian'an writers to borrow the language of romantic love to write about male friendship.

Jian'an writers' emotional and intellectual identification with the beautiful woman results in the assumption of her voice, especially in their five-syllable poems. Because of a ubiquitous pessimism about the passions (*qing* 情) expressed in Jian'an writings, women's voices in their poems are often characterized by melancholy and lament over the ephemerality of love.

This chapter uses the term "Jian'an literati/writers" to refer to a group of literati who served the Cao family and frequented their courts. This group includes Yang Xiu 楊修 (175–219), Wang Can, Chen Lin 陳琳 (d. 217), Ruan Yu 阮瑀 (d. 217), Liu Zhen 劉楨 (d. 217), Xu Gan 徐幹 (171–218), Ying Yang 應瑒 (d. 217), and Po Qin 繁欽 (d. 218), among others. It also includes the three Caos, especially Cao Pi and Cao Zhi, who were not only hosts and patrons, but also avid participants in literary activity at their courts. The Caos had not yet claimed the throne during the Jian'an period, but they exerted de facto control over state affairs.[6] For the sake of convenience, terms such as "court," "ruler," and "subjects" are used here to discuss literature composed at the parties and gatherings they hosted. Some works discussed in this chapter were written after the Jian'an period, such as Cao Zhi's "*Fu* on the Luo Goddess," and some can only be approximately dated to the Jian'an period. They are included under the umbrella of Jian'an writing primarily because they belong to a shared discourse on women.

1 The Fall of the Empire and a New Environment for Court Writing

As the unified empire declined in the final decades of the Eastern Han, court literary writing changed remarkably in the Jian'an period. Compositions in the forms of *fu* and poetry were still an important component of literary activities at court, but the centralized political setting of earlier times no longer existed. This is clearly shown in the dynamics between the ruler and the court literati. Xie Lingyun 謝靈運 (385–433), writing in the voice of Cao Pi, describes the unprecedented flourishing of group literary composition at the Cao courts in the city of Ye:

6 Cao Cao never made a claim to the throne during his lifetime. After his death in 220, his son Cao Pi forced Emperor Xian of Han to abdicate the throne and became Emperor Wen of the Wei dynasty 魏文帝.

天下良辰美景，賞心樂事，四者難並。今昆弟友朋，二三諸彥，共盡之矣。古來此娛，書籍未見，何者？楚襄王時有宋玉、唐、景，梁孝王時有鄒、枚、嚴、馬，游者美矣，而其主不文；漢武帝徐樂諸才，備應對之能，而雄猜多忌，豈獲晤言之適？

In this world, fine moments and lovely scenes, hearts capable of appreciation and events of delight—these four things are hard to come by conjoined; but with a small group of talented men like my brother and my friends, we have experienced them to the utmost. Since the ancient times joys like ours have never been seen in any record. Why do I say this? At the time of King Xiang of Chu, there were Song Yu, Tang [Le], and Jing [Cuo]. At the time of Prince Xiao of Liang, there were Zou Yang, Mei Sheng, Yan Ji, and Sima Xiangru. Those who went on excursions were indeed wonderful, yet their lords were not themselves literary. Xu Yue and the other talented men at the time of Emperor Wu of the Han were quite competent in responding [to the emperor], and yet their ruler was suspicious and took offense easily, and how could they have felt at ease in face-to-face conversations?[7]

Xie sees two major obstacles to court literary activity. First, rulers who had talented literati at their courts, such as King Xiang of Chu and Prince Xiao of Liang, were not themselves skilled at literary composition and could not fully appreciate its value. Second, the ruler–subject dynamics were not encouraging or nurturing for court literati. In Xie's view, Cao Cao, Cao Pi, and Cao Zhi formed a sharp contrast to earlier rulers, and their encouragement and participation contributed to the great success of Jian'an literature. Similar ideas are stated in the following passage from the *Wenxin diaolong*:

魏武以相王之尊，雅愛詩章；文帝以副君之重，妙善辭賦；陳思以公子之豪，下筆琳琅。並體貌英逸，故俊才雲蒸。

Emperor Wu of Wei [Cao Cao], in his honored capacity of regent, was always fond of poetry. Emperor Wen [Cao Pi], in the important position of the heir apparent, was versed in rhetoric. Prince Chensi [Cao Zhi], with

7 Xie Lingyun, "Imitations of the Crown Prince of Wei's Gathering in Ye" (Ni Wei taizi Ye zhong ji 擬魏太子鄴中集), *Wen xuan* 30.1432–40. I use Tian's translation in *The Halberd at Red Cliff*, p. 31. With an analysis of this preface and individual poems in this series, Tian shows how Xie Lingyun carefully constructs the "Jian'an moment" that best reflects not the historical period, but Xie's own vision of it as a literary and cultural ideal. Tian, *The Halberd at Red Cliff*, pp. 30–58.

> his extraordinary spirit as the son of a prince, wrote in a splendid style. All three of them treated men with outstanding talents with respect, so talented writers gathered around them like vapors and clouds.[8]

In contrast to previous rulers, the Caos were both recipients and contributors of literature composed at their courts. Their dual role, along with the loss of the centralized imperial authority, deeply affected the relationship between the ruler and the literati at their courts. At the Western Han courts, a hierarchy between the ruler—the only audience and recipient—and the court literati, the composers, and the performers, was meticulously maintained and repeatedly stressed. The presentation of court literature was comparable to stage performance, with the ruler observing and supervising from a superior position. Court writers of *fu* were compared, with contempt, to entertainers and jesters and criticized for exerting a negative influence on the emperor.[9] This comparison speaks both to the performance setting of the court literary activity and to the strict hierarchy between its presenter and recipient. But the situation was different at the Cao courts. Lin Wenyue 林文月 goes as far as to say that the Caos created "a general environment of freedom, openness and equality" 自由開放平等的大環境.[10] This "free, open and equal" relationship between the ruler and writers is probably anachronistic and romanticized, yet Lin is right about the unique environment of Jian'an court writing in comparison with earlier times. In the following passage, Cao Pi gives a firsthand depiction of literary gatherings at his court:

> 昔日遊處，行則連輿，止則接席，何曾須臾相失。每至觴酌流行，絲竹並奏，酒酣耳熱，仰而賦詩。

> In days past if we went roaming, we went with our carriages one after another; if we stayed in, we sat on mats placed together. We would not be separated for an instant. Whenever the wine goblets and ladles were

8 *Wenxin diaolong zhu* 文心雕龍註, ed. Fan Wenlan 范文瀾 (Beijing: Renmin wenxue chubanshe, 1962) 9.673.

9 For example, Mei Gao 枚皋 (fl. 128 BCE) laments being treated like a jester: *Han shu* 51.2367. Ban Gu criticizes Mei Gao and Dongfang Shuo 東方朔 for their ungraceful roles at court; see *Han shu* 51.2366 and 64a.2775. Kern argues that in the Western Han, *fu* writers were never thought of as political or moral advisors to the ruler. The goal of "political remonstrance" was a later construction that was retrospectively imposed on early *fu*. See Kern, "Western Han Aesthetics and the Genesis of the *Fu*," pp. 405–07.

10 Lin Wenyue, "Penglai wenzhang Jian'an gu—shilun zhongshiji shitan fenggu zhi shiwei yu fuxing" 蓬萊文章建安骨——試論中世紀詩壇風骨之式微與復興, in *Zhonggu wenxue luncong* 中古文學論叢 (Taipei: Da'an chubanshe, 1989), pp. 1–54, esp. p. 8.

> moving freely, and the strings and bamboos played together, we felt tipsy from the wine and warm about the ears and, lifting our heads, composed poems.[11]

Cao Pi, in the capacity of "the leader of court gentlemen for miscellaneous uses" (*Wuguan zhonglang jiang* 五官中郎將),[12] hosted many gatherings of this kind. Extant Jian'an literary works are mostly products of group compositions on such occasions.[13] The setting of literary writing described here is friendly and relaxed, showing no apparent hierarchical distinction between presenters and recipients. The ruler and his subjects are closely connected, not just by linking carriages (*lianyu* 連輿) or mats (*jiexi* 接席), but also by a common literary experience. The strictly delineated hierarchical structure in early court literature was dissolved as the presenter of literature situated himself side by side with the audience, physically as well as emotionally. The audience was no longer just the ruler but included all the literati present. Meanwhile, with the ruler's active participation in the group composition, the roles of presenter and audience or recipient of literature were no longer fixed. In his "*Fu* on Entertaining Guests" (Yubin fu 娛賓賦), Cao Zhi gives a description of a lively banquet:

辦中廚之豐膳兮	The bountiful foods of the inner kitchen are made;
作齊鄭之妍倡	alluring singing girls from Qi and Zheng perform.
文人騁其妙說兮	Literati spew their marvelous talk,
飛輕翰而成章	set flying light quills and complete compositions.[14]

---

11 Cao Pi, "A Letter to Wu Zhi" (Yu Wu Zhi shu 與吳質書), *Wen xuan* 42.1896–98. I use Cutter's translation in "Cao Zhi's Symposium Poems," p. 5.

12 I follow Charles O. Hucker's *A Dictionary of Official Titles in Imperial China* (Stanford, CA: Stanford University Press, 1985) for the translation of official titles.

13 Many scholars have convincingly proved this aspect of Jian'an literature. See, for example, Cheng Liang-shu 鄭良樹, "Chu ti feng zuo—Cao Wei jituan de fuzuo huodong" 出題奉作——曹魏集團的賦作活動, in *Wei Jin Nanbeichao wenxue lunji* 魏晉南北朝文學論集, ed. Xianggang zhongwen daxue zhongguo yuyan wenxue xi (Taipei: Wenshizhe chubanshe, 1994), pp. 181–290; and Liao Guodong 廖國棟, *Jian'an cifu zhi chuancheng yu tuoxin: yi ticai ji zhuti wei fanwei* 建安辭賦之傳承與拓新：以題材及主題為範圍 (Taipei: Wenjin chubanshe, 2000). More recently, Knechtges provides a thorough examination of the group composition of the Jian'an period in an unpublished article "Group Literary Composition in the Court of Ye in the Later Eastern Han." I would like to thank him for generously giving permission to cite.

14 Cao Zhi, *Cao Zhi ji jiaozhu* 曹植集校註, ed. Zhao Youwen 趙幼文 (Beijing: Renmin wenxue chubanshe, 1984), p. 47. I use Cutter's translation in "Cao Zhi's Symposium Poems," p. 11, with modifications.

Robert Joe Cutter reads Cao Zhi's *fu* as "a kind of literary thank-you note, perhaps written on the spot."[15] The "compositions" (*zhang* 章) in the last line include Cao Zhi's own *fu*. Cao Zhi sees himself as a member of the group of "literati" (*wenren* 文人) attending the banquet, entertaining (*yu* 娱) his fellow literati with his own "marvelous talk" (*miaoshuo* 妙说) and compositions as well as being entertained by others. Cao Zhi portrays court literati in an utterly different light than court jesters. The performative and entertaining function of literature at previous Han courts is replaced by professional performance of music and dance that the ruler and the court literati enjoy together.[16] Clearly, group literary composition in the Cao courts served to form a community that included both the ruler and the court literati.[17] This sense of community contrasts sharply with the emphasis on the ruler's exclusive ownership of experience in earlier court literature. At a time when the Cao family was expanding its political influence by attracting able men—many of them literati—to join their courts, these gatherings served a serious political function beyond mere merrymaking. Lacking established sovereignty, the Caos had to prove their worth to the literati, just as much as the reverse was true.[18] The construction of this literary and political community, therefore, was a collective effort from above as well as below.[19]

---

15 Cutter, "Cao Zhi's Symposium Poems," p. 11.

16 The presence of female entertainers was common at these gatherings, as indicated in many Jian'an poems on this topic. For example, Cao Pi's "Ballad on Grand!" (Shanzai xing 善哉行), Cao Zhi's "I Am Unfortunate" (Qie boming 妾薄命), and "Sitting in the Company of the Crown Prince" (Shi taizi zuo 侍太子坐) all describe female singers and/or dancers at banquets: *XianQin Han Wei Jin Nanbeichao shi* 1.391, 436, and 450.

17 Cao Pi was the first person to group the literati in his "A Discourse on Writing" (Lunwen 論文) and to create the notion of the "Seven Masters of Jian'an" (*Jian'an qizi* 建安七子), in *Wen xuan* 52.2270–72. A translation and close analysis of the essay can be found in Stephen Owen, ed. and trans., *Readings in Chinese Literary Thought* (Cambridge, MA: Harvard University Asia Center, 1992), pp. 57–72. Almost all contemporary accounts of their group activities mention writing and reciting literary works.

18 Many Jian'an writers served other warlords before switching allegiance to the Caos. For example, Chen Lin was Yuan Shao's secretary, and Wang Can served Liu Biao 劉表 (d. 208). Both surrendered to Cao Cao after the death of their previous lords. For a study of the political trajectories of Jian'an writers as shown in their writings, see Shih, "Jian'an Literature Revisited." Speaking of the power dynamic at the Jian'an courts, Tian notes that "although in the end the vassals must show deference to their lord, the lord depends on his vassals as much as they on him, and there are always different sources of power that compete and negotiate with each other": Tian, *The Halberd at Red Cliff*, p. 149.

19 There was still a strict hierarchy between rulers and subjects, as well as between subjects of different official ranks. And the relationships among the Jian'an literati, like their relationships with the Caos, were not always as harmonious and friendly as their writings suggest. In fact, the situation of literati in their courts, especially Cao Cao's, was often

Cao Zhi's "*Fu* on Entertaining Guests" also highlights a new, textual aspect of court composition in the Jian'an period with the mention of writing literary works with "flying light quills." This textuality distinguishes Jian'an group composition from the oral performativity of early court *fu*. According to the *Sanguo zhi*, when the construction of the Bronze Bird Terrace (*tongque tai* 銅雀臺) was completed, Cao Cao asked his sons to compose *fu* to commemorate the occasion:

> 時鄴銅雀台新成，太祖率諸子登台，令各為賦。植援筆立成，太祖甚異之。
>
> At that time, the construction of the Bronze Bird Terrace at Ye had just been completed. Taizu [Cao Cao] led his sons to ascend the terrace and ordered them to each compose a *fu*. Cao Zhi took his brush and finished in no time. Taizu greatly marveled at him.[20]

It is not clear whether Cao Zhi's *fu* was orally recited on the occasion, but it was perceived and preserved as a written text. Jian'an literati often praised each other's ability to improvise, in front of a watching crowd and within a short time span, lengthy and high-quality texts in writing. The above account, for example, was meant to prove Cao Zhi's talent of "writing entire chapters promptly" (*xiabi chengzhang* 下筆成章).[21] Cao Zhi's dirge for Wang Can notes Wang's similar talent: "Whenever he uttered words, he could [immediately] chant them; whenever he put words down, they came in chapters" 發言可詠，下筆成篇.[22] This new attention to textual aspects of court literary composition is significant, especially in the genre of *fu*. As a form of oral performance, the creation of *fu* at the Western Han courts, like singing and dancing,

dangerous and turbulent, as indicated by the deaths of Kong Rong 孔融 (153–208) and the Ding brothers (Ding Yi 丁廙 [d. 220] and Ding Yi 丁儀 [d. 220]). This chapter is more interested in the shifting *ideas* about court writing and its functions. There were closer and slightly more equal relationships between the rulers and the court literati in terms of the composition and enjoyment of literature, especially with Cao Pi and Cao Zhi.

20 *Sanguo zhi* 19.557.

21 Ibid.

22 Cao Zhi, "Dirge for Wang Zhongxuan" (Wang Zhongxuan lei 王仲宣誄), *Wen xuan* 56.2435. This line might indicate that an oral recitation preceded the textual rendition. This does not mean that oral recitation of *fu* did not exist at the Cao courts, as Cao Pi's account of literary banquets shows otherwise. Cao Zhi's lines from the "*Fu* on Entertaining Guests" may also indicate that the "completion of compositions" happened after an oral presentation of "marvelous talk."

was meant for temporary enjoyment and not expected to hold a lasting value beyond its designated occasion and audience. In contrast, written works have permanent appeal and the potential for a wider audience once they enter textual transmission. Building on extant ideas, Cao Pi discusses the power of writing in achieving posthumous immortality (*buxiu* 不朽) for the writer in "A Discourse on Writing":

> 蓋文章經國之大業，不朽之盛事。年壽有時而盡，榮樂止乎其身，二者必至之常期，未若文章之無窮。是以古之作者，寄身於翰墨，見意於篇籍，不假良史之辭，不託飛馳之勢，而聲名自傳於后。
>
> I would say that literary works are the supreme achievement in the business of state, a splendor that does not decay. A time will come when a person's life ends; glory and pleasure go no further than this body. To carry both to eternity, there is nothing to compare with the unending permanence of the literary work. So writers of ancient times entrusted their persons to ink and the brush, and let their thoughts be seen in their compositions; depending neither on a good historian nor on momentum from a powerful patron, their reputations are handed down to posterity on their own force.[23]

The lasting influence of writing (*wen*) depends on its textuality. Among the three means to attain immortality listed in the *Zuo Zhuan*, "to establish words" (*liyan* 立言) occupies the last position, after "to establish deeds" (*ligong* 立功) and "to establish virtue" (*lide* 立德).[24] Cao Pi elevated the significance of writing for its unique ability to exert a longer-term and wider influence on the generations to come. Cao Pi's recognition of the power of writing may also have to do with the premature death of his many talented literati friends in the devastating plague of 217. He laments the brevity of their lives in contrast to their textual legacy in a letter to Wu Zhi 吳質:

> 間者歷覽諸子之文, 對之抆淚，既痛逝者，行自念也。…… 觀其姓名，已為鬼錄。追思昔遊，猶在心目，而此諸子，化為糞壤，可復道哉！

23 *Wen xuan* 52.2271. I use Owen's translation in *Readings in Chinese Literary Thought*, pp. 66–69.

24 Yang Bojun, *Chunqiu Zuo zhuan zhu*, p. 1088.

> At leisure I peruse all writings of those gentlemen and shed tears over them. I am saddened by the deceased and the thought of myself [i.e. my own death] … I look at their names, and they are already on the register of the dead. I recall our past excursions, and they are still in my mind and eyes. But those gentlemen have already turned into dung and soil. How could I say this again![25]

Besides expressing grief over their untimely death, this passage also testifies to the lasting effect of these "gentlemen's" writing on their reader(s): the emotional power is still present even in the writers' absence. Once it was written down, court literature's audience was greatly extended beyond a lone ruler, or those who were present, to a much larger readership including outsiders and latecomers. In this sense, the composition of court literature was no longer meant exclusively for the ruler and instead spoke to a broader audience. This textual aspect of Jian'an literature had a significant impact on its representation of women. It no longer focused solely on satisfying or persuading an individual (ruler) and became a means for lyrical self-expression and community building.

2 The Representation of Women as a Means to Construct a Literary Community

The quest for divine women or women with divine beauty was still a popular topic in Jian'an court writing. Yang Xiu, Chen Lin, Ying Yang, Wang Can, and Cao Zhi all wrote *fu* on the goddess. Unfortunately, with the exception of Cao Zhi's "*Fu* on the Luo Goddess," which is preserved intact in the *Wen xuan*, all other pieces survive only in fragments through their inclusion in the *Yiwen leiju*.[26] Although it is difficult to date them precisely, close examination suggests they are products of the new environment of group composition at the Cao courts.[27] They share distinctive traits in theme, structure, and content. Among the five surviving *fu* on the goddess, Cao Zhi's was written at a much later date, during the Huangchu 黃初 era (220–226), after the other writers had

25 Cao Pi, "A Letter to Wu Zhi," in *Wen xuan* 42.1897.

26 *Yiwen leiju* 79.1351–52.

27 Cheng Liang-shu has ordered all extant Jian'an *fu* writings chronologically. But he assumes that *fu* on the same topic or with the same title were composed on the same occasion, which is likely but not certain. See Cheng, "Chu ti feng zuo—Cao Wei jituan de fuzuo huodong," pp. 203–08. At the very least, Cao Zhi's *fu* on the goddess could not have been written on the same occasion as Chen Lin's.

already passed away. Based on the preface to Chen Lin's *fu*, scholars usually treat the remaining four as composed in a group during Cao Cao's campaign against Liu Biao 劉表 (d. 208) in 208. The *fu* of Chen Lin begins by introducing the background of its composition:

漢三七之建安	In the three-seven year of the Han dynasty, during the Jian'an reign,[28]
荊野蠢而作仇	the barbarians of Jing are impudent and become foes.[29]
贊皇師以南假	Joining the southern campaign of the imperial troop,
濟漢川之清流	I am going to cross the limpid current of the Han River.
慼詩人之攸嘆	Moved by the chant of the [*Shijing*] poet,
想神女之來游	I imagine the goddess coming to roam.[30]

This short "preface" contains something strikingly new compared with previous *fu* on the goddess. Although many early court *fu* begin with a narrative frame for the extensive elaboration on the goddess, the opening plot is always integrated into the world of literary representation. For example, both *fu* on the goddess attributed to Song Yu begin by introducing all the main characters (the speaker Song Yu, his audience the king, and the goddess) and establishing the mediated, performative setting in which Song Yu describes the goddess to the king. There is no clear demarcation between the world of the framing narrative and the main body of the *fu* representation.

The beginning lines of Chen Lin's *fu*, in contrast, set a clear boundary between the represented world in which a goddess comes to roam and the historical moment of the *fu*'s composition: the military campaign in 208. Regardless of whether we take the date and place literally, this preface is given in a matter-of-fact tone from the first-person perspective and avoids a

28 Yu Shaochu 俞紹初 believes that "*sanqi*" is an error for "*shiqi*" 十七 (seventeen). The seventeenth year of Jian'an is 208, the year that Cao Cao led his campaign against Liu Biao. See Yu Shaochu, ed., *Jian'an qizi ji* 建安七子集 (Beijing: Zhonghua shuju, 2005), p. 410. The phrase appears in the biography of Lu Wenshu 路温舒 in the *Han shu*. According to the biography, Lu studied astrology and observed that the fate of the Han dynasty was determined by "*sanqi*," that is, every 210 years. It is approximately a "*sanqi*" from the beginning of the Western Han to the Wang Mang 王莽 (45 BCE–23 CE) usurpation, and another "*sanqi*" after that to the end of the Eastern Han. See *Han shu* 51.2372.

29 This is an allusion to the lines from Mao 178 "Cai qi" 采芑 (Gathering white millet): "Impudent are you, barbarians of Jing; / to a great state you have become foes" 蠢爾荊蠻/大邦為讎. See *Maoshi Zhengyi* 10.755.

30 *Yiwen leiju* 79.1351.

performative setting. The imaginary nature of Chen Lin's writing is marked explicitly with the character "*xiang*" 想 (imagine). His composition is initiated not by a royal command but by an inspiration (*gan* 感) from old texts, which likely includes Song Yu's *fu* on the goddess and Mao 9, "Hanguang" 漢廣 (The Han river is broad), which much of Han exegesis takes to be about a failed courtship of a mysterious woman.[31] By placing his *fu* in a textual tradition rather than the tradition of court performance, Chen Lin identifies himself as an author instead of a performer or entertainer and attaches greater cultural weight to his *fu*. Unlike earlier court *fu* on the goddess, his was not a means to satisfy the ruler's desire to meet the goddess, but a result of the writer's own reading experience and literary imagination. It frames the speaker's encounter with the goddess as a personal experience, with no intention to entertain, impress, or persuade. The lack of an intended (royal) audience in the representation changes its structure from a mediated triangle (object–speaker–audience) to a one-on-one, direct relationship (object–speaker). It results in a very different kind of interaction between the poet and the goddess:

申握椒以貽予	Repeatedly [she] holds the fragrant grass to me as a gift;
請同宴乎奧房	and asks me to dine with her in the secluded chamber.[32]

The presentation or exchange of gifts in early literature often indicates love and affection.[33] Without someone in a powerful position initiating and overseeing the *fu* representation, the object of the goddess's romantic interest is none other than her seeker—the poet. The goddess is no longer unfathomable.

---

31 *Maoshi Zhengyi* 1.63–67; Zhang Shubo 張樹波, ed., *Guofeng jishuo* 國風集說 (Shijiazhuang: Hebeirenmin chubanshe, 1993), pp. 83–91. For a study of the Han exegesis of the poem, see Qiulei Hu, "Reading the Conflicting Voices: An Examination of the Interpretative Traditions about 'Han guang'," *Chinese Literature: Essays, Articles and Reviews* 34 (2012): 1–13.

32 *Yiwen leiju* 79.1351.

33 For a detailed study of the presentation of love tokens in early literature, see Madeline Spring, "The Presentation of Love Tokens in the *Shih Ching* and *Ch'u Tz'u*," *Tamkang Review* 9, no. 1 (1978): 1–31. In the story about Zheng Jiaofu's 鄭交甫 encounter with two goddesses in the Han River, the failure to exchange gifts signifies his unsuccessful tryst. A version of this story is preserved in the *Liexian zhuan* 列仙傳 (Biographies of immortals) attributed to Liu Xiang 劉向 (*c.*77–6 BCE); see Wang Xianqian 王先謙 (1842–1918), ed., *Shi sanjia yi jishu* 詩三家義集疏 (Shanghai: Shanghai guji chubanshe, 1995), p. 51. The story was used to interpret "Hanguang" in Han dynasty exegesis. For further discussion of the motif of gift exchange in *Shijing* poems, see Hu, "Reading the Conflicting Voices," p. 7.

The *fu* not only reveals her admiration for the poet but also provides a reason for it:

既嘆爾以豔采	[The goddess] admires you [the poet] for your alluring words.
又悅我之長期	she [the goddess] also is pleased by my [the poet's] long waiting.[34]

The goddess is attracted to the speaker's superior literary skills and his enduring faith. There is ambiguity in the first line regarding who is admiring whom. The subject of the second line is no doubt the goddess, because it is the poet who is waiting for her. The expression "not only ... but also" (*ji ... you* 既 … 又) typically connects two lines that maintain the same subject unless explicitly marked otherwise, so the subject of the first line should be the goddess as well. The first line is in the goddess's voice speaking to the poet, directly addressing him with the second-person pronoun "*er*" 爾 (you). Furthermore, the phrase "*yancai*" 豔采 (alluring words) commonly refers to the beauty of *fu* rhetoric.[35] It forms an interesting parallel to the "alluring demeanors" (*yanzi* 豔姿) used earlier in the same piece to describe the goddess. Now the poet and the goddess are both "alluring" (*yan* 豔), albeit in different ways. The lovely goddess is the creation of the poet's literary imagination, so her beauty is the external manifestation of the poet's talent. This accounts for the ambiguity in the references: the goddess and the poet are indeed one and the same. If the goddess is a symbol of the ruler's absolute authority and beyond the poet's reach in earlier court *fu*, here she has become the perfect match for the poet.

Almost all Jian'an *fu* on the goddess establish an identification between the poet and the goddess based on mutual recognition and appreciation—so much so that the portrayal of the goddess is at times indistinguishable from that of the poet.[36] In Wang Can's "*Fu* on the Goddess," for example, after an

34 *Yiwen leiju* 79.1352.

35 For example, "Wearing the splendid feather of literary embellishment; / completing the emerald radiance of beautiful words" 服文藻之華羽/被豔采之翠英, in Jin dynasty literati Cai Hong's 蔡洪 "*Fu* on Fighting Teals" (Dou fu fu 鬥鳧賦), in *Yiwen leiju* 91.1582. "With his talents he has exhausted beautiful words; / with his pen he has used up charming rhetoric" 才罄豔采/筆盡麗辭, in Jiang Yan's 江淹 (444–505) "Dirge for Emperor Taizu of Qi" (Qi Taizu gao huangdi lei 齊太祖高皇帝誄), in Hu Zhiji 胡之驥 (16th/17th century), ed., *Jiang Wentong ji huizhu* 江文通集彙註 (Beijing: Zhonghua shuju, 1984) 10.353.

36 Wai-yee Li observes a "confusion of the human and the divine-numinous realms" in Cao Zhi's "*Fu* on the Luo Goddess"; see Li, *Enchantment and Disenchantment*, p. 35.

extravagant depiction of the goddess's stunning appearance, the speaker suddenly turns to describing her "voice":

稱詩表志	She recites the *Shi* to express her intent;
安氣和聲	pacifies the spirit and harmonizes the sound.
探懷授心	She probes her feelings and presents her mind;
發露幽情	and reveals her hidden affection.[37]

There is again ambiguity about the subject of these lines. The context dictates that they describe the goddess, but here she takes the role of a poet to "speak the intent." Compared with Chen Lin's *fu*, the speaker has come even closer to the goddess and gained access to her hidden affection (*youqing* 幽情), further stressing the poet's sympathy for and identification with the goddess. Cao Zhi depicts the Luo goddess in a similar fashion:

嗟佳人之信修	Oh, the fair one, how truly good she is!
羌習禮而明詩	She is well versed in the Rites and understands the *Shi*.[38]

The quest for the goddess in Jian'an *fu*, therefore, is the pursuit of a personal ideal, a sympathetic friend, or an "appreciative mind" (*shangxin* 賞心), as Xie Lingyun states in his preface. The goddess moves beyond being an object of desire to become the exterior manifestation of the poet's literary talent and moral virtue.

As explained earlier, Jian'an court compositions largely abandoned the ruler-centered, mediated structure pervasive in early court literature. The poetic "I," rather than an audience in a superior position, occupies the center of representation. At the Cao courts, this "I" went beyond individual poets and became a collective identity, representing a community of literati (including the Caos themselves) who arrived from various places to serve a rising political power with literary talents and political ambitions. With her extraordinary beauty, poetic talent, and sympathetic mind, the image of the goddess became the perfect embodiment of this community. As literary talent was the primary means by which this community defined itself, the representation of a goddess

37 *Yiwen leiju* 79.1352.

38 *Wen xuan* 19.898. I use Knechtges's translation in *Wen xuan or Selections of Refined Literature*, Vol. 3, p. 361, with modifications.

well versed in literature and admiring of literary skills was an apt means to create a shared identity and common values.[39]

Besides goddesses, mortal women of extraordinary beauty also epitomize talent and virtue in Jian'an writings. The first of Cao Zhi's two poems titled "I Am Unfortunate" describes a pleasant excursion with his fellow literati, during which some charming female entertainers inspire everyone to chant poetry:

想彼宓妃洛河	We imagine Fu Fei of the Luo River;
退詠漢女湘娥	when we return, we chant about the Han-river girls and the Xiang Goddess.[40]

In the second poem, the poet specifically mentions one girl who serves delicious dishes at the banquet:

進者何人齊姜	Who presents them but Lady Jiang of Qi,
恩重愛深難忘	her devotion so strong and love so deep—they're unforgettable.[41]

Some scholars read this "Lady Jiang of Qi" as a hidden reference to Empress Zhen and thereby understand this poem as Cao Zhi's lament for his secret love affair with her.[42] Cutter has convincingly disputed this and other biographical readings of Cao Zhi's writing and traced the creation and development of the legend surrounding the empress.[43] There is, however, something telling about the connection these interpretations, from traditional to modern, all try to make. There is indeed something in common between the Luo goddess and Lady Jiang of Qi. They are both images of beautiful women that Cao Zhi created in his works to symbolize his personal ideal and sympathetic companionship. One should not, however, assign to these women a real historical identity, precisely because of the idealized nature of such images.

---

39 Extant writings by Jian'an literati often mention their literary activities and speak highly of other members' literary talents. For example, Cao Pi's "A Discourse on Writing" appraises individual writers' strengths and weaknesses, while letters exchanged between Wu Zhi, Cao Pi, and Cao Zhi also focus on the literary aspects of their group activities.

40 *XianQin Han Wei Jin Nanbeichao shi* 1.436.

41 Ibid. 1.437.

42 The Qing dynasty critic Zhu Qian believes the poems are about a palace lady who lost imperial favor and became a court performer: *San Cao ziliao huibian*, p. 200. K. P. K. Whitaker identifies the woman as Empress Zhen; see K. P. K. Whitaker, "Tsaur Jyr's Song of the Ill-fated Lady," *Bulletin of the School of Oriental and African Studies, University of London* 17, no. 3 (1955): 526–34, esp. pp. 531–32.

43 Cutter, "The Death of Empress Zhen."

Cao Zhi was not the only Jian'an writer who created female images as sympathetic companions in his works. Cao Pi's "Ballad on Grand!" depicts a beautiful female musician:

有美一人	There is a fair lady,
婉如清揚	delicate and graceful.
妍姿巧笑	Beautiful form, delightful smiles,
和媚心腸	soothe and beguile the heart.
知音識曲	She knows the tune and understands melody,
善為樂方	and is good at making music.
哀弦微妙	Her sorrowful strings are subtle and marvelous,
清氣含芳	the clear air harbors fragrance.
流鄭激楚	Dissolute music of Zheng, the stirring Chu,
度宮中商	play the note *gong*, then strike *shang*.
感心動耳	it stirs my heart and moves my ear,
綺麗難忘	an intricate beauty hard to forget.
離鳥夕宿	The bird, separated, rests for the evening
在彼中洲	on the isle midstream.
延頸鼓翼	It stretches its neck and beats its wings,
悲鳴相求	singing out sadly, seeking.
眷然顧之	With longing I turn to look on it,
使我心愁	making my heart feel grief.
嗟爾昔人	Ah, you persons of the past—
何以忘憂	how can I forget my cares?[44]

The relationship between the poetic speaker and the woman is compared, through the phrase "*zhiyin*," to Boya and Ziqi's friendship built on mutual understanding and appreciation. The bird metaphor in lines 13–16 brings about familiar ambiguity in the object and subject of the seeking (*qiu* 求). The interpretation is left open because at this point the perspectives of the speaker and the "fair lady" have merged into one. Like most Jian'an *fu* on the quest for the goddess, this "seeking" ends on a grievous note. In the last four lines, the speaker yearns in sorrow for the "persons of the past" (*xiren* 昔人), who are likely the companions he seeks. If the poetic voice is understood as belonging to Cao

44 *XianQin Han Wei Jin Nanbeichao shi* 1.391. I use Owen's translation in *The Making of Early Chinese Classical Poetry*, pp. 125–26, with modifications. Liu Zhen's five-syllable "Poem on the Lord's Feast" (Gongyan shi 公宴詩) describes a musical performance at a banquet with many similar expressions, including the image of birds by the pond and the lingering effect of music as "intricately beautiful and hard to forget" 綺麗不可忘: *XianQin Han Wei Jin Nanbeichao* shi 1.369.

Pi himself, these "persons of the past" might refer to his literary friends who used to frequent his court banquets but who died prematurely in the plague. In the passage from "A Discourse on Writing" quoted earlier, Cao Pi speaks of past gatherings with these friends in the same nostalgic tone and even uses the same word for "the past" (*xi* 昔) in "the past excursion" (*xiyou* 昔遊) when recalling the wonderful time they shared. In "A Letter to Wu Zhi," Cao Pi again invokes the story of Boya and Ziqi to express his grief over the loss of friends "who know the tune":

> 昔伯牙绝弦於鍾期，仲尼覆醢於子路，痛知音之難遇，傷門人之莫逮。
>
> In the past, Boya broke the zither after the death of Zhong Ziqi. Confucius discarded minced meat after the death of Zilu. They were pained by the difficulty of meeting "someone who knows the tune" and lamented that the other disciples could never emulate him.[45]

The sentiment in this passage resonates strongly with the "Ballad on Grand!" Both works could have been inspired by the same grief and longing for lost friends and happy times. Without further information about the compositional background, this cannot be considered the "correct" reading of the poem, but the search for like-minded companions is a common theme in Jian'an writings about women, and the romantic pursuit often leads to a yearning for friendship.

It is also not uncommon for Jian'an literati to apply expressions of romantic love to male friendship, as in Cao Zhi's "Poem Presented to Wang Can" (Zeng Wang Can shi 贈王粲詩):

> 端坐苦愁思 Sitting straight, I am pained by sorrowful thoughts,
> 攬衣起西游 I gather my clothes, get up, and roam to the west.
> 樹木發春華 Trees and bushes bring forth the spring flowers;
> 清池激長流 In the lucid pool, the long currents flow rapidly.
> 中有孤鴛鴦 In the middle there is a lonely mandarin duck.

45 *Wen xuan*, 42.1896. Zilu lost his life in a coup while serving the ruler of Wei 魏. His body was chopped into pieces. Since then Confucius would not eat minced meat to show grief and respect for Zilu's death. Although Zilu was Confucius' disciple, his seniority and blunt personality made him more like an equal to Confucius than a student. Their relationship is quite fitting to this situation: Cao Pi was both a patron/ruler and a friend to the Jian'an literati at his court.

哀鳴求匹儔　Chirping in grief, it seeks a match.
我願執此鳥　I wish to hold this bird,
惜哉無輕舟　What a pity to not have a swift boat!
欲歸忘故道　I want to return but forget the old path;
顧望但懷愁　I turn back to gaze out, and my heart is filled with pain.
悲風鳴我側　The sorrowful wind blows by my side;
羲和逝不留　Xihe gallops always and does not stay.[46]
重陰潤萬物　The double *yin* moisturizes a myriad of things.[47]
何懼澤不周　Why fear the insufficiency of its grace?
誰令君多念　Who makes you worry so much?
自使懷百憂　You let yourself harbor hundreds of anxieties.[48]

The imagery of a lonely mandarin duck seeking its mate in the third couplet strongly calls for a romantic interpretation, which in Cao Zhi's poems is often understood as a plea for political recognition. But because of its title, some scholars view it as a special metaphor for friendship, or even evidence of Cao Zhi's literary creativity and originality.[49] Line 10, "I turn back to gaze out, and my heart filled with pain" 顧望但懷愁, uses the same expression of the poet's romantic feelings about the goddess as Cao Zhi's "*Fu* on the Luo Goddess":

遺情想象　My love remains, and I visualize her appearance in my mind;
顧望懷愁　I turn back to gaze out, and my heart filled with pain.[50]

Similarly, the second poem of Cao Zhi's "Two Poems Sent to Mr. Ying [Ying Qu 應璩]" (Song Yingshi ershou 送應氏二首) combines the description of

46 Xihe is the god of the sun, who drives a chariot through the sky.

47 The "double *yin*" refers to the rain.

48 *XianQin Han Wei Jin Nanbeichao shi* 1.451.

49 For example, Yu Xianhao 郁賢浩 and Zhang Caimin 張采民 comment on this couplet: "Mandarin ducks refer to Wang Can. It is common for pre-modern poets to use the imagery of a pair of mandarin ducks to symbolize the faithful love between a man and a woman. But here Cao Zhi uses it in a novel way and makes a lonely mandarin duck seeking a mate into the analogy of the deep affection between good friends." 鴛鴦，喻王粲。用雌雄鴛鴦形影不離象徵男女之間忠貞不渝的愛情，是古代詩人常用的手法。而這裡另翻新意，用"孤鴛鴦"求偶來比喻好友之間的刻骨相思. In Wu Xiaoru 吳小如, ed., *Han Wei Liuchao shi jianshang cidian* 漢魏六朝詩鑒賞辭典 (Shanghai: Shanghai cishu chubanshe, 1992), p. 276.

50 *Wen xuan* 19.900.

friendship with a wish to transform into "a pair of birds flying side by side" (*biyi niao* 比翼鳥), a symbol of love.[51]

Xiaofei Tian observes "a generalized language of desire" in the expression of the relationship between lord and vassal at this time. She juxtaposes Cao Zhi's "Poem Presented to Wang Can" with Wang Can's "Miscellaneous Poem" to show how this language of desire could add multiple dimensions to the relationship of the two poets, including dominance and submission, friendship and mutual dependency, as well as negotiation and competition.[52] Though this analysis is certainly valid, it is also necessary to note that among these dimensions, the mutual dependency and friendship between the ruler and his subjects is a unique feature of the Jian'an literary community.

Other Jian'an literati applied romantic discourse to male friendship as well. In the poem "Presented to the Leader of Court Gentlemen for Miscellaneous Uses [Cao Pi]" (Zeng Wuguan zhonglang jiang 贈五官中郎將), for example, Liu Zhen writes about his longing for Cao Pi in the language of a wife's yearning for her absent husband:

秋日多悲懷	On an autumn day, I harbor many sorrowful thoughts.
感慨以長嘆	Filled with regretful thoughts, I sigh for a long while.
終夜不遑寐	I cannot sleep all night,
叙意于濡翰	and express my feelings with the soaked brush.
明燈曜閨中	The light lamp illuminates the inner chamber;
清風凄已寒	the clear wind is chilly and cold.
白露塗前庭	White dew covers the front courtyard,
應門重其關	and the front gate is doubly barred.
四節相推斥	Four seasons push each other;
歲月忽已殫	the time is suddenly late.
壯士遠出征	The soldier goes far away for the campaign.
戎事將獨難	The military affair will be extremely difficult.
涕泣灑衣裳	Tears go down and sprinkle my clothes:
能不懷所歡	how can I not miss the person I take delight in?[53]

This is one of four poems Liu Zhen sent to Cao Pi. The setting of the doubly barred (*chong qi guan* 重其關) inner chamber (*guizhong* 閨中), an acute sensitivity to the change of season, the longing for an absent soldier (*zhuangshi*

51 *XianQin Han Wei Jin Nanbeichao shi* 1.454–55.

52 Tian, *The Halberd at Red Cliff*, pp. 148–56.

53 *XianQin Han Wei Jin Nanbeichao shi* 1. 370.

壯士), and the address to "the person I take delight in" (*suohuan* 所歡) all have strong romantic connotations.[54] One may attempt to read Liu Zhen's expression of romantic longing in the allegorical tradition of comparing the subject–ruler relationship to that of wife and husband. Yet this poem describes the relationship between the speaker and her lover as being equal, marked by the informal and intimate address "*suohuan*." The romantic sentiment here can be understood as a metaphor for friendship and personal intimacy, rather than as a hierarchical relationship between and ruler and the subject.[55]

A proud sense of community is vividly present in Jian'an poems on the "lord's feast" and in poems exchanged between members of the literary community (*zengda shi* 贈答詩).[56] The following are some examples:

高會君子堂	We gather in grandeur in the hall of the gentlemen;
並坐蔭華榱	sit together in the shade of the carved rafter.

WANG CAN, "Poem on the Lord's Feast"[57]

穆穆眾君子	Sublime are all these gentlemen;
好合同歡康	friendly and harmoniously, they share the joy and peace.

YING YANG, "Poem on the Lord's Feast"[58]

54 In southern *yuefu* songs, *huan* is a specific reference to the beloved. One can certainly read elements of homosexuality in these expressions, but there is no other extratextual evidence to verify or evaluate this assertion. This discussion only concerns the literary/textual level: the romantic discourse is used to describe the relationship between two men.

55 Tian discusses this poem as another example in which a "generalized language of desire" is used to express the relationship between lord and vassal and maintains that "the perception of femininity is a later, anachronistic one": Tian, *The Halberd at Red Cliff*, p. 152.

56 Connery traces the origin of this kind of literary community to the Eastern Han and discusses them mostly in political terms. See Connery, *The Empire of the Text*, pp. 79–109. Cheng Yu-yu observes a shared sense of pride in literary accomplishments in Jian'an poems on the lord's feast. She argues that Jian'an literati consciously distinguished themselves from other groups at the Cao–Wei courts that served a political or military function. See Cheng Yu-yu, "Shilun gongyanshi zhiyu Yexia wenshi jituan de xiangzheng yiyi" 試論公讌詩之於鄴下文士集團的象徵意義 in *Liuchao qingjing meixue zonglun* 六朝情境美學綜論 (Taipei: Xuesheng shuju, 1996), pp. 171–218. It is, however, hard to draw a definite line between "literary groups" and "political groups," since their members overlap considerably, and literary writing often serves clearly political or military purposes.

57 *XianQin Han Wei Jin Nanbeichao shi* 1.360.

58 Ibid., 383.

志士營世業 The man with high aims is busy with his achievements;
小人亦不閒 the lesser man too is not at leisure.

CAO ZHI, "Poem Presented to Xu Gan" (Zeng Xu Gan shi 贈徐幹詩)[59]

烈士多悲心 The ardent knight has many sad thoughts;
小人媮自閒 the lesser man takes pleasure in his own ease.

CAO ZHI, "Miscellaneous Poem" (Zashi 雜詩) VI[60]

君子通大道 The gentleman understands the Great Way,
無願為世儒 and does not wish to be a mundane scholar.

CAO ZHI, "Poem Presented to Ding Yi" (Zeng Ding Yi shi 贈丁翼詩)[61]

This vein of poetic writing collectively defined a community and its shared values while claiming a superior position for its members in contemporary society. The poems perfectly demonstrate the Confucian idea regarding the social function of poetry found in the *Analects*: "Poetry is the means by which people form groups" (*shi keyi qun* 詩可以群).[62] Some scholars read the last three poems by Cao Zhi as complaints, of his own and on behalf of his friends, about their talents not being recognized and appreciated by the ruler.[63] In the context of group composition at the Cao courts, however, the "lesser men" are often set in contrast with the "gentlemen." In this setting they do not need to

59 Ibid., 451. Some scholars read the expression "*xiaoren*" 小人 (lesser man) in this and the following poems as Cao Zhi referring himself to show modesty, in a similar way to Ying Yang's use of "*xiaozi*" 小子 (minor person) in his "Poem Attending the Leader of Court Gentlemen for Miscellaneous Uses at a Gathering at the Jianzhang Terrace" (Shi Wuguan zhonglangjiang jianzhangtai ji shi 侍五官中郎將建章臺集詩); see *Han Wei Liuchao shi jianshang cidian*, pp. 272–73. However, "lesser man" carries a negative association due to its frequent use in contrast with the "gentlemen" in the *Analects*. Moreover, unlike Ying Yang, Cao Zhi is writing to someone below him in social status, which makes a display of modesty unusual and unnecessary.

60 *XianQin Han Wei Jin Nanbeichao shi* 1.457.

61 Ibid., 452. In his discussion of Cao Zhi's "Poem Presented to Ding Yi," Cutter argues that Cao Zhi echoes Wang Chong's 王充 (25–100) critique of the "word-for-word parroting of the words of former teachers by Confucian scholars" and expresses a "general attitude of the period toward the ineffectiveness of current Confucian pursuits in dealing with real problems": Cutter, "Cao Zhi's Symposium Poems," p. 18.

62 *Lun yu ji shi* 35.1212.

63 For example, Liu Lü understands Cao Zhi's "Poem Presented to Xu Gan" as a critique of Cao Cao's promotion of "the evil and flattering" (*xie ning* 邪佞) and his failure to recognize "virtuous gentlemen" (*youde zhishi* 有德之士). He also believes the poem conveys Cao Zhi's own feelings of "not realizing his ambitions" (*bu dezhi* 不得志). Wu Qi reads "Miscellaneous Poem" VI as Cao Zhi's complaint that Cao Pi intentionally distanced him from state affairs. *San Cao ziliao huibian*, pp. 122–23; 151–52.

have a particular identity but may signify any men who are inferior and do not share the poets' values. Other readers have theorized these "lesser men" as a veiled insult to Cao Pi or his subordinates. But Pi, as an important member of the Jian'an literary community, more likely belonged to the "gentlemen."

Similar ideas about superior values and incompatibility with the vulgar masses are often found in Jian'an literati's representations of the fair lady. Cao Zhi's "Miscellaneous Poem" IV describes such an image:

南國有佳人	In the southland there is a fair lady;
容華若桃李	her flowery appearance is as beautiful as peach and plum.
朝遊江北岸	In dawn she roams along the northern bank of the River;
夕宿瀟湘沚	In dusk she dwells on an isle in the Xiaoxiang River.
時俗薄朱顏	Vulgar people of the time disdain beautiful appearance;
誰為發皓齒	for whom could she open her mouth?
俯仰歲將暮	Within a short moment, the year is about to come to an end;
榮耀難久恃	the dazzling glory is hard to rely on long.[64]

The contrast between the lonely "fair lady" and the "vulgar people of the time" is essentially the same as that between "gentlemen" and "lesser men." Both define by contrast and comparison a social community rising to significance in a disordered world.[65]

Later readers, however, have often understood Cao Zhi's poems on the beautiful woman in the context of his political frustration later in life.[66] Many read them as the poet's laments of his talents not being valued by the ruler, Cao Pi. Both Liu Lü and Zhang Yugu 張玉穀 (1721–1780) believe that Cao Zhi wrote "Miscellaneous Poem" IV to express his resentment and sorrow during his exile in a remote fief after Cao Pi ascended the throne.[67] Guo Maoqian remarks on the image of a beautiful woman in "Song on a Beauty" that "the beautiful woman is a metaphor for a gentleman. [The poem] speaks of a gentleman

---

64 *XianQin Han Wei Jin Nanbeichao shi* 1.457.

65 A peerless yet lonely beauty is the central image in Cao Zhi's "Song on a Beauty," "Ballad of Resentment" (Yuange xing 怨歌行), and "Miscellaneous Poem" III, as well as many more.

66 For a study of the political struggle between Cao Zhi and Cao Pi and possible reasons for Cao Zhi's loss in the competition to become the heir to Cao Cao, see Robert Joe Cutter, "The Incident at the Gate: Cao Zhi, the Succession, and Literary Fame," *T'oung Pao* 71 (1985): 228–62.

67 *San Cao ziliao huibian*, pp. 120–21; 208–09.

with fair qualities who wishes to serve a wise lord. If he does not meet the right opportunity, he will not be subdued even when recruited" 美女者，以喻君子。言君子有美行，願得明君而事之。若不遇時，雖見徵求，終不屈也.[68] Chia-Ling Mei views this image as a metaphor for the frustration felt by Jian'an poets, particularly Cao Zhi.[69] These interpretations narrow the significance of the beautiful woman without considering her prevalence in the overall Jian'an literary discourse. In the absence of information about the compositional context, why place Cao Zhi in the position of a subject seeking employment? He was, after all, once a competitive candidate for the role of future ruler. The image of Cao Zhi as an ill-fated and mistreated talent is itself a cultural construct dating probably no earlier than the 5th century. Moreover, if we interpret Cao Zhi's portrayal of the woman this way, how do we understand similar images of a beautiful woman seeking a match in Cao Pi's poem? It is more plausible to compare the beautiful woman's longing for a match to a talented gentleman's search for worthy companions. The yearning for an opportunity to realize political ambitions with like-minded friends drew many Jian'an literati away from their previous alliances and patrons to join the Cao courts. Sentiments of longing for peers are common in their writing, often expressed through the image of a beautiful woman, as in Wang Can's "*Fu* on Stilling Evil Passions" (Xianxie fu 閑邪賦):

橫四海而無仇	Nowhere within the four seas has she an equal;
超遐世而秀出	surpassing all ages, she stands out pre-eminent.
發唐棣之春華	She resembles the spring flowers of the *tangdi* tree.
當盛年而處室	In her prime years, she stays in her chamber.
恨年歲之方暮	She regrets that the year is drawing to a close,
哀獨立而無依	and grieves to be alone with no one to rely on.[70]

The beautiful woman cannot find a worthy companion because her extraordinary beauty and talent see "no match" (*wuchou* 無仇) in this world. Her

---

68 *XianQin Han Wei Jin Nanbeichao shi* 1.431–32; *San Cao ziliao huibian*, p. 114.

69 Mei, "Han Jin shige zhong 'sifu wenben' de xingcheng ji xiangguan wenti," pp. 76–77. For a discussion of the political allegory in Cao Zhi's poetry, see David Roy, "The Theme of the Neglected Wife in the Poetry of Ts'ao Chih," *Journal of Asian Studies* 19, no. 1 (1959): 25–31. The autobiographical reading of Cao Zhi's poems was questioned by Hans H. Frankel in his article "Fifteen Poems by Ts'ao Chih: An Attempt at a New Approach," *Journal of the American Oriental Society* 84 (1964): 1–14. Frankel suggests treating Cao's poetry as "an imaginative work of art."

70 *Yiwen leiju* 18.332. I use James Hightower's translation in "The *Fu* of T'ao Ch'ien," *Harvard Journal of Asiatic Studies* 17, no. 1/2 (1954): 169–230, esp. pp. 174–75, with modifications.

loneliness is not a desperate situation born of lack of recognition, but rather the result of high self-esteem and a refusal to compromise.

Comparing the images of beautiful women in Jian'an *fu* with those in previous works, including "Encountering Sorrow" (Li sao 離騷), "*Fu* on Gaotang," "*Fu* on the Goddess," and "*Fu* on Master Dengtu the Lecher," Cheng Yu-yu argues that the former lost allegorical or political connotations and became playful literary practices.[71] While it is true that from "Li Sao" to "Master Dengtu the Lecher" the role of the woman became increasingly subordinate and the *fu*'s function increasingly entertaining, Jian'an *fu* on beautiful women are certainly not devoid of any political and social implications.[72] The image of the beautiful woman in Jian'an literature, while profoundly influenced by earlier works, especially Western Han court *fu*, developed distinctive features within new cultural and historical environments. As the primary function of court writing shifted from providing entertainment and pleasure exclusively to the ruler to defining a collective identity for participating literati, the woman was transformed from a symbol of centralized imperial power to a shared ideal of the literary community. By writing about the woman's sympathetic interaction with their poetic selves, Jian'an writers made her an external manifestation of their own virtue, ambition, and talents. The woman's steadfast integrity and firm refusal to follow the crowd stands for their unbending pride and uncompromised virtue in an unsettling world. Her longing for a commensurate match signifies their yearning for worthy companions, that is, their fellow literati at the Cao courts.

3 "Such Joy Cannot Endure": Jian'an Discourse of *Qing* 情

In the writings of Jian'an literati, the man's pursuit of a beautiful woman, or the woman's search for a good match, almost always ends in failure and regret. Why can the romantic pursuit not have a happy ending? If the beautiful woman is a symbol of the Jian'an literati's idealized personality and companionship, why is she always lonely and sorrowful? The answer lies in the lack of confidence in human passions (*qing*) among Jian'an literati. The pessimistic attitude toward *qing* shaped the feminine image and voice in Jian'an writing and set it apart from previous court writing about women.

---

71 Cheng, "Meili de zhouxuan—Shennü lunshu yu xingbie yanyi," pp. 23–35.

72 I discuss political and military functions of Jian'an *fu* and poetry, including several *fu* on the goddess written on the military campaign against Liu Biao, in "Following the Troops, Carrying Along our Brushes: Jian'an (196–220 AD) *Fu* and *Shi* Written for Military Campaigns," *Asia Major* (2020) 3d ser. Vol. 33.2: 61–91.

Jian'an literati's writings about women often adopt a melancholic tone. This is evident in Cao Zhi's "*Fu* on the Luo Goddess," which, like Chen Lin's *fu* on the goddess, is set in the context of the writer's personal experience:

> 黃初三年，余朝京師，還濟洛川。古人有言，斯水之神，名曰宓妃。感宋玉對楚王神女之事，遂作斯賦。
>
> In the third year of Huangchu, I attended court in the capital. Upon my return I crossed the Luo River. The ancients say that the goddess of this river is called Fufei. Inspired by Song Yu's response to the king of Chu on the matter of the goddess, I have composed this *fu*.[73]

Like Chen Lin, Cao Zhi places his composition in the textual lineage of Song Yu's *fu* on the goddess and claims it is the product of his literary imagination. His reading experience has also familiarized him with the inevitable failure of the quest. Unlike the optimistic beginning (the king's eager expectation or Song Yu's positive encouragement) in Song Yu's "*Fu* on Gaotang" and "*Fu* on the Goddess," the speaker's experience is overshadowed by ominous signs from the start:

日既西傾	The sun has already inclined toward the west,
車殆馬煩	my chariot is tipping precariously, the horses are tired.
…	
於是精移神駭	And then my spirit is shaken, my soul startled,
忽焉思散	and suddenly my thoughts scatter.
俯則未察	Looking down, I perceive nothing;
仰以殊觀	looking up, I behold an unusual sight.
覩一麗人	I see a beautiful person,
于崖之畔	on the bank below the cliffs.[74]

Like other beautiful women in Jian'an writings, Cao Zhi's goddess demonstrates strong sympathy with the speaker. Unlike the elusive divine women in the "Li Sao" and Song Yu's *fu*, who remain untouched and aloof despite the speaker's diligent pursuit, she does not terminate the communication for no reason. It is, instead, the poet's suspicion and hesitation that lead to the ending of the relationship:

---

73 *Wen xuan* 19.896. I use Knechtges's translation in *Wen xuan, or Selections of Refined Literature*, Vol. 3, pp. 355–65, with modifications.

74 *Wen xuan* 19.896; *Wen xuan, or Selections of Refined Literature*, Vol. 3, p. 357.

感交甫之棄言兮	Moved by the broken promise made to Jiaofu,
悵猶豫而狐疑	I disconsolately pause, doubtful and uncertain.[75]

The speaker's lack of confidence in the consummation of *qing* comes from the familiarity with earlier texts about the goddess. Despite writing in the tradition of the elusive goddess, this voluntary distancing from the woman resonates more with the tradition of *dingqing*, pacifying the passions. Xie Lingyun's preface to the "*Fu* on the River Goddess" (Jiangfei fu 江妃賦) summarizes the central message of Cao Zhi's "*Fu* on the Luo Goddess" as "purifying thoughts" (*qingsi* 清思) and points to the merger of the motif of the quest for the goddess with that of pacifying the passions. It is in fact quite common in Jian'an writings on the goddess to combine the two motifs, precisely because of the ubiquitous distrust and despair in *qing*. In Wang Can's "*Fu* on the Goddess," although the goddess shows romantic interest in the speaker and discloses her innermost feelings, he fights against his passions in the most determined way:

顧大罰之淫愆	I worry that the grand punishment would be excessive;
亦終身而不滅	and that it would also last my whole life and never extinguish.
心交戰而貞勝	My heart fights within, yet chastity wins.
乃回意而自絕	Then I change my mind and alienate myself [from her.][76]

The speakers in both Cao Zhi's and Wang Can's *fu* are attracted to the goddess, yet they turn away from her for fear of the dangerous consequences their passions might bring. This negativity toward *qing* is distinct from the representation of women in early court *fu* that conveys total confidence in bringing *qing* under firm control or directing it to moral or political causes. As discussed in the previous chapter, the confidence lies in the conviction of "using sex to illustrate ritual." In contrast, "sex" (*se* 色) and "ritual" (*li* 禮) occur in Wang Can's and Cao Zhi's *fu* as rival concepts. It is to the restriction of *li* that Cao Zhi's speaker resorts when he needs to suppress his feelings toward the beautiful goddess:

收和顏而靜志兮	Then, assuming a mild expression, I calm my feelings,
申禮防以自持	and control myself with the restraints of the ritual.[77]

75 *Wen xuan* 19.898; *Wen xuan, or Selections of Refined Literature*, Vol. 3, p. 361.
76 *Yiwen leiju* 79.1352.
77 *Wen xuan* 19.898.

The comforting belief that the indulgence in *qing* naturally leads to ritual and political order is no longer present.

Jian'an discourse on *qing* finds its fullest expression in several *fu* on pacifying the passions, fragments of which survived through inclusion in the *Yiwen leiju*. In an article on Tao Qian's 陶潛 (*c*.365–427) "*Fu* on Stilling the Passions" (Xianqing fu 閒情賦), James Hightower delineates the tradition of this motif and translates all extant works since Zhang Heng's 張衡 (78–139) "*Fu* on Pacifying the Passions" (Dingqing fu 定情賦), concluding that their expressions are highly conventional and formulaic.[78] Notably, except for Zhang Heng and Cai Yong 蔡邕 (133–192), all other writers, including Ruan Yu, Wang Can, Ying Yang, Chen Lin, and Cao Zhi, were active members of the Jian'an literary circle. Given the limited number of works on this topic after Jian'an, it is fair to say that Jian'an literati had a special interest in the concept of *qing* and its consequences. These *fu* are probably the result of a group composition initiated by Cao Pi. As Knechtges states, the occasion was the court banquet described in Cao Pi's "*Fu* on Warning Against Self-Satisfaction" (Jieying fu 戒盈賦):

> 避暑東閣，延賓高會，酒酣樂作，悵然懷盈滿之戒，乃作斯賦。
>
> I escaped the heat in the Eastern Pavilion and invited guests to a formal gathering. We were deep in our cups and music was played. I sadly recalled the warning about self-satisfaction. I then composed this *fu*.[79]

In the *fu*, Cao Pi invites his guests to offer him "admonition and warning" (*zhengui* 箴規):

何今日之延賓	Why have we invited guests today?
君子紛其集庭	Gentlemen in great numbers gather in the courtyard.
信臨高而增懼	Truly looking down from a high place increases fear,
獨處滿而懷愁	Dwelling alone in self-satisfaction one harbors sadness.
願羣士之箴規	I wish all you gentlemen to give me admonition and warning,
博納我以良謀	And broadly present me good plans.[80]

This anxiety about satisfaction (*man* 滿), voiced by a ruler, is unheard of in the Western Han court *fu*, which serve to evoke the ruler's feeling of satisfaction

78 Hightower, "The *Fu* of T'ao Ch'ien," pp. 170–89.

79 *Yiwen leiju* 23.417. I use Knechtges's translation in "Group Literary Composition at the Court of Ye in the Later Eastern Han," pp. 15–16.

80 Ibid.

with the celebration of his absolute authority. Sima Xiangru's "*Fu* on the Great Man" (Daren fu 大人賦), for example, brought the "elevating/floating" (*piaopiao* 飄飄) sentiment to Emperor Wu.[81] But Cao Pi's *fu* presents a ruler with a completely different (self-) image and mindset. He requests the composition of *fu* not to seek emotional satisfaction and fulfillment but to dispel them.[82]

The *fu* composed on this occasion include Ruan Yu's and Chen Lin's "*Fu* on Putting a Stop to Desires" (Zhiyu fu 止欲賦), Wang Can's "*Fu* on Stilling Evil Passions," Ying Yang's "*Fu* on Rectifying Passions" (Zhengqing fu 正情賦), Liu Zhen's "*Fu* on Clarifying Thoughts" (Qinglü fu 清慮賦), Cao Zhi's "*Fu* on Stilling Thoughts" (Jingsi fu 靜思賦), and Po Qin's "*Fu* on Stilling Sorrows" (Michou fu 弭愁賦).[83] Extant fragments have a similar plot and structure, which Knechtges summarizes as follows:

(1) description of the beauty of a lovely lady;
(2) the poet's expression of his attraction to the beauty;
(3) the poet's unsuccessful quest to obtain the beauty usually culminating in a dream journey;[84]
(4) cessation of erotic desire.[85]

At first glance, Jian'an *fu* on pacifying the passions closely follow their literary precedents, such as the "*Fu* on Master Dengtu the Lecher," but further

81 After Sima Xiangru's presentation of the "*Fu* on the Great Man," "the Son of Heaven greatly rejoiced and had the intent of floating on the clouds and roaming between heaven and earth." 天子大悅，飄飄有凌雲氣遊天地之間意. *Han shu* 57b.2600.

82 Another notable fact is that the ruler himself called for admonition and persuasion against his own indulgence in superior power, which is very different from early court *fu* in which the speaker/subject tries to warn or remonstrate with his pleasure-loving ruler. Cao Pi solicits advice in a modest and almost humble tone that is quite different from the condescending and commanding position the ruler usually occupies in early court *fu*.

83 All these *fu* are preserved in the category "beautiful women" (*mei furen* 美婦人) in *Yiwen leiju* 18.331–33. All are translated in Hightower's "The *Fu* of T'ao Ch'ien," except for Liu Zhen's and Po Qin's *fu*. Moreover, Po Qin's five-syllable "Poem on Pacifying the Passions" (Dingqing shi 定情詩), which Hightower mentions briefly, treats the same topic and could have been composed on the same occasion. Chapter 4 gives a detailed discussion of the gendered voice in Po Qin's poem.

84 In a few pieces love is consummated, but only in a dream.

85 Knechtges, "Group Literary Composition at the Court of Ye in the Later Eastern Han," p. 16. Hightower summarizes the plots: "There is a woman of beauty whose equal cannot be found in times past or present. She is good and wise, a model of decorum. I am irresistibly attracted to her, but alas! I have no way to approach her. I try to meet her soul in my dreams, but here too I am frustrated. I imagine the bliss of being some inanimate object which she has constantly about her, but realize that all of these are used only to be cast aside. I despair. Finally, I resolve to pull myself together, and, by resigning myself to the inevitable, gain some measure of control over my feelings": Hightower, "The *Fu* of T'ao Ch'ien," p. 194.

examination reveals some fundamental differences. The rejection of the passions in the "*Fu* on Master Dengtu the Lecher" serves to demonstrate the speaker's loyalty to the ruler. Like early court *fu* on the goddess, there is no gap between *se* and *li*, desire and order. The passions aroused by the encounter with a beautiful woman are proven to be not only harmless—because they can be subdued—but also a necessary testimony to the speaker's chastity and loyalty. The optimistic view of the passions is closely related to the *fu*'s political function. Its message to the royal audience is that the speaker would gain more satisfaction by serving the ruler than by consummating his passions with a beautiful woman.

But this confidence in bringing the passions under control is absent in Jian'an *fu*. In contrast to the explicit political or moral agenda in earlier *fu*, the speaker does not provide a clear motivation for the termination of passions. For that reason, the transition between the speaker's active quest and his decision to stop, that is, from step three to four in Knechtges's summary, is rather abrupt.[86] There is, however, always an acute awareness of the swift passage of time:

忽日月之徐邁　May the sun and moon move slowly on their courses,
庶枯楊之生稊　So that the leafless poplar may put forth sprouts.

CHEN LIN, "*Fu* on Putting a Stop to Desires"[87]

恨年歲之方暮　I regret that the year is drawing to a close,
哀獨立而無依　Grieved to be alone with no one to rely on.

WANG CAN, "*Fu* on Stilling Evil Passions"[88]

86 It is true that these *fu* only exist in fragments. But as Hightower argues, the extant portions of these *fu* show a consistent structure that is the same as Tao Qian's "*Fu* on Stilling the Passions." Tao's *fu* survives in its entirety. See Hightower, "The *Fu* of T'ao Ch'ien," pp. 189–90. Lin Xiaoguang reconstructs the lost texts of Jian'an *fu* on pacifying the passions, using Tao Qian's *fu* as a model. He tries to detect the "gist" (*zhuzhi* 主旨) of these *fu* through this reconstruction. He believes they are about an old man's admiration for a beautiful woman who is significantly younger. See Lin Xiaoguang, "'Xianqing fu' puxi de wenxian huanyuan—jiyu zhongshi wenxian gouzao yu wentixing de zonghe yanjiu"《閒情賦》譜系的文獻還原——基於中世文獻構造與文體性的綜合研究, *Wenxue pinglun* 3 (2014): 204–14. I doubt his final discovery about the meaning of these *fu* and have reservations about such a mechanical comparison and breakdown of literary texts. But his close comparison between the lexicon and narrative patterns of these *fu* show that they follow a certain sequence and structure and share rhetorical features such as topics, styles, and expressions. For that reason, it is not too far-fetched to discuss the overall structure based on common features in the surviving fragments.

87 *Yiwen leiju* 18.332, I use Hightower's translation in "The *Fu* of Tao Ch'ien," pp. 178–79.

88 *Yiwen leiju* 18.332, Hightower, "The *Fu* of Tao Ch'ien," p. 174.

遂終夜而靡見	At last the night is past, nor have I seen her;
東方旭以既晨	The rising sun in the east marks the dawn.

RUAN YU, "*Fu* on Putting a Stop to Desires"[89]

傷往禽之無隅	It grieves me that the passing bird has no mate,
悼流光之不歸	I am sorry that the flowing light cannot be stayed.
愍伏辰之方逝	Too bad the lucky conjunction is just now past,
哀吾願之多違	I regret that my wishes are all thwarted.

YING YANG, "*Fu* on Rectifying Passions"[90]

These sad realizations about time elapsing occur at the end of the dream journey in step three and before the final decision to pacify the passions. The negative attitude toward the passions in Jian'an *fu* arose more from an awareness of their impermanence than from fear of the moral destruction or other ill consequences they might cause. Several *fu* contain a section about the speaker's wish to transform into items on the woman's body, only to be dismissed by a fear of abandonment after use. For example:

思在體為素粉	I long to be the plain powder on your body,
悲隨衣以消除	but I grieve that it will disappear when you remove the clothes.

RUAN YU, "*Fu* on Putting a Stop to Desires"[91]

思在前為明鏡	I imagine myself to be the bright mirror before her,
哀既往于替？	but I grieve once it has gone ...

YING YANG, "*Fu* on Rectifying Passions"[92]

願為環以約腕	I would like to be the bracelet that binds your arm,
...	

WANG CAN, "*Fu* on Stilling Evil Passions"[93]

89 Ibid.

90 *Yiwen leiju* 18.333, Hightower, "The *Fu* of Tao Ch'ien," pp. 176–77.

91 These two lines are not included in the *Yiwen leiju* but are quoted in the 9th-century *Bunkyō hifu ron* 文鏡秘府論 (The secret treasury of poetic mirrors). Yu, *Jian'an qizi ji*, p. 164.

92 These two lines are missing in the *Yiwen leiju* and is quoted in another 7th-century encyclopedia *Beitang shuchao* 北堂書鈔 (Book excerpts from the Northern Hall, completed *c.*610) 136. Yu, *Jian'an qizi ji*, p. 176. I use Hightower's translation in "The *Fu* of Tao Ch'ien," p. 177, with modifications.

93 This line is missing in the *Yiwen leiju* and is quoted in *Beitang shuchao*.Yu, *Jian'an qizi ji*, p. 100. Hightower, "The *Fu* of Tao Ch'ien," p. 175.

This listing of wishes and fears is inherited by the speaker's ten "wishes" (*yuan* 願) in Tao Qian's "*Fu* on Stilling the Passions." The intense longing for intimacy, followed immediately by frustration, creates an impression of the predestined failure of the passions due to their ephemerality. Such strong sensitivity to time is nowhere to be found in early court *fu* on pacifying the passions. The speaker's confidence about the passions is replaced by a sense of insecurity and anxiety in the Jian'an *fu*. Written at Cao Pi's request, they sufficiently accomplished their intended goal: to send an effective warning against the passions. Opposite to the idea of "using sex to illustrate ritual," these *fu* convey the message that the indulgence in *qing* would inevitably lead to disturbance and loss.[94] This drastic change in perception reflected the changing political environment at court after the collapse of a once powerful and unified empire.

This fateful view of human emotions is evident in Cao Pi's account of a past banquet:

> 清風夜起，悲笳微吟，樂往哀來，愴然傷懷。余顧而言，茲樂難常。足下之徒，咸以為然。
>
> Cool breezes arose in the night, and a sad reed whistle softly moaned. Happiness left and sorrow came, leaving us woeful and melancholy. I would look back and say that such joy cannot endure. You and the others thought I was right.[95]

Writing at a time when he had lost many of those friends to the plague, Cao Pi's recounting of the event was overshadowed by nostalgia. This sad recognition of the fleeting nature of human passions was also shared among Jian'an literati, as suggested by the unanimous consent to his statement "this joy cannot endure." Cutter observes in Jian'an poems on the lord's feast "a kind of *carpe diem* mentality" caused by a recognition of the ephemerality of life.[96] Human passions were perceived as the cause of loss and grief from this perspective.

---

94 Cao Zhi expresses similar opinions about the dire effects of the passions—especially those associated with female beauty and sexuality—and a wish to eliminate them elsewhere in his writing. For example, he states that "relishing wealth and taking delight in beautiful women; these are also scorpions to the gentlemen" 甘財悅色，此亦君子之蠍也, in the "Explication on the Imperial Field" (Jitian shuo 籍田說); also, "I only regret that I cannot restrain myself completely from music and beauty, to concentrate on learning the Way of longevity" 但恨不能絕聲色，專心以學長生之道也, in "On Explaining Skepticism" (Shiyi lun 釋疑論). See *Cao Zhi ji jiaozhu*, p. 428 and p. 396.

95 Cao Pi's "Letter to Wu Zhi, Prefect of Zhaoge" (Yu Zhaoge ling Wu Zhi shu 與朝歌令吳質書), *Wen xuan* 42.1895. I use Cutter's translation in "Cao Zhi's Symposium Poems," p. 4.

96 Cutter, "Cao Zhi's Symposium Poems," p. 32.

The ubiquitous distrust of *qing* is not limited to certain topics, genres, or literary images and voices. In addition to the pursuit of the goddess or beautiful women narrated from a man's perspective, another trope to convey this distrust is the resentment felt by ill-fated women, expressed in their voices. Although this literary trope exists as early as in the *Shijing*, it is Jian'an literati who first brought it to prominence. Some of these *fu* were evidently composed in a group setting. Cao Pi wrote the "*Fu* on a Widow" (Guafu fu 寡婦賦) about Ruan Yu's widow. Its preface states: "I ordered Wang Can and others to compose *fu* on the subject together" 命王粲等並作之.[97] The fragments of three separate "*Fu* on a Widow," by Cao Pi, Wang Can, and Ding Yi's 丁廙 wife, are preserved in the *Yiwen leiju*.[98] This subject's appeal probably lies in a combination of the ephemerality of *qing* and the transient nature of human life, two major and closely related motifs in Jian'an literature.

Another, more prevalent, type of ill-fated woman is the abandoned wife as victim of a change of heart by her lover and the impermanence of the passions. Cai Pi, Cao Zhi, and Wang Can all wrote "*Fu* on a Divorced Wife" (Chufu fu 出婦賦). Like their *fu* on pacifying the passions, their writing on abandoned wives often contrasts the past and the present to convey an acute sense of change and loss, for example:

思在昔之恩好	I think of your favor and kindness in the past;
似比翼之相親	we were as intimate as a pair of love birds.
惟方今之疏絕	Now you are estranged and broke off [from me],
若驚風之吹塵	like rapid wind blowing away the dusts.

CAI PI, "*Fu* on a Divorced Wife"

恨無愆而見棄	I resent being abandoned without doing anything wrong;
悼君施之不終	I lament that your favor failed to persist.

CAO ZHI, "*Fu* on a Divorced Wife"

97 Quoted in Li Shan's commentary to Pan Yue's 潘岳 (247–300) "*Fu* on a Widow." *Wen xuan* 16.735.

98 *Yiwen leiju* 34.600–01. The authorship of Ding Yi's wife's *fu* has long been the subject of debate. It is also attributed to Ding Yi's 丁儀 wife and Ding Yi 丁儀 in different sources. For a discussion of this issue, see Zhuang Xinxia 莊新霞, "Ding Yi qi 'Guafu fu' zuozhe ji xiangguan wenti kaolun" 丁儀妻《寡婦賦》作者及相關問題考論, *Zhongguo dianji yu wenhua* 2 (2001): 6–12.

君不篤兮終始	You, my lord, do not keep consistency from the start to end,
樂枯荑兮一時	and take temporary pleasure in your new lover.
心搖蕩兮變易	Your heart sways and changes;
忘舊姻兮棄之	you have forgotten and abandoned the former marital bond.

WANG CAN, "*Fu* on a Divorced Wife"[99]

These *fu* all accentuate the passage of time and its devastating impact on the emotional bond between lovers. Cao Pi's *fu* fittingly compares the lover's unpredictable change of heart to a mysterious force of nature, thus presenting the loss of passion as unavoidable and irrational. Cao Zhi's and Wang Can's *fu* criticize the husband, first and foremost, for not sustaining his initial feelings toward his wife and for betraying their marital commitment. The "lack of persistence" (*buzhong* 不終) over time is the cause of his "unfaithfulness" (*buzhong* 不忠) and the eventual loss of passion. This lament on abandonment echoes the sentiments in Jian'an *fu* on pacifying the passions but with the gender roles reversed.

Cao Zhi's collected works include a five-syllable poem with the title "Song on an Abandoned Wife" (Qifu pian 棄婦篇), which, along with his other poems about lonely and abandoned women, has often been read as political allegory.[100] Again, it is important to understand individual works in the context of the prevalent distrust of human passions in Jian'an writing. This distrust is not even a gender-specific feeling. Cao Zhi's five-syllable "Song on Planting Hemp" (Zhongge pian 種葛篇), for example, conveys the same disappointment in the lack of consistency of love in a man's voice.[101] Conditions and causes may vary, but the impermanence of *qing* is constant.

Some scholars see Jian'an literati's interest in women's sorrowful fate as an indicator of the increasing cases of divorce and untimely deaths in their historical moment. Some view it as evidence of a newly emerging sympathy toward women among Jian'an literati.[102] While the end of the Han did witness many

---

99 *Yiwen leiju* 30.528–29.

100 Cao Zhi's five-syllable "Song on Duckweeds" (Fuping pian 浮萍篇) is also about a divorced wife. *XianQin Han Wei Jin Nanbeichao shi* 1. 455–56 and 424.

101 Ibid. 1.435–36.

102 For a summary and discussion of views on the reason for the popularity of female representations in the Jian'an period, see Wu Congxiang 吳從祥, "Lun Jian'an shiqi nüxing wenxue xingsheng de yuanyin" 論建安時期女性文學興盛的原因, *Zhongnan minzu daxue xuebao* 26, no. 2 (2006): 147–50. Cutter mentions traditional explanations "ranging from the influence from earlier literature, through the harsh realities of the time, to

family separations and much loss of human life, there is no scientific or statistical evidence that the rate was especially high in comparison with other periods of disorder. The elevated number of literary works on unfortunate women also did not necessarily correspond to an increase in actual events, given that many were composed in a group on the same subject matter. Jian'an literati's pessimistic view of the passions was primarily tied to their awareness of the brevity of life and the fragility of emotional bonds, both of which are universal human conditions, as accurately expressed in Cao Pi's "*Fu* on a Widow":

惟生民兮艱危	[The life] of common people is difficult and dangerous;
於孤寡兮常悲	For orphans and widows it is constantly sorrowful.[103]

The lament is really on the hardships experienced by all human beings, and the subjects of widows and abandoned women provide especially effective outlets for its articulation.[104]

One may wonder if this pessimism toward *qing* was at odds with Jian'an writers' frequent expressions of longing for idealized companionship in their representations of women. This question should be considered in contemporary social and political contexts. Most Jian'an writers had abandoned or been abandoned by their previous patrons before joining the Caos and had seen a great deal of intrigues, betrayals, and uncertainties in their lives. Even this new environment in which they found themselves was not a safe haven. Political intrigues, power struggles, and killings occurred no less frequently than in other parts of the world.[105] Jian'an writers lived in an era full of potential and

---

the allegorical usefulness of such poems in lamenting the loyal subject's alienation from his ruler." While accepting all of these as possible inspirations for Jian'an writings about women, he views the primary reason to be that the "Jian'an era falls within a time of extraordinary interest in what it was, or what literati imagined it was, to be a woman": Cutter, "To Make Her Mine," p. 44.

103 *Yiwen leiju* 34.600.

104 In his first "Poem on Seven Sorrows" (Qi ai shi 七哀詩), of which there are three, for example, Wang Can describes a young mother forced to abandon her baby (here both "orphans" and "widows") as an illustration of the dire situation faced by all during the chaotic time after the fall of the Han. *XianQin Han Wei Jin Nanbeichao shi* 1.365–66.

105 To name just a few, Kong Rong, Yang Xiu, and the Ding brothers were all executed as the result of the power struggles and factionalism at the Cao courts. Nicholas Morrow Williams describes the constant danger of offending the Caos at court. See Nicholas Morrow Williams, "Irony and Death in the Writings of Liu Zhen," *The Bulletin of Jao Tsung-I Academy of Sinology* 4 (2014): 325–52. Tian also demonstrates the "complicated power dynamics between lord and vassal" that often involved the former's claim of authority and ownership under the veneer of congeniality: Tian, *The Halberd at Red Cliff*, p. 140.

ambition, yet also of danger and uncertainty. While taking delight in friendship and companionship in a community of like-minded literati, they were not so naive as to overlook the dark side of human relations and emotions, between the ruler and subjects as well as among themselves. Despite showing strong interest in personal emotions and human passions, their writings are often tainted by the awareness of their limitations and impermanence.

4 Conclusion

The image of the beautiful woman in Jian'an literature, while profoundly influenced by earlier works, developed many distinctive features in this new cultural and historical environment. As the primary function of court writing shifted from providing entertainment and satisfaction exclusively to the ruler to defining a collective identity for participating literati, the female image was transformed from a symbol of centralized imperial power to a shared ideal of a literary community. By writing about the woman's sympathetic interaction with their poetic selves, Jian'an writers made her an external manifestation of their own virtue, talents, and longing. The woman's steadfast moral integrity and firm rejection of the vulgar crowd equate to their unbending pride and uncompromised virtue in an unsettled world. Jian'an literati express a yearning for worthy companions—that is, their fellow literati at the Cao courts—through the woman's longing for a commensurate match. At the same time, the general lack of confidence in human passions and anxiety about their impermanence and vulnerability among Jian'an writers are often expressed through the melancholic sentiment and voice of women. It is through Jian'an literati's writings that the image of a lonely beauty lamenting the impermanence of love and the sentiments of sorrow and resentment first became essential components of the archetypical feminine voice in literature.

CHAPTER 3

Gender, Genre, and Historical Narrative

Jian'an literati depicted women in their writings in many different genres, including *fu*, four-syllable, and five-syllable poetry. But they most commonly chose five-syllable poetry when assuming the persona of a woman and speaking in her voice. Is there a link between this poetic genre and the voices of women? Five-syllable poetry has enjoyed immense popularity and acclaim among literati writers since the Jian'an period. This genre is the focus of two important works compiled in the 6th century: the *Yutai xinyong*, an anthology of poetry, and the *Shi pin*, a work of literary criticism. However, only a very small number of recent or contemporary women writers of five-syllable poetry are mentioned in these two works.[1] Women writers of five-syllable poems are equally poorly represented in the *Wen xuan* and *Wenxin diaolong*, two other works of literary anthology and criticism compiled in the 6th century. Therefore, it is compelling that accounts of this genre's early history feature quite a few women writers. Zhong Rong, the compiler of the *Shi pin*, marvels at the disproportionate number of women among early writers of five-syllable poetry:

> 二漢為五言者，不過數家，而婦人居二。
>
> The number of people who wrote five-syllable poems during the two Hans [i.e. Western and Eastern Han] does not exceed a handful. Yet among them there were two women.[2]

The "two women" are Lady Ban 班婕妤, concubine of Emperor Cheng of Han 漢成帝 (r. 33–7 BCE), to whom the famous "Poem on Resentment" (Yuan shi 怨詩) is attributed; and Xu Shu 徐淑 (mid-2nd century), who is known for a poem in reply to her husband. Both are ranked and discussed in the *Shi pin*. Yet Lady Ban and Xu Shu are not the only women to whom early five-syllable poems are attributed. Other names include Lady Yu 虞姬, concubine of Xiang Yu 項羽 (232–202 BCE); Lady Qi 戚夫人, concubine of Xiang Yu's rival Liu Bang

1 It is especially significant for the *Yutai xinyong* because of its emphasis on including recent and contemporary writers and its general interest in poems about women. See the discussion in Chapter 5.

2 Cao Xu, *Shi pin jizhu*, pp. 249–50.

 DOI:10.1163/9789004546455_005

劉邦 (256–195 BCE); Zhuo Wenjun 卓文君, wife of the Western Han *fu* writer Sima Xiangru; Empress Zhen; and Cai Yan 蔡琰 (*c.*177–239). This list is surprisingly long in comparison with the small number of known pre-Jian'an writers of five-syllable poetry, both male and female. For this reason, some scholars maintain that five-syllable poetry originated in women's writing.[3] Such an assertion is questionable for it is based on the uncritical acceptance of the attribution of authorship in received accounts of literary history. Thanks to scholars including Lu Qinli, Hans Frankel, Diény, Donald Holzman, Knechtges, and Owen, there is now scholarly consensus that most, if not all, of these attributions to women are unreliable and most likely false.[4] But the question remains why women's voices and authorship were disproportionally found in early five-syllable poems.

The central questions this chapter attempts to answer are: why, when, and how did five-syllable poetry become the genre for the conventional feminine voice? It explores the connections between the conventional feminine voice, five-syllable poetry, and romanticized historical stories circulated in the 4th and 5th centuries. Poems are often attributed to female figures in these stories as expressions of their intense feelings at a crucial moment in life. The five-syllable poetic genre, for its association with performance and impersonation, becomes a suitable carrier of women's voices in these stories. Through analysis and comparison of women's voices in the Han historiography, Jian'an literati writings, and romanticized historical narratives of the 4th and 5th centuries, I demonstrate how the feelings of abandonment and resentment and the five-syllable poetic genre became essential features of the feminine voice. Many poems examined here are discussed in Owen's *The Making of*

3 See, for example, Wu Shichang 吳世昌 (1908–1986), "Lun wuyan shi qiyuan yu funü wenxue" 論五言詩起源於婦女文學, *Wenshi zhishi* 11 (1985): 35. Qian Zhixi 錢志熙 states that "before the formal establishment of literati poetry, women had a more intimate relationship with the newly developing five-syllable poetry and *yuefu*" 在文人詩歌正式形成之前，女性與新興的五言及樂府之間具有更加親密的關係: Qian Zhixi, "Shidafu wenhua shijiao zhong de Zhongguo gudai nüxing shige fazhan shi" 士大夫文化視角中的中國古代女性詩歌發展史, *Zhongguo gaoxiao shehui kexue* 5 (2019): 95–107, esp. p. 97.

4 See Lu Qinli's notes on the origins and authenticity of attributions of these poems in *XianQin Han Weijin Nanbeichao shi*; Hans H. Frankel, "Cai Yan and the Poems Attributed to Her," *Chinese Literature: Essays, Articles and Reviews* 5 (1983): 133–56; Jean-Pierre Diény, *Aux Origines de la poésie classique en Chine* (Leiden: Brill, 1968); Donald Holzman, "Les premiers vers pentasyllabuques datés dans la poésie chinoise," in *Mélanges de sinologies offerts à Monsieur Paul Demiéville, II* (Paris: Presses universitaires de France, 1974), pp. 77–116; David R. Knechtges, "The Poetry of an Imperial Concubine: The Favorite Beauty Ban," *Oriens Extremus* 36, no. 2 (1993): 127–44; and Owen, *The Making of Early Classical Chinese Poetry*, especially chapter 5, "Author and Speaker," pp. 214–59.

Early Chinese Classical Poetry, especially in the fifth chapter, "Author and Speaker." Owen shows that the concept of authorship was a historical development, and a large number of anonymous early five-syllable poems acquired an "author" over time, mostly through an uncritical equalization of a plausible identity of the poetic speaker with the author.[5] His discussion provides a thought-provoking point of departure for this chapter. But my interest is not in the process of attribution of authorship. Instead, I want to explore the reasons why certain poems, sentiments, and literary genres became associated with women's voices. What can these attributions tell us about the changing views of gendered voices? How did accounts of the early history of five-syllable poetry, many of which are from the early medieval period, come to be populated with women authors? These questions need to be answered in the historical context of the genre's development, starting with a close look at the genre's history before the Jian'an period.

1 The Five-Syllable Line and Women's Literary Voices before Jian'an

There are few scholarly discussions about the perception of five-syllable poetry before the Jian'an period. What kind of people composed five-syllable poetry? What occasions called for its composition? How was it received by contemporary audiences? Did it have a particularly close association with women's voices? The reason that few have attempted to answer these questions has much to do with the scarcity of available sources regarding the genre's early history. Many poems with the "Han" (not including the Jian'an period) label are from much later sources and their dating cannot be accepted with full credibility. These include poems attributed to Li Ling 李陵 (d. 74 BCE), Ban Gu 班固 (32–92), Zhang Heng, Li Yan 酈炎 (150–177), Zhao Yi 趙壹 (fl. *c.*168–189), and Cai Yong, among others. Yet we can be relatively certain that the four poems entirely or mostly in the five-syllable line quoted in the *Han shu* were composed before the book's completion at the end of the 1st century, even though much caution still needs to be taken in their alleged authorship and exact dates of composition.[6] Therefore the following analysis of these poems shows how

5 Owen, *The Making of Early Chinese Classical Poetry*, pp. 214–59.

6 This is not to suggest that the compilers of the *Han shu* biographies intentionally forged these poems and the events around them. In compiling the history, they may have consulted and incorporated a variety of sources, many of which are probably not strictly "historical" in the modern sense of the word.

five-syllable poetry was perceived in Ban Gu's time, rather than at the putative time of their composition.

Compared with the *Shi ji*, its Western Han predecessor, the *Han shu* incorporates many more verses in its narration of history.[7] It inherits most poems cited in the *Shi ji* and adds many that are not found in the earlier source. Notably, the *Shi ji* does not include any five-syllable poems, whereas the *Han shu* quotes four of them. Although this is not an indication that five-syllable poetry did not exist at the time of the *Shi ji*'s compilation in the 1st century BCE, the difference could at least suggest an elevated interest in the new poetic genre by Ban Gu's time.[8]

Two of the four five-syllable poems, both dating to the reign of Emperor Cheng 成帝 (r. 33–7 BCE), are presented as omen songs, prevalent in early historiography, which describe political or natural catastrophes as warnings or results of the ruler's failure.[9] One is found in the biography of Yin Shang 尹賞, a reputed "cruel official" (*kuli* 酷吏), about a mass execution of hundreds of reckless young evildoers (*qingbo shaonian ezi* 輕薄少年惡子) in Chang'an under his command. Residents of Chang'an took pity on their mourning relatives and made the following song:

安所求子死	Which place did you meet your death?
桓東少年場	"Young men's field" to the east of the Pillar.
生時諒不謹	When alive, you were probably imprudent,
枯骨後何葬	after [you die], where will your skeleton be buried?[10]

The other five-syllable omen song predicted Wang Mang's usurpation of the Han through a series of ominous signs:

7 Two articles discuss verses in the Han historiography: David Schaberg, "Song and the Historical Imagination in Early China," *Harvard Journal of Asiatic Studies* 59, no. 2 (1999): 305–61; and Martin Kern, "Poetry of Han Historiography," *Early Medieval China* 10–11, no. 1 (2004): 23–65. Both examine verses in all forms, including five-syllable ones, for the relationship between the narration of historical events and the citation of poetry.

8 Ban Gu's personal interest in the genre may have played a role too. Ban Gu is the alleged author of a five-syllable "Poem on History" (*yongshi shi* 詠史詩) that tells the story of Tiying 緹縈, a filial girl who avenged the death of her father; *XianQin Han Wei Jin Nanbeichao shi* 1.170.

9 See Schaberg's discussion of omen songs in early historical writings in "Song and the Historical Imagination in Early China," p. 339. These songs make comments on social and historical events that are about to happen and almost always accurately "predict" the future.

10 *Han shu* 90.3674; *XianQin Han Wei Jin Nanbeichao shi* 1.123.

邪徑敗良田	Crooked paths ruin fine fields;
讒口害善人	slandering mouths harm good people.
桂樹華不實	Cinnamon trees bloom but do not bear fruit;
黃雀巢其顛	Yellow sparrows build nests on its top.
故為人所羨	In the past people envied you;
今為人所憐	now people take pity on you.[11]

Like the previous poem, it is said to have been sung by commoners at the time. There is no way to identify the actual writer or composer, and the significance of such poems lies precisely in their anonymity. They were supposed to unveil the unfolding or forthcoming truth and purposefully avoided any personal or emotional connection. Their blunt style suits the immediacy and straightforwardness of truism: even an unsophisticated commoner could put it in verse, comprehend the message upon hearing it, and pass it on.

The other two poems, mostly in the five-syllable line, are each attached to a named author in the *Han shu* accounts. One is Lady Qi, a concubine of the founding emperor Liu Bang and rival of his principal wife, the powerful Empress Lü 呂后 (d. 180 BCE). Lady Qi attempted to depose the Crown Prince, Empress Lü's son, and replace him with her own son, Ruyi 如意. But the plan failed despite Liu Bang's support. After Liu Bang died, Empress Lü, now the empress dowager, retaliated by putting Lady Qi in prison, cutting off her hair, and ordering her to pound grain all day. The account quotes the following song by Lady Qi:

子為王	The son is a prince;[12]
母為虜	the mother is a slave.
終日舂薄暮	All day long I pound the grain [until] it approaches dusk.
常與死為伍	I am always in company of death.
相離八千里	Separated from you for eight thousand *li*,
當使誰告女	whom shall I send to inform you [of my situation]![13]

The song is a five-syllable poem except for the beginning couplet. Given the context of Lady Qi's tragic story, one might expect this song to be a heartbroken lament for her sorrowful fate or a bitter complaint about the mistreatment

11 *Han shu* 27.1396; *XianQin Han Wei Jin Nanbeichao shi* 1.126.

12 Her son Ruyi was enfeoffed as the Prince of Zhao 趙王 at birth.

13 *Han shu* 97a.3937; *XianQin Han Wei Jin Nanbeichao shi* 1.91. The *Shi ji* tells the same story without quoting the song.

she received. But it does not convey much personal feeling and describes the situation in a matter-of-fact manner. According to the *Han shu*, the empress dowager was greatly enraged (*danu* 大怒) upon hearing this song. She immediately killed the Prince of Zhao, chopped off Lady Qi's four limbs, and made her into a "human pig" (*renzhi* 人彘). One wonders what in this short song could have unleashed such horrifying hatred. The reason lies precisely in its matter-of-fact tone. Although cast in Lady Qi's voice about her personal adversity, the first two lines take on an impersonal perspective, as if stating a fact from a third person's viewpoint. This unsentimental voice, if not the impersonal perspective, is present throughout the song. It turns the song from one person's lament into a statement of facts about the terrible disorder and injustice in the reign of the empress dowager. In many ways this song is also an omen song, with its social commentary and prediction (of Lady Qi's death). The downplay of personal emotion makes Lady Qi a performer or deliverer of truth rather than an author of a poem. The empress dowager's rage and decision to kill the mother and son could have been born of fear of the truth being revealed and spread.

Another five-syllable poem that *Han shu* associated with an individual is Li Yannian's "Song on a Fair Lady." Li Yannian was a musician at the court of Emperor Wu. Once at a court banquet he performed a song for the emperor:

北方有佳人	In the north there is a fair lady;
絕世而獨立	Out of this world, she stands alone.
一顧傾人城	With one glance she could topple a city,
再顧傾人國	With another she could topple a state.
寧不知傾城與傾國	Don't you know, toppling cities and states,
佳人難再得	A fair lady will never be found again!

The account continues:

> 上嘆息曰：“世豈有此人乎？”平陽主因言延年有女弟，上乃召見之，實妙麗善舞。由是得幸。
>
> The emperor heaved a sigh and said, "Could there be a person like this in this world?" Thereupon Princess Pingyang said that Yannian had a younger sister. The emperor then summoned her for an audience. She was indeed beautiful and skilled at dancing. Since then [Lady Li] had received imperial favor.[14]

14 *Han shu* 97a.3951; *XianQin Han WeiJin Nanbeichao shi* 1.102.

While enjoying the performance, the emperor apparently did not realize that Li Yannian was singing about his own sister, or any person in particular. He was under the impression that the lady in the song was from a different realm and beyond his reach, like a goddess in the court *fu*. So he was pleasantly surprised by the princess's revelation of her identity and availability. The emperor's reaction is understandable because Li's song does not contain anything personal. The song narrates a situation from the perspective of a third-person observer and could be performed by any court musician about any beautiful person, male or female. Put in the context of Lady Li's biography, its plain language also hides a prophetic message. The lines about toppling a city and a state imply something portentous about Lady Li's beauty that is soon attested by her manipulation of imperial favor for the speedy advance of her own family. The lament at the end of the poem also foreshadows her untimely death and the emperor's profound grief afterward. After Li's death, the emperor sought solace from and became emotionally dependent upon court musicians and Daoist adepts, men of humble and suspicious status. This violation of social propriety and hierarchy again proves the prophecy about the lady's ability to "topple a state" or subvert imperial power even after her death.[15] This short song is an uncanny prediction of Lady Li's entire life and its impact on the emperor, that is, an omen song.

All four five-syllable poems/songs in the *Han shu* have something in common, especially when compared with other poetic genres quoted in the *Han shu* narrative, such as four-syllable poetry and Chu songs (*chuge* 楚歌). First, their articulators are members of the lower class, including singers, entertainers, and commoners. Lady Qi was an imperial consort, but neither the *Shi ji* nor the *Han shu* provides much information regarding her family background. Her humble origin is indicated by the fact that she was a skilled entertainer when Liu Bang met her. Second, due in large part to their association with the lower class, the language of these poems is plain and unadorned. Finally, all four poems are more descriptive than expressive, and they state facts or truisms rather than conveying personal sentiments. The people who articulate them—Lady Qi, Li Yannian, and commoners in Chang'an—are "performers" of certain events or facts. They say very little or nothing about the feelings of the person. Instead of *yanzhi* (speaking one's intent), these poems are characterized by performativity. The speaker maintains a certain emotional distance

15 *Han shu* 97a.3951. For a close reading of Lady Li's biography and its hidden moral message, see Stephen Owen, "One Sight: The *Han shu* Biography of Lady Li" in *Rhetoric and the Discourses of Power in Court Culture: China, Europe and Japan*, ed. David Knechtges and Eugene Vance (Seattle and London: University of Washington Press, 2004), pp. 239–59.

and the same poem could easily be voiced by a different individual. Even in Lady Qi's case, where the song indeed contains exclusive details about her story, the lack of emotional involvement is notable.

This performative feature seems to belong specifically to five-syllable poetry at the time of the *Han shu* compilation. Four-syllable poems, as a well-established genre among elite literati, are rooted in the specific circumstances of their composition and routinely trace the author's personal and family history leading up to that compositional point.[16] There is no distance between the poetic persona and the authorial voice. Performativity also distinguishes five-syllable poems from Chu songs cited in the *Han shu*. An example is the song attributed to Princess Wusun 烏孫公主, the daughter of a Han prince who was married to the king of the Wusun tribe during Emperor Wu's reign. She "made a song herself" (*zizuo ge yue* 自作歌曰) to lament her misfortune:

吾家嫁我兮天一方	My family marries me, alas, to the other end of the world,
遠託異國兮烏孫王	far away, they entrust me to a foreign land, alas, to the King of Wusun.
廬為室兮旃為牆	Cottages are their chambers, alas, felt their walls;
以肉為食兮酪為漿	they have meat for meal, alas, fermented milk for drink.
居常土思兮心內傷	I always miss my homeland, alas, my heart pains within,
願為黃鵠兮還故鄉	I wish to be a yellow swan, alas, to return to my hometown.[17]

Even without the account, there is little doubt regarding who is supposed to have composed this song and the circumstance of its creation. This poem was written to convey the princess's longing and desperation at a unique moment in her life. This is not to suggest that the princess was the actual author of this poem; in fact, the alleged circumstance of the poem's composition led to questions regarding how it was recorded and transmitted. The point is rather the speaker's emotional involvement in the poetic expression. Although both express sorrow and desperation, this Chu song takes on a poignant first-person perspective that is very different from the matter-of-fact tone in Lady Qi's song.

16 See Zeb Raft, "Four-Syllable Poetry in Early Medieval China" (PhD diss., Harvard University, 2007), pp. 1–32.

17 *Han shu* 96b.3903; *XianQin Han Wei Jin Nanbeichao shi* 1.111–12.

If the five-syllable poems in the *Han shu* drive forward the narrative by recounting a past event or foreshadowing a future one, Chu songs pause the story at a climactic moment to dive deep into the character's emotion. Examples also include Xiang Yu's "Song of Gaixia" (Gaixia ge 垓下歌),[18] Liu Bang's "Song of the Great Wind" (Dafeng ge 大風歌),[19] and Li Ling's song performed at the parting banquet for Su Wu 蘇武,[20] among others. These Chu songs show a close link between their content and their articulators' emotions and thoughts. The Chu song in Li Ling's voice included in his biography speaks of his tragic experience after being captured by the Xiongnu and conveys highly personal emotions related to this experience. It sharply contrasts with the generic expressions in the group of five-syllable parting poems later attributed to him. Most of those five-syllable poems lack a specific and close bond with Li Ling's story, and some even contain conflicted elements.[21] It appears that in the *Han shu*, the Chu song, more than any other poetic genre, serves the function of conveying intense personal sentiments at a critical moment in its speaker's life.[22]

In terms of women's voices, no particularly tight connection with the five-syllable genre can be detected in the *Han shu*. Only one of the four five-syllable poems is in the voice of a woman. Most women writers mentioned in the *Han shu* came from the imperial family, including Lady Ban; Princess Wusun; Lady Tangshan 唐山夫人, concubine of Liu Bang;[23] and Lady Huarong 華容夫人, consort of Emperor Wu's son Liu Dan 劉旦 (d. 80 BCE).[24] Their genres of choice are *fu* or Chu songs, which is consistent with a general preference for Chu songs among members of the royal Liu family that hailed from the Chu area. Their lack of interest in five-syllable poetry, or in recording their works in the genre, probably has to do with its association with the lower class at the time.

In sum, five-syllable poetry in the *Han shu* is characterized by the presentation of facts (rather than emotion), unadorned style, and lower-class people.

---

18 *Shi ji* 7.333; *Han shu* 31.1817; *XianQin Han Wei Jin Nanbeichao shi* 1.89.

19 *Shi ji* 8.389; *Han shu* 1.74; *XianQin Han Wei Jin Nanbeichao shi* 1.87.

20 *Han shu* 54.2466; *XianQin Han Wei Jin Nanbeichao shi* 1.109.

21 *XianQin Han Wei Jin Nanbeichao shi* 1.336–42. Chapter 4 further discusses this group of poems.

22 Wang Ping argues that the Chu song style, probably accompanied by the music from Chu, was particularly effective in conveying sad sentiments. See Wang Ping, "Plaint, Lyricism and the South," in *Southern Identity and Southern Estrangement in Medieval Chinese Poetry*, ed. Ping Wang and Nicholas Morrow Williams (Hong Kong: Hong Kong University Press, 2015), pp. 79–108.

23 *Han shu* 22.1046–51; *XianQin Han Wei Jin Nanbeichao shi* 1.145–47.

24 *Han shu* 63.257; *XianQin Han Wei Jin Nanbeichao shi* 1.109.

These associations are distinct from the common recognition of the genre's superiority in conveying personal emotions in the early medieval period. In his preface to the *Shi pin*, Zhong Rong asserts that the genre is "the most flavorful among all genres of writing" 眾作之有滋味者 and "the most comprehensive and precise when it comes to referring to what really happens, creating images, exhausting emotions and depicting objects" 指事造形，窮情寫物，最為詳切者.[25]

In addition to the *Shi pin*, other extant representations of five-syllable poems in anthologies and discussions in works of literary criticism from the 6th century predominantly focus on the expressive instead of descriptive function of this genre. Between the 1st and 6th centuries, how did five-syllable poetry come to be seen as the most efficient genre for expressing emotions? And when did it become associated specifically with women's voices? A pivotal moment is the Jian'an period.

2 The Transformation of Five-Syllable Poetry and Persona Composition in Jian'an

The significance of the Jian'an period in the development of five-syllable poetry is acknowledged in both the *Shi pin* and *Wenxin diaolong*:

> 暨建安之初，五言騰踴，文帝陳思，蹤轡以騁節；王徐應劉，望路而爭驅；並憐風月，狎池苑，述恩榮，敘酣宴；慷慨以任氣，磊落以使才，造懷指事，不求纖密之巧；驅辭逐貌，唯取昭晰之能；此其所同也。

25 *Shi pin jizhu*, p. 43. Some scholars see a teleological evolution of literature from *fu* and four-syllable poetry to five-syllable poetry. See, for example, Zhao Minli 趙敏俐, "Lun Handai wenren wuyanshi de yishu tezheng" 論漢代文人五言詩的藝術特徵, *Wenxue yichan* 2 (1995): 14–22; Ge Xiaoyin 葛曉音, "Zaoqi wuyanshi de shengcheng tujing jiqi dui Hanshi yishu de yingxiang" 早期五言詩的生成途徑及其對漢詩藝術的影響, *Wenxue yichan* 6 (2006): 15–27; and Cai Zong-qi, "A New Exploration of Early Pentasyllabic Poetry: Rhythms, Syntax, Structures, and Visions," *Bulletin of the Institute of Chinese Literature and Philosophy* 44 (2014): 1–56. Recently Zeb Raft disputed this linear narrative about four-syllable poetry being replaced or eclipsed by five-syllable poetry in the early medieval period. Raft points out that instead of disappearing from the literary scene completely, four-syllable poetry was still a prominent genre of writing among early medieval literati and served different social functions from that of five-syllable poetry: Raft, "Four-Syllable Poetry in Early Medieval China," pp. 1–3.

> At the beginning of the Jian'an poetry in five syllable lines bounded upward: Emperor Wen [Cao Pi] and Prince Chensi [Cao Zhi] let the reins go and set a galloping pace. Wang Can, Xu Gan, Ying Yang and Liu Zhen set their eyes on the course and raced each other. In each other's company they were fond of the breeze and moonlight, felt easy familiarity with pond and park, gave account of the glories of enjoying favor, told of festively tipsy banquets. Moved to passion, they gave free rein to their energies; and they employed their talents with expansive grandeur. Without trying to achieve a dense and delicate artfulness, they fashioned their concerns in reference to what really happened; they employed phrasing to catch the appearances of things, preferring only skill in luminous lucidity. In these things they were the same.[26]

> 降及建安，曹公父子，篤好斯文；平原兄弟，鬱為文棟；劉楨王粲，為其羽翼。次有攀龍托鳳，自致於屬車者，蓋將百計。彬彬之盛，大備於時矣。

> When we come down to the Jian'an Reign, the lord Cao, father and sons, were steadfastly fond of literary culture. Pingyuan [Cao Zhi] and his brother burgeoned as a beam of letters. Liu Zhen and Wang Can formed the wings. Beyond that there were those who "clung to the dragon and rode the phoenix" [rose by the power of their masters], and those who brought themselves to the level of attendants can be reckoned at almost a hundred. The glory of pattern and substance in balance was fully achieved in those times.[27]

Jian'an literati's writing of five-syllable poetry not only elevated its social status and disassociated the genre from lower-class authors, but also made it the literati's preferred choice for lyrical self-expression. As suggested in the *Wenxin diaolong* passage, Jian'an literati made the genre into a significant platform for conveying personal feelings in private or semi-private settings, such as banquets and communications with friends. Extant five-syllable poems by Jian'an literati confirm Zhong Rong's and Liu Xie's observations. In contrast to their predecessors, most Jian'an poems in the five-syllable line establish an emotional connection to the author with specific information regarding the

---

26 *Wenxin diaolong zhu* 2.66–67. I use Owen's translation in *The Making of Early Chinese Classical Poetry*, p. 50.

27 *Shi pin jizhu*, p. 20. I use Owen's translation in *The Making of Early Chinese Classical Poetry*, p. 53.

occasion of composition. For example, Wang Can's "Poem on Seven Sorrows" (Qi ai shi) II recounts a sorrowful journey that the speaker undertook, with a description of various geographic sites he passed en route:

荊蠻非我鄉	The barbarian Jing is not my home,
何為久滯淫	So why do I linger here so long?
方舟溯大江	In a double boat I went upriver,
日暮愁我心	The sunset saddened my heart.
山崗有餘暎	The lingering light hung on the ridges of hills,
巖阿增重陰	In the folds of cliffs the shadows increased.
狐狸馳赴穴	Foxes went scurrying to their lairs,
飛鳥翔故林	Birds flew circling native groves.
流波激清響	Rolling waves stirred clear echoes;
猴猿臨岸吟	monkeys and gibbons howled from high on shore.
迅風拂裳袂	A sudden breeze ruffled my skirt and sleeves,
白露霑衣衿	and silver dew soaked the folds of my gown.
獨夜不能寐	Alone that night I could not sleep,
攝衣起撫琴	then lifting my robe, I stroked the zither.
絲桐感人情	Its silk and beechwood stir passions,
為我發悲音	and bring forth sad melody on behalf of me.
羈旅無終極	This wayfaring will never end;
憂思壯難任	My sorrowful thoughts too strong to endure.[28]

The highly personal expressions and emotions in this poetic account of the journey in the first-person voice naturally inspire the identification of the speaking voice with the author Wang Can's own. One could even trace the poet's flight from the war-ravaged Chang'an to the southern city Jingzhou in 192 through his series "Poem on Seven Sorrows."[29] The problem with using literary texts as historical evidence notwithstanding, the possibility of establishing a close emotional bond between the poetic expression and the (individual) literary voice (and thereby with the author's identity) was rare in previous five-syllable poems. Poems such as this mark a new development in five-syllable poetry.

---

28 *XianQin Han Wei Jin Nanbeichao shi* 1.366. I use Owen's translation in *An Anthology of Chinese Literature*, p. 256, with modifications.

29 Besides Wang Can, other Jian'an writers wrote five-syllable poems that could be closely connected to their personal experiences. Hsiang-Lin Shih's dissertation "Jian'an Literature Revisited" reconstructs the historical background of many Jian'an poems based on the information found in them. She discusses many different genres, yet a large proportion of the works are five-syllable poems.

These changes in five-syllable poetry, however, happened mostly among a small circle of writers, that is, the group of literati surrounding the Cao family and frequenting their courts. Despite the enthusiastic tone of Zhong Rong and Liu Xie, their discussions of actual writers of five-syllable poetry are curiously limited to members of this literary circle. Zhong Rong mentions "hundreds of people" who wrote five-syllable poems yet remains vague regarding who they were. His comments on individual writers in the book fail to supply a substantial number of writers. Based on extant materials, contemporary literati outside this circle still wrote primarily in the four-syllable line, with the archaic and ornate style reminiscent of earlier poets such as Wei Xuancheng 韋玄成 (d. 36 BCE) and Fu Yi 傅毅 (fl. second half of the 1st century).[30] Moreover, members of the Jian'an literati often adopted the four-syllable line when exchanging poems with "outsiders." Wang Can's "Poem Presented to Cai Zidu" 贈蔡子篤詩, "Presented to Shisun Wenshi" 贈士孫文始, "Presented to Wen Shuliang" 贈文書良, and Ying Yang's "Poem in Reply to Zhao Shuli" 報趙淑麗詩 are some notable examples.[31] Four-syllable poetry was still the poetic genre used on stately occasions and it carried a political and public tone distinct from the five-syllable form. In his "A Discourse on Branches and Categories of Writings" (*Wenzhang liubie lun* 文章流別論),[32] Zhi Yu 摯虞 (d. 311) discusses the nature and primary functions of different poetic genres. He views the four-syllable form to be the only "correct/orthodox genre" (*siyan wei zheng* 四言为正) and the "refined sound" (*yayin* 雅音). The two extant versions of this essay diverge in his remarks on the common usage of the five-syllable line. The version preserved in the encyclopedia *Taiping yulan* 太平御覽 (Imperial overview from the *Taiping* [*xingguo*] reign [976–983], completed in 983) reads "it is also used in *yuefu*" (*yuefu yi yongzhi* 樂府亦用之). The *Quan Jin Wen* 全晉文 version has "it is often used in comic and entertaining music" (*yu paixie changyue duo yongzhi* 於俳諧倡樂多用之).[33] It is difficult to determine which version is closer to the original or what the stylistic or functional difference is between "*yuefu*" and "comic and entertaining music," but both

30 See, for example, Handan Chun's 邯鄲淳 "To Wu Chuxuan" 贈吳處玄詩, *XianQin Han Wei Jin Nanbeichao shi* 1.409.

31 Ibid. 1.357–59 and 382.

32 For a translation and an introduction to Zhi Yu and this work, see Joseph Allen, "Chih Yü's Discussions of Different Types of Literature: A Translation and Brief Comment," *Parerga 3: Two Studies in Chinese Literary Criticism* (Seattle: Institute for Comparative and Foreign Area Studies, University of Washington, 1976), pp. 3–36.

33 Li Fang 李昉 (925–996) et al., eds., *Taiping yulan* (Beijing: Zhonghua shuju, 1960) 586.2639; Yan Kejun 嚴可均 (1762–1843), ed., *Quan Jin wen* 全晉文 in *Quan Shanggu Sandai Qin Han Sanguo Liuchao wen* 全上古三代秦漢三國六朝文 (Shanghai: Shanghai guji chubanshe, 2009) 77.477.

have the aspect of performativity and impersonation. It is by this aspect that five-syllable poetry was first and foremost known in the early 4th century. This conviction about the function of five-syllable poetry resonates with how the four five-syllable poems are used in the *Han shu*. Although only the "Song on a Fair Lady" is explicitly performative, the other three contain performative elements in their impersonality.

Because it incorporates both performativity and expressivity of personal feelings, five-syllable poetry became a suitable medium for Jian'an poets to speak across boundaries of identity and convey intense feelings on someone else's behalf. Xu Gan's "Poem on Seeing a Boatman Bidding Farewell to His New Wife at Qinghe" (Yu Qinghe jian wanchuanshi xinhun yuqibie shi 於清河見挽船士新婚與妻別詩) articulates sorrow upon parting with his newly wed wife in the voice of a young boatman.[34] Cao Zhi's "Song of Sighing" (Xujie pian 吁嗟篇) assumes the voice of swirling weeds (*zhuanpeng* 轉蓬) to lament its disoriented and unsettled life.[35] Its alternative title, "Zither Song" (Qin se ge 琴瑟歌), suggests that it may have been performed with zither. Since the poetic impersonation often involves the crossing of gender boundaries, five-syllable poetry became the genre of choice for Jian'an literati to take on a woman's voice and to speak her mind, examples of which are discussed in Chapter 2. In contrast, Jian'an literati's four-syllable poems about women tend to be descriptive and written from the third-person perspective, such as Cao Zhi's four-syllable "Encomium on Lady Ban" (Ban Jieyu zan 班婕妤贊):

有德有言	Having virtue and writings;[36]
實惟班婕	indeed there is only Lady Ban.
盈冲其驕	In fullness, she guarded against arrogancy;
窮悅其厭	In despair, she took delight in [the emperor's] rejection.
在夷貞艱	At the time of waning, she remained chaste and steadfast,[37]
在晉正接	When she received the imperial favor, she remained proper in her reception [of the emperor].[38]

34 *XianQin Han Wei Jin Nanbeichao shi* 1.378.

35 Ibid. 1.423.

36 This alludes to Confucius' saying "Those who have virtue must also have writings" 有德者必有言 in the *Analects*.

37 *Yi* 夷 was *mingyi* 明夷, a trigram in the *Yijing* 易經 (The book of changes), which means that during a dark time, one should cultivate one's virtue of chastity and rectitude and should not follow the common people.

38 *Jin* 晉 is a trigram that means promotion and advance.

臨飈端幹　Facing strong wind, the tree stands still,
衝霜振葉　Its leaves hold up while enduring frosts.[39]

Lady Ban was a virtuous consort of Emperor Cheng of Han who lost imperial favor to the seductive and vicious Zhao sisters. The Zhao sisters accused Lady Ban, along with Empress Xu, of witchcraft and caused Empress Xu to be deposed. Lady Ban was only pardoned thanks to her eloquent defense.[40] The last two lines of the poem probably refer to her reaction to the slander. The didactic nature of the "encomium" dictates that the poem emphasizes the person's virtue and deeds. The poem makes an interesting contrast with Cao Zhi's five-syllable poems about women, which tend to delve into the depths of emotion and, either partially or entirely, assume her voice.

The most well-known poem associated with Lady Ban, however, is the five-syllable "Poem on Resentment," attributed to her in both the *Wen xuan* and *Yutai xinyong*. The earliest source for Lady Ban's life story—her biography in the *Han shu*—although citing a *fu* lamenting her fate, does not mention this poem at all.[41] Questions were raised about the validity of Lady Ban's authorship as early as the 6th century.[42] But the poem has always been celebrated as one of the earliest five-syllable poems in the tradition:

新裂齊紈素　Newly cut, fine plain silk from Qi;
鮮潔如霜雪　as fresh and pure as frost and snow.
裁為合歡扇　It was cut into a fan with "double-joy" patterns,[43]
團團似明月　perfectly round like the bright moon.
出入君懷袖　It goes in and out of your bosom and sleeves,
動搖微風發　When moving, it stirs up a gentle breeze.
常恐秋節至　I ever fear the arrival of the autumn season,
涼飆奪炎熱　when cool gusts eliminate blazing heat.
棄捐篋笥中　I will be cast away in a storage box;
恩情中道絕　your favor and love will disappear midway.[44]

39 *Cao Zhi ji jiaozhu*, pp. 86–87.

40 *Han shu* 97b.3984.

41 Ibid. 97b.3985–87.

42 Liu Xie mentions the skepticism regarding the authorship of Lady Ban and Li Ling in the *Wenxin diaolong*: Fan Wenlan, *Wenxin diaolong zhu* 2.22.

43 "*Hehuan*" is the Chinese name for acacia. The plant is often featured on clothing, utensils, and furniture because of the auspicious meaning of its name.

44 *XianQin Han Wei Jin Nanbeichao shi* 1.116–17. I consulted Owen's translation in *The Making of Early Chinese Classical Poetry*, p. 223.

The poem portrays a lovely round fan. It starts with a description of the fan's material, appearance, and function. The "double-joy" pattern on the fan indicate a romantic relationship between the owner and the "*jun*" (you) in line 5. Yet in the middle of the poem it turns into an anxious anticipation of the loss of favor and a lament on the inevitable abandonment. The helpless and powerless tone of the speaking voice unmistakably translates into the voice of the owner of the fan, a forsaken woman.

Most scholars now agree that "Poem on Resentment" was not actually written by Lady Ban. First, there is no mention of her being a writer of (five-syllable) poetry in sources before the 5th century, including the *Han shu*; second, there is no evidence of any other five-syllable poems with such a mature style in Lady Ban's time. It is possible that the poem was originally composed some time during the Jian'an era, along with many other Jian'an persona compositions in the five-syllable line. Lady Ban, as one of the most famous abandoned women in history, became an appealing voice of this poem and then later the "author."[45] This theory cannot be verified for lack of textual evidence, but the textual history of another poem may shed some light on it. It is the "Miscellaneous Poem Written on behalf of Mrs. Wang, Divorced Wife of Liu Xun" (Dai Liu Xun chuqi Wangshi zashi 代劉勳出妻王氏雜詩), attributed to Cao Pi in the *Yiwen leiju*:

翩翩床前帳　Fluttering, a curtain in front of the bed;
張以蔽光輝　hung up to shield the gleaming light.
昔將爾同去　In the past, I took you with me and left [for his home],
今將爾同歸　Now I bring you with me to return [to my home].
緘藏篋笥裏　Sealed and stored inside a box,
當復何時披　When will you be spread out again?[46]

The title clearly marks the poem as a persona composition in the voice of a divorced wife. As part of the dowry that she took to her husband's household, the bed curtain is a perfect analogy for the abandoned woman. Originally a

45 Knechtges believes the poem was written in the Eastern Han period and "belongs to the same anonymous song tradition as the *gushi* and *yuefu*. It may have originally been a folksong about an abandoned lady. Later, probably in the Wei–Jin period, it was attached to the story of Favorite Beauty Ban, to whom the piece then was attributed": Knechtges, "The Poetry of an Imperial Concubine," p. 136. Owen uses the authorship attribution of this poem to illustrate the complex relationship between the concepts of "author" and "speaker" in early five-syllable poems. He maintains that the poem was attributed to Lady Ban around the mid-3rd century: Owen, *The Making of Early Chinese Classical Poetry*, pp. 223–25.

46 *XianQin Han Wei Jin Nanbeichao shi* 1.402.

symbol of marital bliss, similar to the "double-joy" pattern on the round fan, it is now forsaken, stored away, and taken with the woman to her natal home. The agony shared between the woman and the curtain is accentuated by the way she addresses it, with the personified pronoun "you" (*er* 爾) in lines 3 and 4. The female persona's heartbroken revelation of her misfortune is made possible only by the poem's assumption of the first-person voice. The poem follows the same narrative sequence found in the "Poem on Resentment," starting with the description of a lovely object and turning into a sad lament about it being cast off in the middle. The object even ends up in the same place—the "storage box" (*qiesi* 篋笥).

Listed as Cao Pi's poem in a woman's voice in the *Yiwen leiju*, the poem is included in the *Yutai xinyong* under the name Wang Song 王宋, with the title "Miscellaneous Poem by Mrs. Wang, Wife of Liu Xun" (Liu Xun qi Wangshi zashi 劉勳妻王氏雜詩) and a short preface:

> 王宋者。平虜將軍劉勳妻也。入門二十餘年。後勳悅山陽司馬氏女。以宋無子出之。還于道中作詩。
>
> Wang Song was the wife of the General of Pacifying Salvage Liu Xun. She was married to Liu for over twenty years. Later Xun took delight in the daughter of the Sima clan in Shanyang and divorced Song for bearing no son. When she returned [to her natal family], she composed this poem in the middle of her journey.[47]

The story told in this preface is almost the same as Lady Ban's: some years into a happy marriage, the husband took a fancy to another woman and abandoned his wife on the grounds of a malicious accusation. But this story and the name Wang Song are nowhere to be found in any other sources. Liu Xun was a real historical figure, appearing in the *Sanguo zhi*, but there is no record of his wife anywhere. Neither Zhong Rong nor Liu Xie mentions her in their discussions of early five-syllable poems. At the same time, persona writing in the voice of an abandoned woman was common among Jian'an poets. Cao Pi, Cao Zhi, Wang Can, and Xu Gan all wrote poems and/or *fu* on widows and abandoned wives.[48] It was also a common practice among Jian'an writers to write both *fu* and poetry on the same topic. For example, Cao Zhi wrote a five-syllable poem in the voice of an abandoned wife entitled "Song on an Abandoned Wife" and

47 *Yutai xinyong jianzhu* 2.58.

48 *Yiwen leiju* 30.514 and 528. See the discussion in Chapter 2.

a "*Fu* on a Divorced Wife" (Chufu fu 出婦賦).[49] Since Cao Pi wrote a "*Fu* on a Divorced Wife," it would not be surprising if he also wrote a five-syllable poem on the topic. What likely happened is that the persona of the poem was taken to be the "author," and a story was created to explain the context of its composition. The point here is not to argue for Cao Pi's authorship, but to show how easily the persona "Wang Song" could become the author and, by extension, how easily such misattribution could happen for many persona writings in the feminine voice.[50]

We have reason to reconstruct a similar scenario regarding the authorship of "Poem on Resentment," a 3rd-century poem in the voice of an abandoned woman that was later attributed to a historical woman whose story resonated with the sentiments expressed in the poem. Mu Zhai 木齋 takes Xu Gan to be the real author of "Poem on Resentment," on the grounds that Xu wrote "*Fu* on a Circular Fan" (Yuan shan fu 圓扇賦).[51] Mu Zhai does not offer more solid evidence for his theory. But considering the practice of writing both poetry and *fu* on the same topic, Xu Gan is indeed a possible candidate for its authorship.

Unlike Lady Ban, the authorship of Wang Song was never sustained in the tradition. No existing sources other than the *Yutai xinyong* list the poem under her name. Feng Weine's 馮維訥 (1513–1572) *Gushi ji* 古詩紀 (Records of ancient poems), for example, still attributes the poem to Cao Pi.[52] The name Wang Song rarely if ever appears in anthologies or accounts of literary history made in pre-modern and modern times. The reasons are twofold: (1) there is another, more feasible candidate for authorship; and (2) the name Wang Song, unlike Lady Ban, fails to offer a compelling or historically significant backstory for the poem. Its association with one of the most virtuous and talented palace ladies in early history secured a prominent place for the "Poem on Resentment" in cultural and literary history: it has thus become the earliest five-syllable poem

49 *XianQin Han WeiJin Nanbeichao shi* 1.455–56; *Yiwen leiju* 30.528–29.

50 I am aware that in extant sources the attribution to Cao Pi appeared at a later time (*Yiwen leiju*) than that to Wang Song (*Yutai xinyong*). But the *Yutai xinyong* is known for dubious attributions, especially to women writers, given the anthology's pronounced interest in female authorship and readership. The case regarding the authorship of the "Ballad on a Pond" discussed in the Introduction is a good example. In comparison, the *Yiwen leiju* is mostly conservative in its preservation of texts. It is not uncommon to find the earliest version of a five-syllable poem in the *Yiwen leiju*.

51 See Mu Zhai's discussion in "Lun Jian'an nüxing ticai de xingqi—Jianlun 'Yuan shi' de zuozhe" 論建安五言詩女性題材的興起—兼論《怨詩》的作者, *Shanxi daxue xuebao* 29, no. 2 (2009): 36–41. Xu Gan's *fu* is now lost but its title is mentioned in Cao Pi's "A Discourse on Writing," *Wen xuan* 52.2271.

52 *XianQin Han WeiJin Nanbeichao shi* 1.402.

by a known author and a moving articulation of her pathos. The attribution to Lady Ban is also backed up by records of her literary talent and wifely virtue in the official history *Han shu*. The name Wang Song, on the other hand, carries no such historical or cultural weight.

As in the choice of Empress Zhen over Cao Cao for the authorship of the "Ballad on a Pond,"[53] the attribution to a female author often has to do with the belief that the sentiments of loss, abandonment, and desperation belong exclusively to women and that the sincere expression of such sentiments could only come from personal experience. In the "Nineteen Old Poems" v, upon hearing the sorrowful zither music from a high tower, the speaker speculates on the gender and identity of the player:

上有弦歌聲	From above came song and the sound of a zither,
音響一何悲	how sad the echoes are!
誰能為此曲	Who could make this song?
無乃杞梁妻	It *must* be Qiliang's wife![54]

The query and answer are formed as an unquestioned inference with the conjunction "it must be" (*wunai* 無乃): if a song sounds deeply sad, it must have been made by a lonely, abandoned woman. In this case, she is a wife who lost her husband in battle. This couplet provides the zither song with a plausible speaker and a contextual story. The same logic that "it must be [composed by]" was behind the attribution of poems about abandonment and resentment to Wang Song, Lady Ban, and Empress Zhen.

3 Five-Syllable Poetry and Women's Voices in Romanticized Historical Narratives of the Fourth and Fifth Centuries

As demonstrated in the previous section, an enticing contextual story is the key element for a poem to be attached to the voice of a woman and read as a genuine expression of her feelings. It is not a coincidence, therefore, that most women writers of early five-syllable poems, including Lady Ban and Empress Zhen, are well known historical figures with dramatic and tragic life stories. Stories of women, with the exception of members of the royal family, are largely absent from official historical records, but they are often told in romanticized accounts of historical events. Such accounts were very popular in the 4th and

53 See the discussion in the Introduction.

54 *XianQin Han Wei Jin Nanbeichao shi* 1.330. See the discussion in Chapter 1.

5th centuries. Based on extant texts and records, *Chu Han chunqiu* 楚漢春秋 (Spring and autumn of Chu and Han), *Han Wudi gushi* 漢武帝故事 (Stories of Emperor Wu of the Han), *Yezhong ji* 鄴中記 (Records of Ye), *Yedu gushi* 鄴都故事 (Stories of the capital Ye), *Cai Yan biezhuan* 蔡琰別傳 (Informal biography of Cai Yan), and *Xijing zaji* 西京雜記 (Miscellaneous records of the Western Capital) are among the titles that were widely circulated.[55] Unfortunately, most of these texts have been lost except for fragments surviving in encyclopedic and historical sources. Some of them are the earliest sources to attribute five-syllable poems to women writers, such as the *Yedu gushi*, which attributes the "Ballad on a Pond" to Empress Zhen. In these texts, a five-syllable poem is often quoted at the climactic moment in a female character's life—sometimes right before her death—as a direct expression of her most intense emotions. Another example is the following poem as the final words of Lady Yu, the beloved concubine of Xiang Yu:

漢兵已略地	Han troops have already approached our lands,
四面楚歌聲	From all four sides comes the sound of Chu songs.
大王意氣盡	My lord, your spirit is at the end,
賤妾何樂生	For me, your humble concubine, what joy is there to live?[56]

Zhang Shoujie's 張守節 (fl. 730) commentary to the *Shi ji* quotes this poem from a certain *Chu Han chunqiu*. This title is included in the *Han shu* bibliography as the work of the early Han scholar Lu Jia 陸賈 (*c*.240–170 BCE).[57] But it is quite unlikely that an early Han work would contain a five-syllable poem in such mature form. Moreover, if the five-syllable poem were indeed in Lu Jia's book, it would have been strange for it to be absent in both the *Shi ji* and *Han shu*, especially given that both histories quote Xiang Yu's song to which it is supposed to respond. The most plausible explanation is that this *Chu Han chunqiu* was not Lu Jia's book, but a later work with the same title.[58]

55 Some stories from these accounts found their way into dynastic histories. For example, the biography of Cai Yan that quotes her two poems in the *Hou Han shu* 後漢書 draws extensively from popular stories such as *Cai Yan Biezhuan*.

56 *XianQin Han Wei Jin Nanbeichao shi* 1.89.

57 *Han shu* 30.1714. The *Han shu* biography of Sima Qian 司馬遷 (*c*.145–86 BCE) also mentions the *Chu Han chunqiu* as one of the sources for the *Shi ji*: *Han shu* 62.2737.

58 The title resembles Xi Zaochi's 習鑿齒 (d. 384) *Han Jin chunqiu* 漢晉春秋 (Spring and autumn of the Han and Jin), a historical account that, unlike the *Sanguo zhi*, recognizes the legitimacy of Shu-Han. Xi's book has also been lost since the Song dynasty.

As mentioned previously, both the *Shi ji* and *Han shu* record Xiang Yu's "Song of Gaixia" about his desperation and grief under the besiegement of Liu Bang's troops. Here I quote the passage from the *Shi ji*. *Han shu*'s account is similar, with minor variants:

> 項王則夜起，飲帳中。有美人名虞，常幸從；駿馬名騅，常騎之。於是項王乃悲歌忼慨，自為詩曰：力拔山兮氣蓋世，時不利兮騅不逝，騅不逝兮可奈何？虞兮虞兮奈若何！歌數闋，美人和之。項王泣數行下，左右皆泣，莫能仰視。
>
> King Xiang [Xiang Yu] then rose at night and drank in his tent. He had a Lady whose name was Yu. She was always favored and in his company. There was [also] a fine steed named Zui that Xiang always rode. Thereupon King Xiang sang with sorrow and fervency, and made the following poem by himself: "My strength could lift a mountain; alas, my spirit sees no parallel in this world; / Time is not on my side; alas, my steed would not proceed. / My steed would not proceed; alas, what can I do? / Lady Yu, Lady Yu! Alas, what should I do about you?" He sang for a few stanzas and *the lady sang in harmony*. King Xiang's tears fell in streams and his retainers were all weeping. None bore to look up [at him].[59]

Although both the *Shi ji* and *Han shu* mention that the lady "sang in harmony," neither includes the matching song. Depending on the meaning of the character *he* 和, Lady Yu might have composed another song or sung the same "Song of Gaixia." But this account leaves ample room for imagination and creativity. It is also noteworthy that Xiang Yu's poem is in the form of Chu song, which is the most common poetic form to express intense personal feelings in Han historiography, as shown in the previous section. But when the lady's "matching song" was added to the story later, it appeared in the five-syllable line, a genre that was not commonly used for conveying individual emotions until the Jian'an period.[60]

The attribution of the "Chant of White Hair" (Baitou yin 白頭吟) to Zhuo Wenjun, Sima Xiangru's wife, is similarly integrated in a romanticized historical

59 *Shi ji* 7.333 and *Han shu* 31.1817; *XianQin Han Wei Jin Nanbeichao shi* 1.89.

60 Note that it is unusual for a matching poem to be in a different genre/style from the original. The employment of the five-syllable line to express personal emotion is another reason to date the *Chu Han chunqiu* after the Jian'an period, when the function of five-syllable poetry was increasingly seen as more expressive than descriptive.

story. Its earliest source, the "Treatise on Music" of the *Song shu*, includes it as an anonymous Han *yuefu*:

皚如山上雪	Clear like snow on the mountain,
皎若雲間月	shining like the moon among clouds.
聞君有兩意	I have heard you have feelings for another,
故來相決絕	therefore I come to break off with you.
平生共城中	Our lives spent in the same city,
何嘗斗酒會	when have we ever met over a jug of ale?
今日斗酒會	This day we meet over a jug of ale.
明旦溝水頭	tomorrow morning, by the waters of the moat.
躞蹀御溝上	Slowly pacing by the royal moat,
溝水東西流	the moat's waters flow off east and west.
郭東亦有樵	East of the town there is a woodsman,
郭西亦有樵	west of the town there is also a woodsman.
兩樵相推與	The two woodsmen each defer to the other,
無親為誰驕	without kin, to whom can one show off?
淒淒重淒淒	Dreary, and again dreary,
嫁娶亦不啼	in marrying there is no need to weep.
願得一心人	I want someone with a faithful heart,
白頭不相離	never separating until hair turns white.
竹竿何嫋嫋	How the bamboo pole sways!
魚尾何離簁	how the fishtails swish to and fro!
男兒欲相知	When a man wants someone who knows him,
何用錢刀為	What use is coin and cash?
齕如馬噉箕	Munching, the horse chews its straw,
川上高士嬉	by the river fine gentlemen sport.
今日相對樂	This day we face each other and have pleasure.
延年萬歲期	May your years extend to ten thousand.[61]

Like the *Song shu* version of the "Ballad on a Pond," this poem contains too many conflicting elements to offer a cohesive storyline or narrative voice. It mentions a range of different relationships including those between friends, married couples, woodsmen, gentlemen, and so forth, with no clear connection or transition in between. But an anecdote in the *Xijing zaji*, conventionally

61 *XianQin Han Wei Jin Nanbeichao shi* 1.274–75. I use Owen's translation in *The Making of Early Classical Chinese Poetry*, p. 229, with modifications.

attributed to Ge Hong 葛洪 (283–343),[62] associates the poem with Zhuo Wenjun:

> 相如將聘茂陵人女為妾，卓文君作《白頭吟》以自絕，相如乃止。
>
> Xiangru was about to take the daughter of a person from Maoling as concubine. Zhuo Wenjun wrote the "Chant of White Hair" to break up with him. Xiangru thereupon stopped.[63]

The poem's only tangible connection with Zhuo Wenjun's story is the first two couplets, which speak about breaking off a relationship, and lines 15–18, about the wish to have "someone with a faithful heart" in marriage. But as we will see in the next chapter, such an ill match between a poem and its alleged articulator is not uncommon in early five-syllable poems. In a similar way that Chu songs are quoted in the *Shi ji* and *Han shu*, five-syllable poems are introduced in romanticized historical accounts in the early medieval period to convey strong personal emotions at a pivotal point in a person's, especially a woman's, life. In the popular imagination of the time, they must have (*wunai* 無乃) written these poems in response to the extreme situations they were experiencing.

Two versions of "Zither Song" (Qin ge 琴歌) in the Chu song style are attributed to Sima Xiangru in the *Yutai xinyong*. The preceding preface reads, "Sima Xiangru traveled to Linqiong. The wealthy man Zhuo Wangsun had a daughter who recently widowed. She secretly peeped at Sima Xiangru through the wall. Xiangru plucked the zither and sang to seduce her" 司馬相如遊臨邛，富人卓王孫有女文君新寡，竊於壁間窺之，相如鼓琴歌挑之.[64] It is telling that in both Xiang Yu/Lady Yu and Sima Xiangru/Zhuo Wenjun stories, while the male character was accredited with a Chu song, the five-syllable poem was the genre of choice in the woman's voice.

Cao Yan's 蔡琰 five-syllable "Poem on Grief and Anger" (Beifen shi 悲憤詩) is another poem associated with a woman's voice in a romanticized historical

62 For debates surrounding the dating of the *Xijing zaji*, see William H. Nienhauser, "Once Again, the Authorship of the *Hsi-ching tsa-chi*," *Journal of American Oriental Society* 98, no. 3 (1978): 219–36. Nienhauser suggests a later date (550) for its compilation. Owen believes it was compiled "probably in the third or early fourth century": Owen, *The Making of Early Chinese Classical Poetry*, p. 227. We can at least date the book's compilation to the early medieval period.

63 Xiang Xinyang 向新陽 and Liu Keren 劉克任, ed., *Xijing zaji jiaozhu* 西京雜記校註 (Shanghai: Shanghai guji chubanshe, 1991) 3.150.

64 *Yutai xinyong jianzhu* 9.389; *XianQin Han Wei Jin Nanbeichao shi* 1.99–100. These "Zither Songs" do not appear in any sources earlier than the *Yutai xinyong* and might also have once circulated with the story about Sima Xiangru and Zhuo Wenjun.

account. Cai Yan was the daughter of the prominent Eastern Han scholar Cai Yong. According to her biography in the *Hou Han shu* 後漢書 (History of the Later Han), after the death of her first husband, she was abducted by the Xiongnu troops and forced to marry a chieftain. She bore two sons during her 12-year stay in the "barbarian lands," after which Cao Cao, an old acquaintance of her father's, ransomed her back to the Han capital and married her to Dong Si 董祀. This biography quotes a five-syllable poem and a Chu song that she wrote after her return. Both verses recount, in retrospect, her personal tragedy in one of the most chaotic moments in Chinese history.[65] Although she was later celebrated as one of the most talented women in Chinese history, the only occurrence of Cai Yan's name in any sources prior to the 5th century is two "*Fu* on Cai Bojie's Daughter" (Cai Bojie nü fu 蔡伯喈女賦), written by Cao Pi and Ding Yi 丁廙 respectively.[66] Fragments of Ding Yi's *fu* praise Cai Yan's superior understanding of Confucian classics and extraordinary literary talents, which is consistent with her image in the *Hou Han shu* biography. The only record of Cai Yan's writing outside the *Hou Han shu* is the listing of her works in one *juan* 卷 (volume) in the *Sui shu* bibliography.[67] Su Shi 蘇軾 (1037–1101) maintained that the poems in the *Hou Han shu* were written by someone from the Jin or Liu-Song dynasty and were misattributed to Cao Yan due to the negligence and incompetence of the compiler Fan Ye 范曄 (398–445).[68] Since then the authenticity of these two poems has been in doubt. Both the *Yiwen leiju* and *Taiping yulan* cite fragments of the two poems with their provenance in a lost text *Cai Yan biezhuan*.[69] Scholars suggest that Fan Ye consulted the *Cai Yan biezhuan* or other popular romanticized histories circulated in his time and quoted the two poems from it.[70] The "*biezhuan*," informal biography, in the title indicates that the book is a romanticized account, an "unofficial/alternative history," of Cai Yan's life. The fact that the five-syllable poem was quoted

65 *Hou Han shu* 84.2801–02.

66 *Yiwen leiju* 30.542. The text of Cao Pi's *fu* is lost, but its title and a line from its preface survive in the encyclopedia *Taiping yulan* 806.3581.

67 *Sui shu* 35.1059.

68 Su Shi, "Inscribing Cai Yan's Biography" (Ti Cai Yan zhuan 題蔡琰傳), in *Su Shi wenji* 蘇軾文集 (Beijing: Zhonghua shuju, 1986) 67.2094. For studies on the authenticity of Cai Yan's poems, see Frankel, "Cai Yan and the Poems Attributed to Her"; and Liu Yuejin 劉躍進, *Zhonggu wenxue wenxianxue* 中古文学文獻學 (Nanjing: Jiangsu guji chubanshe, 1997), pp. 142–44.

69 *XianQin Han Wei Jin Nanbeichao shi* 1.201.

70 See, for example, Tan Qixiang 譚其驤, "Cai Wenji de shengping jiqi zuopin" 蔡文姬的生平及其作品, in *Hujia shiba pai taolunji* 胡笳十八拍討論集, ed. *Wenxue yichan* bianjibu (Beijing: Zhonghua shuju, 1959), pp. 238–54, esp. p. 250. Owen mentions this possibility too; see Owen, *The Making of Early Chinese Classical Poetry*, p. 233.

alongside the Chu song as a genuine outpouring of Cai Yan's emotion attests to the newly acquired significance of five-syllable poetry in effectively communicating intense personal feelings in the narration of historical events.

The five-syllable poem ends with Cai Yan's lament on her abandonment, even though she was, strictly speaking, not exactly an "abandoned wife":

登高遠眺望	Climbing a high place, I gazed afar,
魂神忽飛逝	my spirit and soul suddenly flew off.
奄若壽命盡	Swiftly my life was gone,
旁人相寬大	those around me encouraged me to take it easy.
為復彊視息	Once again I forced myself to look and breathe for their sake,
雖生何聊賴	Although I lived, what had I to rely on?
託命於新人	I entrusted my life to a new husband,
竭心自勗厲	I did my utmost and exerted myself.
流離成鄙賤	Carried off, I became lowly and base,
常恐復捐廢	I was ever in fear of being cast off and discarded again.
人生幾何時	How long does human life last?—
懷憂終年歲	I will feel grief to the end of my years.[71]

The poetic line "I was ever in fear of being cast off and discarded again" (*changkong fu juanfei* 常恐復捐廢) bears a close resemblance to the line "I ever fear the arrival of the autumn season" (*changkong qiujie zhi* 常恐秋節至) in the "Poem on Resentment" attributed to Lady Ban. The sentimental implications are similar as well. Both express an anticipation of and anxiety about abandonment before its actual occurrence. Notably, this feeling of being abandoned by the husband/lover is absent in the Chu song on the same topic, which focuses on her displacement and misfortune in the Xiongnu. Compared with the five-syllable poem, the Chu song never gained the same status in later tradition as the "authentic" voice of Cai Yan.[72]

Some observations regarding romanticized historical accounts in the early medieval period can be made here. First, these accounts tell dramatic stories about famous historical figures, most of whom were members of the imperial family or of the elite with connections to the court. Female characters

71 *XianQin Han Wei Jin Nanbeichao shi* 1.200. I use Owen's translation in *the Making of Early Chinese Classical Poetry*, p. 237, with modifications.

72 The prominent *yuefu* scholar Yu Guanying 余冠英 (1906–1995) believes the five-syllable poem is authentic but the Chu song is a forgery. This view is very influential and has been accepted by many. See Yu, "Lun Cai Yan 'Beifen shi'" 論蔡琰悲憤詩, in *Han Wei Liuchao shi luncong* 漢魏六朝詩論叢 (Beijing: Shangwu yinshuguan, 2010), pp. 55–64.

with extraordinary, and often tragic, life stories feature prominently in these accounts. Finally, these stories often quote poems in these women's voices to express strong feelings, in the time-honored tradition of using verse to enrich and embellish historical narrative. Most of these poems are in the five-syllable line, a form that has had links to both persona composition and the expression of personal sentiments since the Jian'an period. The sentiments they convey are usually those of abandonment, resentment, and desperation.

If most poems articulated by women in romanticized historical stories were not their own writings, why was there a need in these 4th- and 5th-century texts to provide them with voices? The reason lies in the early medieval literati's strong interest in missing voices in official historical records as well as in alternative perspectives to approach the past. A telling example is the fascination with Wang Zhaojun's 王昭君 story. The *Han shu* gives a very brief account of Wang Zhaojun's marriage to the Xiongnu leader:

> 單于自言願婿漢氏以自親。元帝以後宮良家子王嬙字昭君賜單于。
>
> The Xiongnu Chief proposed to be the son-in-law of the Han royal house. Emperor Yuan bestowed him Wang Qiang, style Zhaojun, who was the daughter of a good family in the rear palace.[73]

Wang Zhaojun is a minor figure in the *Han shu* and is given much less attention than Princess Wusun, another victim of political marriage. Yet the number of stories about Wang grew immensely over the next few centuries. According to the "Biography of Southern Xiongnu" (Nan Xiongnu zhuan 南匈奴傳) in the *Hou Han shu*, Zhaojun volunteered to marry Xiongnu out of resentment over the emperor's neglect. The emperor gave her permission but regretted it after seeing her extraordinary beauty. Anecdotes in the *Xijing zaji* and *Shishuo xinyu* blame Zhaojun's failure to attract the emperor's attention on the court painter's malicious distortion of her appearance in the portrait presented to the throne.[74] Shi Chong's 石崇 (249–300) "Lyric of Wang Mingjun" (Wang Mingjun ci 王明君辭) provides Wang Zhaojun's point of view in her own voice, with a short preface at the beginning:

> 王明君者，本是王昭君。以觸文帝諱，故改之。匈奴盛，請婚于漢。元帝以後宮良家子明君配焉。昔公主嫁烏孫，令琵琶馬上

73 *Han shu* 94b.3803.

74 *Xijing zaji jiaozhu* 2.9; *Shishuo xinyu jianshu* 19.2.665–67.

> 作樂以慰其道路之思。其送明君，亦必爾也。其造新曲，多哀怨之聲，故敘之于紙云爾。
>
> Wang Mingjun's original name was Wang Zhaojun. The name was changed for the violation of the taboo against Emperor Wen's name [Sima Zhao 司馬昭 (211–265)]. Xiongnu was prosperous and proposed a marriage liaison with the Han. Emperor Yuan (r. 49–33 BCE) chose Mingjun, a daughter of a good family in the rear palace, to marry him. In the past, when a princess was married to the Wusun, they ordered that music be played with *pipa* on horseback to console her longing [for home] along the road.[75] When they sent Mingjun off, *there must also have been this*. The new melodies created were mostly grievous and resentful. Therefore I narrate it on paper as follows.[76]

The poem starts with Zhaojun's self-introduction ("I am originally a daughter of the house of Han" 我本漢家子) then relates her marriage to the Xiongnu chieftain and the hardships she endured along the way. The first-person voice reveals, in a deeply personal and heartfelt way, her desperation and loneliness in a strange place and her bitter resentment about being abandoned. The last few couplets read:

願假飛鴻翼	I wish to borrow wings from flying swans,
弃之以遐征	to abandon it all and travel far away.
飛鴻不我顧	Flying swans do not heed me;
佇立以屏營	I stand alone, holding my breath.
昔爲匣中玉	In the past I was a jade in a box;
今爲糞上英	Now I am a flower in filth.
朝華不足歡	Morning flowers are not worthy of joy,
甘與秋草幷	I am willing to be with the autumn grass.
傳語後世人	I send my words to later generations—
遠嫁難爲情	marrying far away, the feelings are hard to bear.[77]

The sentiments in this poem strongly resonate with Cai Yan's five-syllable "Poem on Grief and Anger." Like Cai Yan, Wang Zhaojun is presented first and foremost as an abandoned woman, as she laments being left behind by flying swans and deserted by her homeland. There is no record that Shi Chong ever

75 Princess Wusun and the song attributed to her are discussed earlier in this chapter.

76 *XianQin Han Wei Jin Nanbeichao shi* 1.642.

77 Ibid., 1.642–43.

wrote a story about Wang Zhaojun's marriage to Xiongnu, yet this poem would fit perfectly in such a story.[78] If it did not have an explicitly stated author with a preface declaring his intent, Shi Chong's poem could have been easily attributed to Wang Zhaojun and become part of the cultural narrative about her life. The phrase "there must also have been this" (*yi bi er ye* 亦必爾也) echoes the unquestioned conviction in "*wunai*," or "it must be," in the "Nineteen Old Poems" v. The idea is that a poem must have been written to give voice to the profound feelings of an ill-fated woman under the circumstance. Both expressions show the confidence in matching a poem with an appropriate author/speaker based solely on the feelings expressed in it. And as in the case of the "Ballad on a Pond," the feelings of abandonment and desperation were taken as a marker of femininity.

As shown previously, many early poems attributed to women writers were once circulated with romanticized historical stories. The attribution could occur in different ways: extant poems, anonymous or otherwise, such as the "Chant of White Hair," "Ballad on a Pond," and "Miscellaneous Poem by Mrs. Wang, Wife of Liu Xun," were ascribed to a historical woman; new poems were created to fit a historical story, such as the poems attributed to Lady Yu and Cai Yan. Lastly, Shi Chong's poem in the voice of Wang Zhaojun was intended to provide the voice that was missing from the received historical narrative without trying to pass itself off as her own composition.

Zhong Rong's preface to the *Shi pin* lists several occasions that inspire the composition of five-syllable poetry:

> 至於楚臣去境，漢妾辭宮。或骨横朔野，魂逐飛蓬。或負戈外戍，殺氣雄邊。塞客衣單，孀閨淚盡。或士有解佩出朝，一去忘反。女有颺蛾入寵，再盼傾國。凡斯種種，感盪心靈，非陳詩何以展其義？ 非長歌何以騁其情?
>
> As for the time when the Chu subject left his domain and the Han consort bit farewell to her palace, some left their bones exposed in the deserts of the North, their souls chasing the floating weeds; some carried weapons to fight in the battlefield, their intents to kill holding sway over the

78 Stories of Wang Zhaojun were in wide circulation in early medieval times, including those found in the *Qin cao* 琴操 (Zither tunes, attributed to Cai Yong), *Xijing zaji, Shishuo xinyu*, and *Hou Han shu*. The *Qin cao* quotes a four-syllable poem titled "Song of Resentment, Displacement and Longing" (Yuankuang siwei ge 怨曠思惟歌) as an expression of her resentment about the emperor's decision and her longing for home. *XianQin Han Wei Jin Nanbeichao shi* 1.315–16. For a close examination of the evolution of the Wang Zhaojun stories, see Wang Ping, "Plaint, Lyricism and the South," pp. 91–98.

> border. The clothes of travelers in the frontier were thin; tears of widows in their chambers ran out. There are also retainers who took off their pendants and left the court. Once gone they never returned. There are women who, with brows proudly lifted, received imperial favor. When they gave a second glance, a whole state was toppled. All these various situations moved heart and soul. Without poetry, how could they explicate their intentions? Without long songs, how could they give free rein to their feelings?[79]

These vignettes are commonplaces in extant early works of the five-syllable line, even though it may be hard to locate each reference precisely.[80] Among those that are identifiable, the "Chu minister" in exile could be Qu Yuan or Wu Zixu 伍子胥 (559–484 BCE), although either of them did not leave any five-syllable poems.[81] The "Han consort" most likely refers to Lady Ban, who voluntarily moved out of her palace to take care of the emperor's mother in order to avoid having to compete with the Zhao sisters. Zhong Rong ranks her in the upper gradation (*shang pin* 上品) and speaks highly of her five-syllable "Poem on Resentment." But it could also refer to Wang Zhaojun, who left Emperor Yuan's palace to marry the Xiongnu Chieftain. The woman who "toppled a state" with her glance alludes to Lady Li in Li Yannian's "Song on a Fair Lady." The soldiers fighting on the frontier likely refers to Li Ling, whom Zhong Rong mentions in the preface and places in the upper gradation. What is significant, however, is that they are all melodramatic plots fit for elaboration and imagination in romanticized historical accounts, with narrative elements such as palace intrigues, political struggles, and frontier battles. The agonies of abandoned or left-behind female characters are indispensable factors in almost all these vignettes. The two rhetorical questions at the end—"Without poetry, how could they explicate their intentions? Without long songs, how could they give free rein to their feelings?"—speak to the irreplaceable role of five-syllable poetry in explicating the "intentions" (*yi* 義) and manifesting the "feelings" (*qing*) of characters in these stories. Like the "*wunai*" and "*yi bi er ye*," these two questions convey a firm belief in the expressive power and

79 *Shi pin jizhu*, p. 56.

80 Wang Ping interprets this passage as a summary of a poetic tradition of plaint (*yuan* 怨) that can be traced back to the heritage of Chu songs and the legend of Qu Yuan. She argues that the stereotypical image of plaintive women in five-syllable poetry is derived from the cultural image of Qu Yuan. See Wang Ping, "Plaint, Lyricism and the South," pp. 79–81.

81 Wu Zixu was a Chu minister and fled to the state of Wu 吳 after his father and brother were executed by the Chu King. See his biography in the *Shi ji* 66.2171–83.

irrepressible spontaneity of five-syllable poetry. This belief, along with the general absence of women's voices from official historical accounts, contributed to the establishment and consolidation of the link between five-syllable poetry and women's laments about their abandonment.

4 Xu Shu: The Making of a Woman Writer of Five-Syllable Poetry

Zhong Rong's remark on the disproportionate number of women writers in the Han dynasty quoted at the beginning of this chapter is part of the entry "Poems of the Han Commandery Deputy Qin Jia, Jia's wife Xu Shu" 漢上計秦嘉 嘉妻徐淑詩 in the *Shi pin*. The entry in its entirety reads:

> 夫妻事既可傷，文亦悽怨。二漢為五言者，不過數家，而婦人居二。徐淑敘別之作，亞於《團扇》矣。
>
> The events between the husband and wife are already pitiable, and the writing is indeed miserable and resentful. The number of people who wrote five-syllable poems during the two Hans does not exceed a handful. Yet among them there were two women. Xu Shu's poems relating the parting, is secondary to the "Round Fan."[82]

Although the heading mentions both husband and wife, only Xu Shu's poems are commented on in the entry. Unlike Lady Ban, very little is known about Xu Shu except that her husband Qin Jia 秦嘉 was a low-ranking official during the reign of Emperor Huan of Han 漢桓帝 (r. 146–167). Neither Qin Jia nor Xu Shu is mentioned in the *Hou Han shu*. The *Sui shu* bibliography lists Xu Shu's collection in one *juan* yet says nothing about Qin Jia.[83] The *Yutai xinyong* has Qin Jia's four poems sent to Xu Shu, including three five-syllable poems and one four-syllable poem, along with Xu Shu's five-syllable poem to Qin Jia.[84] It also quotes a preface to Qin Jia's three five-syllable poems, which likely describes the "events" (*shi* 事) Zhong Rong refers to:

> 秦嘉字士會，隴西人也，為郡上掾。其妻徐淑，寢疾還家，不獲面別， 贈詩云爾。

---

82 *Shi pin jizhu*, pp. 249–50. The "Round Fan" refers to the "Poem on Resentment" attributed to Lady Ban.

83 *Sui shu* 33.1059.

84 *Yutai xinyong jianzhu* 1.30–32 and 9.396.

> Qin Jia, courtesy Shihui, was from Longxi. He served as commandery deputy to the capital. His wife Xu Shu was sick and returned to her home. They didn't get a chance to bid farewell with each other face to face. He sent her the following poems.[85]

Lines from their epistolary exchanges are quoted in the *Beitang shuchao*, *Yiwen leiju* and the Dunhuang documents. These letters are, for the most part, prose renditions of the content in the poems.[86] According to them, a few years after parting from his wife, Qin Jia died in his post. A memorial to Emperor Cheng 成帝 of Eastern Jin (r. 325–342) mentions Xu Shu's assumption of the role of mother to Qin Jia's children born to his concubine after his untimely death.[87] The *Taiping yulan* preserves a letter that Xu Shu addresses to her brothers about her determination not to remarry.[88] Like the stories about Empress Zhen, materials surrounding the Xu Shu and Qin Jia story kept expanding: as time went on, more writings in their names emerged to enrich the story with more details. Some of these writings bear visible traces of anachronisms. For example, the letter to her brothers strongly objects to widows' remarriage for the sake of staying chaste. This was more characteristic of the 10th century than the 2nd century.[89]

The only poem under Xu Shu's name—"Poem in Reply to Qin Jia" (Da Qin Jia shi 答秦嘉詩)—showed up in the textual history some 400 years after her death:

妾身兮不令	My body, alas, is not in good shape,
嬰疾兮來歸	encumbered by sickness, alas, I have gone home.
沉滯兮家門	I lie bedridden, alas, in my family's gates,
歷時兮不差	With passing time, alas, I do not mend.
曠廢兮侍覲	I give up, alas, serving and seeing you,
情敬兮有違	In affection and respect, alas, I have missed the mark.

---

85 Ibid.

86 *Beitang shuchao* 136; *Yiwen leiju* 32.571–72; Dunhuang no. 12213. For a comparison between the letters recorded in different sources, see Liu Jingyun 劉景雲, "Hou Han Qin Jia Xu Shu shiwen kao" 後漢秦嘉徐淑詩文考, *Dunhuang yanjiu* 2 (2003): 88–92.

87 Du You 杜佑 (735–812), *Tong Dian* 通典 (Beijing: Zhonghua shuju, 1988) 69.1911.

88 *Taiping yulan* 441.2028.

89 There are stories about filial widows who refused to remarry in order to care for their parents-in-law in the early medieval period; see Keith Knapp's discussion in *Selfless Offspring: Filial Children and Social Order in Medieval China* (Honolulu: University of Hawai'i Press, 2005), pp. 169–74. Yet according to her letter to her brothers, Xu Shu did so to preserve her chastity and to raise her husband's children, which was not a common reason for widows to refuse remarriage at the time.

君今兮奉命	You now, alas, have received a command,
遠邁兮京師	And go afar, alas, to the capital.
悠悠兮離別	Long, alas, will be our separation,
無因兮敘懷	I have no means, alas, to give account of my feelings.
瞻望兮踴躍	I gaze afar, alas, leaping with joy,
佇立兮徘徊	I stand long, alas, faltering.
思君兮慼結	Longing for you, alas, emotions tangle within,
夢想兮容輝	In dream I envisage, alas, the glow of your face.
君發兮引邁	You set forth, alas, faring on,
去我兮日乖	leaving me, alas, farther away each day.
恨無兮羽翼	I regret that I do not have, alas, feathers and wings
高飛兮相追	To fly high, alas, to follow you.
長吟兮永歎	I chant long, alas, and give drawn-out sighs,
淚下兮沾衣	Tears fall, alas, and soak my clothes.[90]

Each line in this poem consists of two two-syllable units connected by the character *xi*, which is very uncommon, if not utterly unique, among extant five-syllable poems.[91] *Xi* is a filling particle of more emotional or rhythmic/musical than semantic significance. For that reason it is prone to variation in textual rendition and transmission. An example is the neatly structured four-syllable "Swan Song" (Honghu 鴻鵠) quoted in both the *Shi ji* and *Han shu*:

鴻鵠高飛	The swan flies high,
一舉千里	with one stroke of the wings it reaches a thousand *li*.
羽翮已就	Once its feathers and quills are full-fledged,
橫絕四海	it travels all across the four seas.
橫絕四海	It travels all across the four seas—
當可奈何	what can be done about it?
雖有矰繳	Even though I have arrows and ropes;
尚安所施	Still, what can be done?[92]

90 *XianQin Han Wei Jin Nanbeichao shi* 1.188. I use Owen's translation in *The Making of Early Classical Chinese poetry*, pp. 249–50, with modifications. The insertion of "alas" (roughly corresponding to the particle *xi* 兮) may read strangely and forcefully in the translation, but it is meant to remain close to the original.

91 The use of *xi* commonly appears in the Chu song style. We also see the insertion of this particle in early poems with uneven lines. But it is rarely used in the same position in each line of an even-lined five-syllable poem.

92 *Shi ji* 55.2047; *Han shu* 40.2036; *XianQin Han Wei Jin Nanbeichao shi* 1.88.

The poem appears in the story about Lady Qi, the miserable rival of Empress Lü. Liu Bang promised Lady Qi to depose the Crown Prince and replace him with her son Ruyi. But he had to abandon his plan after realizing that the Crown Prince had already gained much power and support at court. He told Lady Qi in dismay: "Dance a Chu dance for me while I sing a Chu song for you" 為我楚舞，吾為若楚歌.[93] The song, as quoted in both the *Shi ji* and *Han shu*, has no clear characteristics of a Chu song. But Bai Juyi's 白居易 (772–846) encyclopedia *Baishi liutie shilei ji* 白氏六帖事類集 (Mr. Bai's collection of categorized matters in six tablets) cites a different version of the "Swan Song" that has a *xi* after every odd line, making it into a more typical, nine-syllable Chu song:

> 鴻鵠高飛兮一舉千里
> 羽翮已就兮橫絕四海
> 橫絕四海兮當可奈何
> 雖有矰繳兮尚安所施[94]

Lu Qinli notes that Bai probably quoted the poem from Lu Jia's *Chu Han chunqiu*, yet the extant portion of the book does not have it.[95] Given that the poem is in the four-syllable line in both the *Shi ji* and *Han shu*, another, equally plausible, scenario is that the *xi* was later added to the poem to make it a more recognizable Chu song, either by Bai or by an earlier source he used. Regardless of the textual history of these two versions, it is clear that the character *xi* is a relatively "loose" property of a text and could be easily dropped or added in the transmission.

Like in the "Swan Song," the absence of *xi* does not affect the meaning of Xu Shu's poem but only makes it a standard four-syllable poem. The poem may originally have been in the four-syllable line. Liu Xie, while raising doubts about the authenticity of the poems attributed to Li Ling and Lady Ban, never even mentions Xu Shu or Qin Jia in the *Wenxin diaolong*. The 5th-century poet Jiang Yan wrote a series of "Poems in Various Styles" (Zati shi 雜體詩) to capture the different styles of early five-syllable poems dating from the Han period up to his immediate predecessor Bao Zhao 鮑照 (d. 466).[96] He models his writings

93 *Shi ji* 55.2047; *Han shu* 40.2036.

94 *XianQin Han Wei Jin Nanbeichao shi* 1.88.

95 Ibid.

96 Ibid. 2.1569–81. Owen sees Jiang Yan's imitations as belonging to a scholarly trend to construct a history for poetry in the five-syllable line in the Qi and Liang dynasties: Owen, *The Making of Early Chinese Classical Poetry*, pp. 45–47. Other studies on this series include Wendy Swartz, "Intertextuality and Cultural Memory in Early Medieval China: Jiang Yan's Imitations of Nearly Lost and Lost Writers," in *Memory in Medieval China: Text, Ritual and*

on those of poets before the Jian'an period, including the anonymous poet of the "Nineteen Old Poems," Li Ling, and Lady Ban. It would be curious for Jiang Yan to have left out Xu Shu or Qin Jia if their five-syllable poems had already been in circulation during his time. Less than one generation after Jiang Yan, Zhong Rong added Xu Shu (and possibly also Qin Jia) to the list of pre-Jian'an writers of five-syllable poetry, and the *Yutai xinyong* includes their poems.[97] The reason Jiang Yan did not imitate Xu Shu's poem may be because it was not *yet* in the five-syllable form.

What can be made of the possible transformation of Xu Shu's poem? If this poem was indeed a four-syllable poem in its original form, it might be from an early period, likely Xu Shu's one-*juan* collection listed in the *Sui shu* bibliography. But what is significant is why people *wanted* or *expected* her to write a five-syllable poem, even one with a highly unusual style. The reason lies in the association of five-syllable poetry with women's laments about separation and abandonment. For 6th-century readers, the sentiment conveyed in the poem, and its alleged female author, dictate that it "must be" written in the five-syllable line. Adding a particle *xi* to every line is the easiest way to alter the meter without changing the content. The surviving portion of the encyclopedia *Wenguan cilin* 文館詞林 (Grove of writing from the Academy of Culture, completed in 657) indicates that the entire *juan* 152 is devoted to four-syllable exchange poems, with one subcategory labeled "exchanges between husband and wife" (*fufu zengda* 夫婦贈答).[98] Among the surviving titles (without texts) there is "One Poem Qin Jia of the Later Han Sent to His wife" (Hou Han Qin Jia zeng fu yishou 後漢秦嘉贈婦一首), which could be Qin Jia's four-syllable poem to Xu Shu preserved in the *Yutai xinyong*.[99] Based on the phrase "*zengda*" in the subcategory, the four-syllable poem (her five-syllable poem without *xi* in each line) may indeed have been written by Xu Shu to present to Qin Jia. Moreover, the presence of the subcategory indicates that many women wrote four-syllable poems to their husbands at that time. In received texts, however,

Community, ed. Wendy Swartz and Robert Campany (Leiden: Brill, 2018), pp. 36–62; and Nicholas Morrow Williams, *Imitations of the Self: Jiang Yan and Chinese Poetics* (Leiden: Brill, 2015).

97 Owen also mentions the possibility of Xu Shu's poem being in four-syllable lines and suggests that Zhong Rong includes the poem to "fill in his lacuna of Han writers in the five-syllable line": Owen, *The Making of Early Chinese Classical Poetry*, p. 247.

98 Luo Guowei 羅國威, ed., *Ricang Hongren ben Wenguan cilin jiaozheng* 日藏弘仁本文館詞林校證 (Beijing: Zhonghua shuju, 2001), pp. 19–20.

99 *XianQin Han Wei Jin Nanbeichao shi* 1.186; *Yutai xinyong jianzhu* 9.396.

poems in the feminine voice expressing romantic longing or resentment are seldom, if ever, in four-syllable lines.

Finally, Xu Shu and Qin Jia's tragic story in a chaotic time makes good material for a romanticized historical account. The *Shi pin* entry on Xu Shu's poem begins by commenting on their pitiable "events" and seems to assume contemporary readers' familiarity with them. This could refer to a story circulating with the poem that fits the vignette of "tears of widows in their chambers running out" (*Shuanggui leijin* 霜閨淚盡) in the preface.

5 Conclusion

Since the Jian'an period, certain elements have come to be associated with the feminine voice in male literati's persona writing, including the image of an abandoned woman, the sentiments of longing and resentment, and the genre of five-syllable poetry. They affected the reception of early literary texts and, when necessary, became the criteria by which to determine the gender of the poetic voice and/or the identity of the author. Women authors were assigned to early five-syllable poems with unknown or uncertain authorship, based primarily if not entirely on the sentiments they convey. Five-syllable poems were attributed to famous abandoned women in romanticized narratives of history popular in the 4th and 5th centuries, to demonstrate the intensity and authenticity of their longing and resentment. They not only provided the women's voices that had been missing from received historical accounts but also supplied missing pieces in the early development of five-syllable poetry, a literary genre that had a humble origin yet gained prominence among early medieval writers. By the 6th century, some of these attributions were widely accepted and in turn reinforced these assumptions about the feminine voice by providing literary "precedents" and models.

CHAPTER 4

Is It a Man or a Woman Speaking? Mapping Gender in Early Texts

Discussions in previous chapters have shown early medieval literati's interest in understanding and constructing the cultural and literary past, in particular the history of the five-syllable poetry that gained much popularity and prestige in their times.[1] Xiaofei Tian has demonstrated the large-scale scholarly endeavors to organize received literary texts and create a narrative of literary history at the Liang court.[2] On the individual level, the engagement with earlier texts started as early as the end of the 3rd century, when Lu Ji wrote imitations of the "Nineteen Old Poems" and Fu Xuan composed poems based on received *yuefu* titles and materials.[3] Different views and concepts competed and collided in these close encounters with the past. Chapter 1 discussed 3rd-century literati's "corrections" of what they saw as questionable morality in earlier literary portrayals of women. Chapter 3 provided examples in which poetic voices were given gender and identity in contextual stories created retrospectively. This chapter takes a closer look at how changing views of gender in literary expression led to attempts to "fix" the lack of gender determinacy in early texts, especially five-syllable poems.[4] These changes had much to do with the gradual loss of the performative context in five-syllable poetry over the course of the early medieval period. In a poetic world that values performativity and applicability, the indeterminacy of gender is often taken as an accepted or even desired quality because it allows a poem to be applied to people in different situations

1 An earlier version of this chapter is published under the title "Mapping Gender and Poetic Role in Early Medieval Poetry," *Early Medieval China* 21 (2015): 38–62, © Early Medieval China Group, reprinted by permission of Taylor & Francis Ltd, http://www.tandfonline.com on behalf of Early Medieval China Group.

2 Tian, *Beacon Fire and Shooting Star*, pp. 77–161.

3 Fu Xuan's poems, such as "Ballad: The Prelude" (Yange xing 豔歌行), "Ballad on Qiu Hu" (Qiu Hu xing 秋胡行), and "Ballad on Watering My Horse at the Cave by the Great Wall" (Yinma changcheng ku xing 飲馬長城窟行) use extant *yuefu* titles and incorporate materials from earlier *yuefu* poems: *XianQin Han Wei Jin Nanbeichao shi* 1.554–55; 556; 556–57.

4 This is, no doubt, part of a general tendency toward the increasingly greater weight attached to biography and nonfiction in poetry from the *Shijing* to the medieval period, as discussed by scholars such as Owen and Pauline Yu. See Stephen Owen, *Traditional Chinese Poetry and Poetics: Omen of the World* (Madison: University of Wisconsin Press, 1985); and Pauline Yu, *The Reading of Imagery in the Chinese Poetic Tradition* (Princeton, NJ: Princeton University Press, 1987).

 | DOI:10.1163/9789004546455_006

and ensures its wide appeal and circulation. By the 5th and 6th centuries, however, this lack of determinacy came into conflict with the gender conventions that were being formed and came to be seen as a hindrance to understanding poetry. As anonymity gave way to more individualized and definitive expressions, there arose a need to clarify gendered voices and gender roles in earlier poems. This chapter demonstrates how early medieval writers and readers reduced or eliminated the ambiguity and multiple interpretive possibilities in earlier poems through editing, imitation, rewriting, or interpretation. As a result, relatively indeterminate gendered voices were forced into a "map" of more determinate ones. While establishing the conventions of gender representation, this neatly charted map left little room for certain female images and voices, such as those of elusive and manipulative women.

1 Eliminating Gender Indeterminacy in the "Nineteen Old Poems"

The 6th-century anthology of literature *Wen xuan* includes 19 five-syllable poems collectively titled "Nineteen Old Poems."[5] The dating of these poems has long been a topic of scholarly debate,[6] but when the late 3rd-century poet Lu Ji wrote imitations of these poems, the originals were already considered "ancient" (*gu* 古). Traditional criticism tends to associate them with the turmoil at the end of the Han dynasty and to read them as faithful reflections of the lives and thoughts of people from different social classes and in different situations. Not only do multiple perspectives and mixed voices occur throughout the 19 poems, but they also sometimes coexist within a single poem. The speaker's gender is ambiguous in many poems of this group. The ambiguity in the poetic voice, among other things, gives a generality to the expression of emotion. The most remarkable case is the first poem of the group:[7]

5 *Wen xuan* 29.1343–52. For discussions of these poems, see Jean-Pierre Diény, "Les dix-neuf poèmes anciens 古詩十九首," *Bulletin de la Maison Franco-Japonaise*, Nouvelle série 7, no. 4 (1963): 1–194; Daniel Hsieh, "The Origin and Nature of the 'Nineteen Old Poems'," *Sino-Platonic Papers* 77 (1998): 1–49; and Tian, "Woman in the Tower."

6 The anthology's commentator Li Shan believed that the editor Xiao Tong placed this group of poems at the beginning of the category "Old poems" (*gushi*) out of convenience rather than any solid evidence regarding their chronology. *Wen xuan* 29.1343. Yet this editorial arrangement led later generations to believe that they were "Han poems" and therefore among the earliest works in the five-syllable genre. In the majority of literary histories and textbooks recently written in mainland China, this series of poems is still listed as a "Han" composition or the earliest "poems in the five-syllable line by literati" (*wenren wuyan shi* 文人五言詩).

7 The sequence of poems within the series was probably also Xiao Tong's personal choice. Owen shows that the version of the "Nineteen Old Poems" that Lu Ji had when he wrote his imitations may have differed from Xiao Tong's, including the sequence of individual poems:

行行重行行	On and on, on and on,
與君生別離	I am parted from you in this lifetime.
相去萬餘里	We are away from each other for over ten thousand *li*,
各在天一涯	each at one end of the world.
道路阻且長	The roads are blocked and long;
會面安可知	how can we know if we can meet again?
胡馬依北風	*Hu* horses lean against the northern wind;
越鳥巢南枝	*Yue* birds perch on the southern branches.
相去日已遠	Since we parted, days have passed;
衣帶日已緩	my sash is getting looser every day.
浮雲蔽白日	Floating clouds shadow the bright sun.
遊子不顧返	The traveler does not turn back to return home.
思君令人老	Missing you makes me grow old;
歲月忽已晚	the year suddenly comes to an end.
棄捐勿復道	Forget it, and do not speak of it—
努力加餐飯	do your best and eat more![8]

This poem concerns two persons who are separated from each other. There is not a single passage that specifies the gender or identity of the speaker or addressee, the relationship between them, or the circumstance of their parting. The Ming critic Lu Shiyong 陸時雍 (fl. 17th century) comments on this poem:

> 此詩含情之妙，不見其情；蓄意之深，不知其意.
>
> This poem harbors an emotion so marvelously that it becomes invisible; it embodies a meaning so deeply that it becomes unfathomable.[9]

The difficulty in grasping concrete meanings in this poem may not result from the author's superior poetic skills in purposefully concealing the meaning, as Lu suggests. Rather, the poem deliberately resists specificity or contextualization to convey a general sentiment of separation and longing. As Chia-ying Yeh 葉嘉瑩 has pointed out, the poetic voice could belong to the person leaving or

Owen, *The Making of Early Chinese Classical Poetry*, p. 263. But as the earliest source we have for these "old poems," Xiao Tong's arrangement made the first poem the most celebrated piece among the 19.

8 *XianQin Han Wei Jin Nanbeichao shi* 1.329.

9 Sui Shusen, *Gushi shijiushou jishi*, p. 2.

the one staying.[10] In terms of its relationship with the addressee, it is equally possible for the poem to be spoken by a woman missing her traveling lover, a traveling man missing his wife, a man missing a faraway friend, or a lover missing a lover of the same sex. In sum, it embraces many possibilities in human relations and is relatable and appealing to a wide audience.

Other poems in the group show similar indeterminacy in the gender of the speaker. Poem XIX describes the speaker on a moonlit night and their regret over a long "journey" (*ke xing* 客行):

明月何皎皎	How the bright moon glows so!
照我羅床緯	It shines on the curtain of my silk bed.
憂愁不能寐	Worried and sorrowful, I cannot fall asleep;
攬衣起徘徊	I grasp my clothes, get up and pace about.
客行雖云樂	Although the journey is happy,
不如早旋歸	it is better to return home early.
出戶獨彷徨	I step outside the door and linger alone;
愁思當告誰	to whom shall I tell my melancholy thoughts?
引領還入房	Craning my neck, I go back to the chamber;
淚下沾裳衣	Tears fall, soaking my clothes.[11]

Although the poem is written from a first-person perspective, denoted by the pronoun I (*wo* 我) in line 2, we have trouble determining who is speaking to whom. If we read the poetic *I* as the traveler (*ke* 客 in the third couplet), then this person regrets embarking on the journey and longs to return, despite the note that the journey is quite pleasant (*le* 樂). If the voice belongs to the person left behind at home, then the speaker hopes for an early return of the traveler—and suspects, with jealousy and anxiety, that the traveler might be delayed by some kind of "pleasure" on the road. Both readings are equally plausible and could be supported by elements in the poem. As in Poem I, the different roles of the speaker could also indicate gender. The social reality and cultural roles of the time dictate that the voice of a traveler is usually masculine, whereas the voice of the one left behind is most likely feminine.[12]

---

10 Chia-ying Yeh emphasizes the generality and universality of emotion in these poems. She argues that the emotion has an "eternal validity" (*yongheng de zhenshi xing* 永恒的真實性) that transcends time, literary genre, or identity. See "Yizu yi dong er nan jie de haoshi" 一組易懂而難解的好詩, in Yeh, *Jialing lunshi conggao* 嘉陵論詩叢稿 (Shijiazhuang: Hebei jiaoyu chubanshe, 1997), pp. 126–45.

11 *XianQin Han Wei Jin Nanbeichao shi* 1.334.

12 "Most likely" because we cannot leave out the possibility that a man could be missing his absent friend, or lover of the same sex.

The need for a definite gender and role of the speaker emerges only when one wants to read an individualized "I" behind the poetic expression, but in a good number from this group the presence of such a coherent persona is, at best, vague. Many scholars have pointed out that the "I" in the "Nineteen Old Poems" often represents a collective voice, speaking about a general situation or emotion applicable to any individual, regardless of gender, social class, or identity.[13] The indeterminacy in gendered voice, therefore, contributes to the unique charm of these anonymous poems by maximizing their performativity and applicability, and it could well be deliberate.[14] Literati imitations of the "Nineteen Old Poems" over the subsequent centuries give us a rare opportunity to see how later poets responded to this gender indeterminacy. The concept of "imitation" is complex, evoking different meanings across time and from different poets. Lu Ji's imitations of the "old poems," for example, follow the original closely and rewrite each line in a higher linguistic register, whereas Jiang Yan's 30 "Poems in Various Styles" in imitation of earlier works aim to capture distinctive styles (*ti* 體) of early five-syllable poetry.[15] In most cases, imitation of an early poem indicates a recognition of its classic status and a conscious reworking on the original materials, so it can often tell us much about how later poets understood and interpreted an early poem. In later imitations of the "Nineteen Old Poems" we see an increasing tendency to clarify poetic roles, often starting with the designation of an explicit gender and/or identity for the speaker. Lu Ji's imitation of Poem I, while following the topic and structure of the original quite closely, tells a more cohesive story in the voice of a traveler:

悠悠行邁遠	Ever onward, my journeying goes far,
戚戚憂思深	dismal, my troubled thoughts deepened.
此思亦何思	And what thoughts are these thoughts?—
思君徽與音	They are on your excellence and repute.
音徽日夜離	Separated day and night from your excellence and repute,

13 Hans Frankel discusses the generality and individuality of "I" in Chinese poetry in "The 'I' in Chinese Lyric Poetry," *Oriens* 10, no. 1 (1957): 128–30. Tian analyzes the juxtaposition of both male and female voices in Poem XVI and suggests that it serves as both a hint to and cover for some narrative details deliberately hidden from the reader. The juxtaposition opens the possibility of interpretation and invites the reader to fill in the blanks left between the poetic lines. See Tian, "Woman in the Tower," pp. 13–15.

14 For the concept of performativity and its connotation in this study, please see the discussion in the Introduction.

15 Two studies treat the concept of imitation in the early medieval period: Owen, *The Making of Early Chinese Classical Poetry*, pp. 260–345; and Williams, *Imitations of the Self*, pp. 23–143.

緬邈若飛沈	far asunder, as one flying and the other underwater.
王鮪懷河岫	The royal paddlefish longs for the grotto by the river;
晨風思北林	the dawnwind falcon thinks of the northern forests.
游子眇天末	The traveler is faint at the end of the horizon,
還期不可尋	and a date for return cannot be sought.
驚飈褰反信	Sudden gusts snatch up the returning messenger,
歸雲難寄音	one cannot send word by homing clouds.
佇立想萬里	I stand alone, envisioning thousands of *li* away,
沈憂萃我心	and brooding cares gather in my heart.
攬衣有餘帶	I feel my clothes, there is extra length in the sash;
循形不盈衿	I trace my form: it does not fill the gown's folds.
去去遺情累	Going farther off, I leave the entanglements of feeling,
安處撫清琴	and reside in peace, stroking the clear zither.[16]

Not only does Lu Ji's imitation add the first-person pronoun "I" in line 14, but the poem also presents a distinctive persona of a traveler. In contrast to the original poem, which juxtaposes situations of separation without providing a centralized perspective, Lu Ji's imitation can easily be read as a personal monologue charged with emotion. The image and voice of the male speaker stand out throughout the poem. The animal metaphors in lines 7–8 call for special attention: "The royal paddlefish longs for the grotto by the river; / the dawnwind falcon thinks of the northern forests" 王鮪懷河岫/晨風思北林. In the original poem, two animals appear in the same position in each line: "*Hu* horses lean against the northern wind; / *Yue* birds perch on the southern branches" 胡馬依北風/越鳥巢南枝.[17] "*Hu* horses" and "*Yue* birds" symbolize the idea that all sentient beings are innately bound to their native places. Put in the context of a separation and juxtaposed in a single couplet, these two animals also strongly signify two people separated geographically (north and south) with no chance to be together. Each line tells of a factual situation, and together they represent two creatures living far apart, metaphors for the speaker and the addressee respectively. The animal images in Lu Ji's imitation retain the original sentiments of longing for home but with elevated subjectivity, using two volitive verbs, *huai* 懷 and *si* 思, that draw attention to the same agent: the traveler. The displaced animals in the two lines (paddlefish/falcon) can therefore be read as two different analogues for *the same* homesick traveler

16 *XianQin Han Wei Jin Nanbeichao shi* 1.685–86. I use Owen's translation in *The Making of Early Chinese Classical Poetry*, p. 287, with modifications.

17 *XianQin Han Wei Jin Nanbeichao shi* 1.329.

(who is the subject of the next line).[18] Lu Ji's poem continues to assume the perspective of the traveler in the remaining lines and describes his failure to send a message, as well as his subsequent frustration and grief.[19] The experience of separation and loneliness is articulated in the male traveler's voice throughout the poem.

The original poem ends, somewhat abruptly, with an admonition to eat more: "Forget it, and do not speak of it—/ do your best and eat more!" 棄捐勿復道/努力加餐飯.[20] Such an interlocutory expression is a common ending template in early poems, most likely a remnant of its oral performance context. When the poem is performed in front of an audience, these last lines provide a polite conclusion to the performance. Yet in a written text meant for reading, they cut off the natural flow of emotion and change the tone of expression. In contrast to the original, Lu Ji's imitation ends with an attempt at self-consolation, referencing a highly personal and introspective act—stroking the zither. The sound of zither playing also forms a nice resonance as well as a contrast with the word *yin* 音, which appears earlier in the poem a couple of times, where it means repute and words/message, respectively, and has to do with the other person or communication. Zither playing is a solitary activity and its sound only accentuates the player's loneliness. This ending adds a consistency and continuity that is absent in the "Old Poem." In sum, although Lu Ji's imitation is not entirely devoid of ambiguity,[21] it presents a more tangible poetic subject—a traveler longing for home—and through this identity creates a definitive and coherent masculine voice for poetic expression.

Lu Ji's imitation of Poem XIX again adopts the traveler's voice to express the sorrow of separation:

安寢北堂上	Peacefully I sleep in the northern hall;
明月入我牖	bright moonlight enters my window.
照之有餘輝	It shines with lingering radiance;
攬之不盈手	I hold the light and it does not fill my hand.
凉風繞曲房	Chilly wind circles the tortuous chamber;

18 Williams uses this example to illustrate that "the nature of Lu Ji's imitation (*ni* 擬) ... involves personification (*niren* 擬人) and personalization of his model": Williams, *Imitations of the Self*, p. 85.

19 It also makes more sense for the traveler to send a message home than the other way around.

20 *XianQin Han Wei Jin Nanbeichao shi* 1.329.

21 For example, instead of a personal pronoun such as "*wo*" in line 14, Lu Ji uses "the traveler" (*youzi* 游子) in the fifth couplet, making it uncertain whether the poetic "I" is looking at himself as a third person or addressing someone else.

寒蟬鳴高柳 cold cicadas sing on a high willow branch.
踟躕感節物 I step back and forth, touched by the seasonal objects.
我行永已久 My journey has been eternally long.
游宦會無成 The travel for officialdom has met no success;
離思難常守 it is hard to constantly harbor thoughts of separation.[22]

Unlike the ambiguous phrase "the journey" (*kexing* 客行) in the "Old Poem," "my journey" (*woxing* 我行) in line 8 unmistakably identifies the speaker as the male traveler. The speaker's gender is further confirmed by the last couplet, stating that the purpose of this journey is the pursuit of an official career. This piece of added information also elevates the poem's morality: the traveler is not just pursuing pleasure, as the "Old Poem" suggests. Whereas the "Old Poem" speaks of a separation in a very general sense, Lu Ji offers a specific reason for this situation and a definitive gender for the poetic voice.[23]

Lu Ji's imitations of Poems I and XIX clarify ambiguous elements in the speaker's gender and offer a specific perspective to illustrate the meaning of the poems. Their expressions, however, are still quite generic in many ways. The use of the first-person pronoun *wo*, while offering a general character, does not give any information about the traveler's experience or his longing for home. In other words, Lu Ji's imitations are still about travel and separation in a general sense and could be applied to any man on a journey. The 5th-century poet Liu Shuo's 劉鑠 (431–453) imitation of Poem XIX, however, provides not only a definite gender for the speaker, but also more details of his journey:

落宿半遙城 I take up lodging halfway from the city wall,
浮雲藹層闕 drifting clouds cast a gloom over the layered watchtowers.
玉宇來清風 Into the jade chamber comes a clear breeze;
羅帳延秋月 the silk tent takes in the autumn moon.
結思想伊人 I focus my thoughts on that person,
沈憂懷明發 and think about the next morning in deep sorrow.
誰爲客行久 Who has been on the journey for so long?
屢見流芳歇 For many times I have seen the flowers wither.

22 *XianQin Han Wei Jin Nanbeichao shi* 1.687.

23 It also seems to be a conscious response to the ending couplet in Poem II: "The wanderer left and did not return, / an empty bed is hard to keep alone" 蕩子行不歸/空床難度守. In both couplets, the feeling of loneliness caused by separation is described as hard to maintain. Yet this same loneliness led to an illicit and dangerous desire by the speaker, a wife, for a companion in bed in Poem II, whereas it urged the speaker, a traveling man, to return to his family in Lu Ji's imitation.

河廣川無梁	The rivers are broad, without bridge;
山高路難越	the mountains are high, difficult to cross over.[24]

The original "Old Poem," as well as many poems before the 3rd century on the topic of "sleeplessness at night," narrate a sequence of activities: namely, one is unable to sleep on a bright moonlit night, gets dressed and steps out of the bed chamber, and walks back and forth in the courtyard. Owen believes that this series constitutes part of the "grammar" of early poetry: an indispensable, formulaic component of any poem on this topic, regardless of the real situation of composition.[25] Lu Ji's imitation, while adding some variation and a little personal touch to the sequence, still follows the basic pattern. Liu Shuo's poem forgoes the formula entirely. The first and last couplets locate the speaker between a city he has just passed through and the rivers and mountains he is about to cross the next morning. Together they create a temporal and spatial frame to situate the longing for home. This differs from both the original poem and Lu Ji's imitation, which only give the reader access to an undefined inner space. Stuck in the middle of a journey, Liu Shuo's speaker misses a beloved person (*yiren* 伊人) and regrets the prolonged separation. His anxiety about the hardships ahead in the last couplet offers a more concrete basis for the desire to return. With all its personalized details and a much stronger subjectivity, Liu Shuo's imitation calls for a direct association with the poet's own experience. The phrase "*ke xing*" in line 7 is taken verbatim from the original "Old Poem," yet Liu Shuo's traveler (*ke*) has come a long way from the travelers before him. He consciously defines his individual voice as a homesick traveler in a long tradition of writings about separation and travel. In other words, his poem is about "*the* traveler," not "*a* traveler."

Although they both respond to the ambiguity and indeterminacy in early five-syllable poems, Lu Ji's and Liu Shuo's responses have some evident differences. As one of the first poets to acknowledge the classic status of the "Nineteen Old Poems," Lu Ji tried to bring out the meaning of the poems as he understood them. This includes following the original poetic materials closely yet providing a more distinctive voice for the anonymous speaker. Liu Shuo's imitation shows a strong historical consciousness about the literary tradition before him. Rather than revealing the meaning in the original poem, he rewrote the established tradition with a new, individualized voice. Between the two poets' imitations of the "Nineteen Old Poems," we see increasing

24 *XianQin Han Wei Jin Nanbeichao shi* 2.1214.

25 Owen, *The Making of Early Chinese Classical Poetry*, pp. 77–92.

specificity in the speaker's gender and role. The indeterminacy in the original poems became something to avoid in poetic expression.

2 Explaining the Gender Trouble in the Li Ling Poems

The indeterminacy in the gendered voice of the "Nineteen Old Poems" may be explained by their anonymity.[26] In other words, ambiguity and incoherence are reasonable for poems circulated without an author's name (i.e. as words not articulated by a specific person), such as many poems in the *Shijing*. But even in some poems attributed to the historical person Li Ling, we find a similar absence of determinate gender. If the ambiguity in the "Nineteen Old Poems" results in wide applicability, what we discover in the Li Ling poems is that sometimes the application to a specific situation did not require a strict agreement between gender and its narrative frame.

Li Ling was a Han general. According to his biography in the *Han shu*, he was taken captive in a battle with the Xiongnu in 99 BCE and detained by the Xiongnu. There he formed a friendship with the detained Han envoy Su Wu, who eventually was allowed to return home. Before Su Wu's departure a banquet was held, at which Li Ling bid him farewell.[27] The biography quotes Li Ling's song in the Chu song style, lamenting his tragic fate, but it makes no mention of a group of parting poems in the five-syllable line, which were later attributed to Li Ling as the descriptions of his parting from Su Wu.[28] Many contradictory elements exist in the gender and identity of the speaker and the addressee between the poems and the story. For example, the following poem speaks of a separation between a husband and wife:

結髮爲夫妻	Reaching the hair-binding age, we become husband and wife;
恩愛兩不疑	we love each other without doubt.
歡娛在今夕	Joy and pleasure are present this night;

26 Nine of the 19 poems are listed in the *Yutai xinyong* as the works of Mei Sheng, a famous Western Han writer of rhetorical prose and *fu*: *Yutai xinyong jianzhu* 1.16–21. Zhong Rong also mentions that people "used to suspect" (*jiu yi* 舊疑) they were the works of Jian'an poets: *Shi pin jizhu*, p. 91. But none of these claims of authorship were sustained in the tradition.

27 *Han shu* 54.2439–70. This is the earliest source for this story.

28 It is not clear when the attribution of the poems in the five-syllable line began. It certainly occurred before the early 5th century because Yan Yanzhi 顏延之 (384–456) expresses his doubt about the attribution.

燕婉及良時 our tender love meets the right moment.
征夫懷往路 The traveler thinks about the road home,
起視夜何其 rises up to see how late the night is.
參辰皆已沒 The stars of Shen and Chen both have already disappeared;[29]
去去從此辭 going away, going way, I part from you from now on.
行役在戰場 I leave to serve in the battlefield;
相見未有期 no time is set for us to meet again.
握手一長嘆 Holding your hand, I heave a long sigh;
泪爲生別滋 tears are shed for the parting for a lifetime.
努力愛春華 Do your best and cherish spring flowers;
莫忘歡樂時 do not forget our happy times.
生當復來歸 Alive, I shall return again;
死當長相思 dead, I shall think of you forever.[30]

The phrases "reaching the hair-binding age" (*jiefa* 結髮) in line 1 and "tender love" (*yan wan* 燕婉) in line 4 are both common allusions to marriage.[31] The poem is clearly addressed to the wife of the speaker, who is absent in the Li Ling story. Its only possible link to Li Ling's biography in the *Han shu* is the mention of service on the battlefield in line 9, but in the *Han shu* narrative, neither Su Wu nor Li Ling was going to the battlefield at the time of their parting.

The following poem may better match the historical narrative in certain aspects, but the whole poem contains expressions that point to different relationships between two people and allows multiple possibilities for the gender of the speaker:

骨肉緣枝葉 Flesh and bone join like branch and leaf;
結交亦相因 friends also rely on each other.
四海皆兄弟 Within the four seas men are all brothers;
誰爲行路人 who is a stranger on the road?
况我連枝樹 Even more so, we are like trees with connecting branches;

29 Shen (Orion) and Chen (Antares) are two constellations. Shen appears in the west and Chen in the east. They serve as a common metaphor for separation.

30 *XianQin Han Wei Jin Nanbeichao shi* 1.338. The expression "thinking of you" (*xiangsi* 相思) is traditionally used between lovers.

31 The expression "the pursuit of tender love" (*yanwan zhiqiu* 燕婉之求) appears in Mao 43 "Xin tai" 新臺 (Xin terrace). *Maoshi zhengyi* 2.208–09. Both the Mao commentary and Qi commentaries take it as a reference to marriage or a marriage proposal. See Zhang Shubo, ed., *Guofeng jishuo*, pp. 392–99.

與子同一身	with you I share the same body.
昔爲鴛與鴦	In the past we were a pair of mandarin ducks;
今爲參與辰	now we become the stars of Shen and Chen.
昔者常相近	In the past we were always close;
邈若胡與秦	[now] we are as distant as the barbarian and central lands.
惟念當乖離	Just thinking of how we ought to separate,
恩情日以新	our affection is daily refreshed.
鹿鳴思野草	"Deer cry," longing for wild grasses,
可以喻嘉賓	which can be used as a metaphor for fine guests.
我有一尊酒	I have a goblet of ale,
欲以贈遠人	which I want to send to someone far away.
願子留斟酌	I hope that you can keep it and savor it
慰此平生親	to console this intimate relationship in our life.[32]

The "flesh and bone" (*gurou* 骨肉) and "branch and leaf" (*zhiye* 枝葉) grown from the same tree in the opening couplet are metaphors for kinship. Within the context of the Li Ling–Su Wu story, this could be read as two persons who are as close as brothers. Yet in lines 7–8, the speaker compares the relationship with the other person to that of a pair of mandarin ducks, a symbol of love and marital loyalty.[33] To complicate the reading even further, the poem then depicts a banquet scene, alluding to Mao 161 "Lu ming" 鹿鳴 (Deer cry), a well-known banquet song about receiving worthy guests.[34] The whole poem, therefore, juxtaposes a wide variety of relationships indiscriminately: kinship, romance, patronage, and camaraderie. The gendered voice of the speaker could vary between the feminine and the masculine throughout the poem. Like in the earlier poem, there is no explicit connection to the Li Ling story except for a general theme of parting and a mention of "barbarian and central lands."[35] The expression of the marital bond does not have corresponding

32 *XianQin Han Wei Jin Nanbeichao shi* 1.338.

33 Mandarin ducks do not have an explicit implication of marital loyalty in Mao 216 "Yuanyang" 鴛鴦 (Mandarin ducks), which is a congratulation on the longevity of a prince (*junzi* 君子), but Mao's explication takes them as a symbol of a perfect match (*pi niao* 匹鳥), which came to be the most accepted interpretation of the image. See *Maoshi zhengyi* 14.1011–15. Thus, by the time the attribution to Li Ling was made, mandarin ducks would have been taken primarily as a symbol for love.

34 *Maoshi zhengyi* 9.648–54.

35 Yet the description of two persons separated by geographic distance is common in early poems about parting. We see the description of "*Hu* horses" and "*Yue* birds" in the "Nineteen Old Poems" 1. Another example is a couplet in Fu Xuan's "Song on Bitter Form" (Kuxiang pian 苦相篇): "In the past we were [as close as] body and shadow; / now we are

gender elements in the story. Yet a reader ready to accept the poem as Li Ling's composition can certainly take the inappropriate metaphors (mandarin ducks, branches sharing the same body, and so on) as minor deviations or unconventional references to friendship.

The Li Ling group most likely consists of anonymous parting poems that initially circulated without a clear context, not unlike the individual poems of the "Nineteen Old Poems."[36] Their later association with Li Ling and his parting from Su Wu could be the result of a common concern with separation.[37] Although it is unknown when the attribution to Li Ling was first made, the conflicts in gender apparently did not bother readers at the time.

Due to the general tendency to read poetry within a biographical frame in the early medieval period, questions arose about the lack of coherency in gender in the Li Ling poems by the early 5th century. Yan Yanzhi claimed that these poems were "mixed and heterogeneous. They were [written] in his name, and not all were composed by Li Ling" 總雜不類，是假託，非盡陵制.[38] His remark about these poems being "mixed and heterogeneous" is a general reference to the dissimilarity in themes among the poems, including the indeterminacy of gender. As if to address this suspicion, four poems from this group are attributed to Su Wu in the *Wen xuan*.[39] The attribution of authorship to Su Wu, whether made by Xiao Tong or by some earlier source on which he relied, is questionable since Su Wu was never mentioned as a writer of poetry in earlier sources. The four poems attributed to Su Wu are simply called "Four Poems" (Shi si shou 詩四首) and placed under the category "Unclassified poems" (*za shi* 雜詩), a *Wen xuan* category reserved for poems without a clear compositional context, rather than that of "Exchange poems" (*Zengda shi*). Although it is not

---

[as distant as] the barbarian and central lands" 昔為形與影/今為胡與秦: *XianQin Han WeiJin Nanbeichao shi* 1.555–56. In the poem attributed to Li Ling, the association with the story makes this figurative description somewhat realistic, with Su Wu going back to the central land and Li Ling being left behind in Xiongnu territory.

36 In fact, most of the Li Ling poems would not be out of place if included among the "Nineteen Old Poems" since they share many common topics, expressions, and stock imagery.

37 Chu Hsiao-hai 朱曉海 believes Li Ling had become a "symbol for misfortune and grief" (*qichuang de fuma* 淒愴的符碼) in the early medieval period. When later readers looked for a voice for such sentiments, Li Ling (or sometimes Su Wu) became an appropriate "articulator." This partly results in the attribution of many anonymous early poems about personal catastrophe to him. See Chu Hsiao-hai, "Liang Han Liuchao shiwen zhong de Li Ling xianxiang" 兩漢六朝詩文中的李陵現象, *Gudian wenxian yanjiu* 14 (2011): 1–60.

38 Yan Yanzhi, *Tinggao* 庭誥 (Family instructions), *Taiping yulan* 586.2639. Note that Zhong Rong uses the same phrase "*zongza*" to describe the "Nineteen Old Poems": *Shi pin jizhu*, p. 91.

39 *Wen xuan* 29.1354–56.

entirely clear what this attribution and categorization entail, as a result readers should not feel compelled to read these "Four Poems" as answering poems to Li Ling, nor in the context of the famous parting scene depicted in the *Han shu*. Both of the poems with problematic elements in gender discussed earlier are included among these "Four Poems" attributed to Su Wu. It seems that by the time of their inclusion in the *Wen xuan*, some poems from the Li Ling group had been attributed to Su Wu to clarify the conflicting elements and make up for the missing voice of Su Wu in the story. The "Four Poems" could be read as Su Wu's words to his wife.[40] This is indeed how the poem beginning with "Reaching the hair-binding age, we become husband and wife" (*jiefa wei fuqi* 結髮為夫妻) is presented in the *Yutai xinyong*. In addition to retaining the attribution to Su Wu, the *Yutai xinyong* has an occasional title for the poem, "Parting from My Wife" (Liu bie qi 留別妻), that further defines the gender of the speaker and the addressee. The *Yutai xinyong* also includes Xiao Yan's 蕭衍 (464–549) poem in the voice of Su Wu's wife, "In the Voice of the Wife of Su Wu, Supervisor of Dependent States" (Dai Su shuguo fu 代蘇屬國婦), speaking of her grief over the husband's detention in the north.[41] Together, these two poems form a nice "poetic exchange" between husband and wife that goes far beyond the scope of the *Han shu* narrative.

Although the original *Han shu* story only contains male characters, it is evident that new narrative elements involving female characters were gradually added to the anecdote in the following centuries. In addition to enriching the plot, they also helped reduce conflicts in gender that increasingly troubled readers who tried to read the poems within a biographical frame. There is the same tendency in Jiang Yan's imitation of the Li Ling poems, "Joining the Army by Defender Li Ling" (Li Duwei congjun 李都尉陵從軍). In one version of the poem, the poetic persona Li Ling speaks to his wife:

樽酒送征人 Over a goblet of ale we send off the soldier;
踟躕在親宴 I hesitate at the family banquet.
日暮浮雲滋 Drifting clouds arise at sunset;
握手泪如霰 we hold hands, tears falling like sleet.
悠悠清水川 Long flowing is the river of limpid water,

40 The Qing critic Shen Deqian 沈德潛 (1673–1769) includes these four poems in his collection of early poetry, *Gushi yuan* 古詩源 (The origin of ancient poetry), as Su Wu's works, but he notes the problem with the speaking voice and addressee. He concludes that "Not all [four poems] are about parting from Li Ling" (*feijie bie Li Ling ye* 非皆別李陵也): Shen Deqian, ed., *Gushi yuan* (Beijing: Zhonghua shuju, 1963) 2.46–48.

41 *Yutai xinyong jianzhu* 7.269.

嘉魴得所薦	from which come the fine breams presented at the banquet.
而我在萬里	But I will be ten thousand *li* away,
結髮不相見	Since binding our hair we have not seen each other.
袖中有短書	In my sleeve there is a short letter
願寄雙飛燕	I wish to entrust to a pair of flying swallows.[42]

The poem depicts a banquet—not the one recorded in the *Han shu* but one held by Li Ling's family to send him off to the battlefield. Li Ling laments the separation from his wife in line 8, using the familiar expression *jiefa* 結髮. Together with the shedding of tears in line 4, these lines strongly echo the poem beginning with "Reaching the hair-binding age, we become husband and wife" in the original Li Ling group. Both poems describe a parting scene in which husband and wife shed tears when the husband, who is the speaker, leaves for the battlefield. There is, however, a crucial variant in line 8 among the different versions of this poem. The Li Shan version (which is translated above) has *jiefa*, whereas the Wuchen 五臣 (five officials) edition has *jieyou* 結友, "making friends."[43] The phrase *jieyou* also appears in the version in Jiang Yan's collected works.[44] If we compare these two choices of phrase, *jiefa* provides an explanation for the first line in the original poem by placing it in a new plot: Li Ling's departure from his wife. We may never be able to determine which version is the earliest or which was originally written by Jiang Yan,[45] but the existence of the *jiefa* variant shows traces of female characters being added to the original *Han shu* story by Li Shan's time. The speaker's gender and relationship with the addressee in the poems came to be clarified and defined by these new additions.[46]

---

42 *XianQin Han Wei Jin Nanbeichao shi* 2.1570.

43 This refers to the commentary to the *Wen xuan* collectively compiled by Lü Yanji 呂延濟, Liu Liang 劉良, Zhang Xian 張銑, Lü Xiang 呂向, and Li Zhouhan 李周翰, completed in 718. See *Jingyin Songben Wuchen jizhu Wen xuan* 景印宋本五臣集注文選 (Taipei: Guoli Zhongyang tushuguan, 1981), *juan* 16.

44 Although Jiang Yan's biography in the *Liang shu* 梁書 (History of the Liang dynasty) says that he compiled his own writings into the "former" and "later" collections (*qian hou ji* 前後集), neither of them survived. See *Liang Shu* 14.251. The current collected works are collated from various encyclopedias by scholars in the 18th century.

45 However, we might use the principle of *Lectio difficilior potior* (the more difficult reading is the stronger) to argue for an earlier date for the version with *jieyou* since, unlike *jiefa*, it is a less common phrase in early poetry. In other words, we could easily see people change the former into the latter but not vice versa.

46 In light of the discussions in Chapter 3 on the circulation of early five-syllable poems in women's voices with romanticized historical narratives and extant poems on behalf of Su

Why, then, did the apparent romantic discourse in the Li Ling poems not bother readers prior to the 5th century? This again shows a very different perception of poetic voice or the poetic "I." As discussed previously, performativity or applicability is an important quality in early five-syllable poetry. If the poetic voice is mostly collective and general instead of individualized, it should be understood as being applied to or appropriated by a speaker in a particular case of performance or application rather than belonging to him or her. The same voice could also be provided to different personae in different circumstances. In this kind of poetry, what is at stake is not who first composed or voiced the poem, but what kind of emotion the poem conveys. Even after a poem was attributed or applied to an individual, it did not prevent the same poem from being "used" in other circumstances. The relationship between a poetic voice and its articulator was loose and circumstantial. Another telling example is the attribution of some of the "Nineteen Old Poems" to Mei Sheng. There may have been many other applications that did not survive textual transmission.

3 Regulating the Irregular in Performance Texts

The expression of gender is particularly interesting in the genre of *yuefu*, in which role-playing and performativity are defining attributes. In a way, the indeterminacy of the speaker's gender is easily conceivable in texts meant for performance: this permits easy adaptation to the specific situation of the performer and/or the performance context. Yet there was a similar tendency to "fix" the indeterminacy in the *yuefu* poetry in the early medieval period.[47] The following *yuefu* poem, "Prelude: O When" (Yange hechang xing 艶歌何嘗行), is preserved in the "Treatise on Music" of the *Song shu*. There is an apparent conflict between the two main sections regarding the speaker's gender:

飛來雙白鵠	Pairs of white swans came flying,
乃從西北來	it was from the northwest they came,
十十五五	ten by ten and five by five,
羅列成行	all arrayed in lines.

Wu's wife, such as Xiao Yan's, it is reasonable to suspect that there were stories about Li Ling, Su Wu, and their spouses in circulation that contained poems in the voices of the female characters.

47 As mentioned in Chapter 1, scholars have argued that no clear demarcation can be drawn between the so-called old poems and *yuefu*. The poems discussed in this section are those explicitly preserved as performance texts.

(一解)	(the first stanza)
妻卒被病	Suddenly the wife of one was sick,
行不能相隨	and couldn't keep up.
五里一返顧	Every five *li* [it] looked back once,
六里一徘徊	every six *li* [it] paused.
(二解)	(the second stanza)
吾欲銜汝去	"I want to carry you in my beak,
口噤不能開	but my mouth is closed, I can't open it;
吾欲負汝去	I want to carry you on my back,
毛羽何摧頹	but how ruined my feathers are!"
(三解)	(the third stanza)
樂哉新相知	Happy indeed is a newfound love,
憂來生別離	sorrow comes with parting in life.
躇躊顧群侶	I pause and look around at the flock,
泪下不自知	tears fall without my knowing it."
(四解)	(the fourth stanza)
念與君離別	Thinking on parting with you,
氣結不能言	breath knots within, I cannot speak.
各各重自愛	Let each take heed to take care of self,
道遠歸還難	the journey is long, return will be hard.
妾當守空房	I, your concubine, must keep to my empty chamber,
閑門下重關	the idle gate doubly hinged.
若生當相見	If you live, we shall see each other again;
亡者會重泉	if you die, we shall meet in the world below.
今日樂相樂	Today we enjoy ourselves together,
延年萬歲期	may you live ten thousand years.[48]

The first three stanzas concern a pair of white swans.[49] The personified male bird laments its mate's illness and expresses the wish to carry her along. The last stanza turns to describe a human couple in a similar situation of separation and longing—but it speaks from a distinctive feminine voice, marked by the self-addressing *qie* (I, your concubine) in line 21. Some scholars have noticed this apparent disjunction in the speaker's gender and suggested that the poem might have once been two separate songs. It is common in *yuefu* poetry to combine different segments into one piece, probably for the sake of

48 *XianQin Han Wei Jin Nanbeichao shi* 1.272–73. I use Owen's translation in *The Making of Early Chinese Classical Poetry*, pp. 92–93, with modifications.

49 While the fourth stanza works well as a poetic ending to the topic about two birds, it is disconnected from the bird context and has a different rhyme.

performance.[50] This theory explains the inconsistencies in meter, rhyme, and theme often seen in early *yuefu* poems. In this case, the inconsistency in the speaker's gender could result from such a merger. It is also possible that the two parts in different gendered voices were lyrics intended for two performers. The fact that these two parts with conflicting voices were integrated into one poem attests to the fluidity of the speaker's gender in early poetry. As in the previous examples, what was more important for the poem's audience was probably not who was speaking, but what was being spoken of; that is, the melancholy over separation. This common sentiment is likely the very basis for this combination. However, the fluidity much valued in the performance context became a problem in later textual reception. Another version of this poem in the *Yutai xinyong* with the title "Pairs of White Swans" (Shuang baihu 雙白鵠) contains variants that indicate an attempt to eliminate the contradictory elements in the speaker's gender:

飛來雙白鵠 Pairs of white swans came flying,
乃從西北來 it was from the northwest they came,
十十將五五 Ten by ten, followed by five by five,
羅列行不齊 arrayed in uneven lines.
忽然卒被病 Suddenly one was sick,
不能飛相隨 and couldn't keep flying.
五裏一反顧 Every five *li* it looked back;
六裏一徘徊 every six *li* it paused.
吾欲銜汝去 I want to carry you in my beak,
口噤不能開 but my mouth is closed; I can't open it;
吾欲負汝去 I want to carry you on my back,
羽毛日摧頹 but day by day, how ruined my feathers are!
樂哉新相知 Happy indeed is a newfound love;
憂來生別離 sorrow comes with parting in life.
峙躕顧群侶 I pause and look around at the flock,
泪落縱橫垂 tears fall down all over.

50 See Yu Guanying 余冠英, "Yuefu geci de pincuo he fenge" 樂府歌詞的拼湊和分割, in *Han Wei Liuchao shi luncong*, pp. 17–26. Owen uses "Prelude: O When" to discuss a phenomenon he calls "segmentary composition" that is very common in early *yuefu* poetry. He argues that the *Song shu* version includes two parts of the musical performance: the "prelude" (*yan* 豔) about a pair of birds, and the "coda" (*qu* 趨) about two humans parting from each other. These two parts are combined into a longer hybrid piece, a "great song" (*daqu* 大曲), probably for musical performance. See Owen, *The Making of Early Chinese Classical Poetry*, pp. 97–99.

今日樂相樂	Today we enjoy ourselves together;
延年萬歲期	may you live ten thousand years.[51]

The four-syllable lines in the *Song shu* version are all regularized into standard five-syllable ones by adding a filling word (line 3) or rewriting the line (lines 4 and 5). Line 6, 行不能相隨, has the caesura after the first syllable, whereas the *Yutai xinyong* version has 不能飛相隨 with the caesura after the second syllable, which is its standard position in five-syllable poetry.

The disjunction in the speaker's gender is much less pronounced in the *Yutai xinyong* version. In fact, there is no apparent switch of persona in the middle of the poem as there is in the earlier version. The bird metaphor is carried through the whole poem, and the poem could be read entirely in the voice of a man or a male bird. This version also removes all explicit markers of the speaker's gender, including the mention of the wife at the beginning and the first-person pronoun 妾 toward the end. The *Yutai xinyong* version does not have most of the last stanza of the *Song shu* version, which describes activities and sentiments with strong "feminine qualities," such as locking the gate, missing an absent lover, and so on.[52] This removal contradicts the general regularization of the poetic format in the *Yutai xinyong* version since, compared with other stanzas, the last stanza in the *Song shu* version contains the most standard five-syllable lines in the entire poem.[53] It would be rather strange for the *Yutai xinyong* version to discard this section unless the goal was to reduce contradictory gendered expressions and keep the speaker's voice coherent throughout the poem.[54]

---

51 *Yutai xinyong jianzhu* 1.15–16; *XianQin Han Wei Jin Nanbeichao shi* 1.272.

52 These activities and sentiments are not by themselves "feminine," especially in early poetry without determinacy in gender. As we see in the "Nineteen Old Poems" and other early poems, a man can lock the gate and weep over being separated from the one he loves. But by the 6th century, these actions had become more closely associated with feminine sentiments.

53 It laments the feeling of loneliness and longing as a result of the separation from the beloved person, a very common motif in early poetry in the five-syllable line. Many lines, including line 19 about cherishing each other, line 20 about traveling afar, and line 21 about staying alone in an empty chamber, strongly resonate with lines from the "Nineteen Old Poems" as well as the Li Ling poems.

54 Without the last stanza, the plot is reminiscent of the story about Xu Shu and Qin Jia discussed in Chapter 3. Qin Jia, lamenting the wife's illness and inability to accompany him on his journey, could be a suitable articulator of the poem.

4 Engendering the Discourse of Longing

The discussion so far has revealed a remarkable degree of gender indeterminacy in early poetry. This indeterminacy, once seen as a desirable quality, gradually lost favor over the course of the early medieval period. Relatively indeterminate gendered roles and voices were forced into a "map" of determinate ones by the 5th and 6th centuries. Later readers could never read an early poem with an innocent eye but had to look through the lens of its early medieval audience.[55] In many cases, a definite gender was "assigned" to early poems during this period. An illuminating case is Xu Gan's "Thoughts in a Chamber" (Shi si 室思). This poem was preserved in both the *Yutai xinyong* and, with some variants, in the early Tang encyclopedia *Yiwen leiju*.[56] Here I translate the *Yutai xinyong* version and juxtapose of the two versions side by side, marking their differences in red:

浮雲何洋洋	How vast the floating clouds are!
願因通我辭	I wish that by them I could send my words.
飄遙不可寄	Unsteady and remote, they are impossible to trust.
徙倚徒相思	Lingering in hesitation, I miss you in vain.
人離皆復會	People who are separated all reunite;
君獨無返期	you alone do not have a time set to come back.
自君之出矣	Since you left,
明鏡暗不治	my bright mirror has been dim without polishing.
思君如流水	I miss you like the flowing river—
何有窮已時	How can it have a time to stop?[57]

Yutai xinyong	*Yiwen leiju*
浮雲何洋洋	浮雲何洋洋
願因通吾辭	願因通我辭
飄遙不可寄	一逝不可歸
徙倚徒相思	嘯歌久踟躕[58]

---

55 For a discussion of how the early medieval period shapes our understanding of early poetry, see Owen, *The Making of Early Chinese Classical Poetry*, especially chapter 1, "Han Poetry and the Southern Dynasties," pp. 23–72.

56 The poem is presented in the *Yutai xinyong* as one of a group of six poems collectively titled "Thoughts in a Chamber," *Yutai xinyong jianzhu* 1.36–38. The *Yiwen leiju* only includes this one poem: *Yiwen leiju* 32.563.

57 *Yutai xinyong jianzhu* 1.37; *XianQin Han Wei Jin Nanbeichao shi* 1.377.

58 This couplet in the *Yiwen leiju* version reads: "Once gone, I cannot return; / whistling and singing, I pace back and forth for long."

人離皆復會	人離皆復會
君獨無返期	我獨無返期
自君之出矣	自君之出矣
明鏡暗不治	明鏡開不治
思君如流水	思君如流水
何有窮已時	何有窮已時[59]

This poem has traditionally been read as Xu Gan impersonating a woman longing for her lover.[60] This reading works well with the *Yutai xinyong* version, which presents a consistent speaker's voice lamenting the absence of a beloved person on a prolonged journey, although it does not give any clear indication of the speaker's gender.[61] But the *Yiwen leiju* version of this poem shows some conflicts with regards to the speaker's voice. It has a completely different second couplet, depicting the traveler's longing to return from the first-person perspective. This monologue of the traveler continues in the third couplet, in which the explicit pronoun "I" (*wo* 我) is used in line 6, clearly indicating that the speaker is the one who departs for a journey, not the person who stays in the other version. But the traveler's viewpoint is contradicted in the next two couplets, which apparently lament the other person's departure (*chu* 出) from the perspective of one who stays behind. The *Yutai xinyong* version, most conveniently, has "you" (*jun* 君) instead of "I" in line 6. The variants in the *Yutai xinyong* version therefore keep the speaker's voice consistent throughout the poem. Comparing the two versions, the *Yiwen leiju* text displays much more indeterminacy in the speaker's gender and relationship with the addressee. It could be about a woman missing an absent lover, a man missing an absent lover, or a man missing a friend. These multiple possibilities are significantly reduced in the *Yutai xinyong* version, which involves deliberate editing or selection of variants in order to eliminate conflicts in the speaker's voice.

If there existed multiple possibilities for the speaker's gender in Xu Gan's poem, why is the feminine voice traditionally favored? A crucial reason is the popularity of quatrains starting with the line "Since you left" 自君之出矣 in

59 *Yiwen leiju* 32.563.

60 For example, Shen Deqian believes this poem is "in the voice of a woman in the boudoir" 此託言閨人之詞也: *Gushi yuan* 6.131. Modern scholar Zhao Qijun 趙其均 believes that it is a "persona composition, about a wife's longing for her husband who left home" 這是一組代言體的詩，寫的是妻子對離家丈夫的思念. In Wu Xiaoru, ed., *Han Wei Liuchao shi jianshang cidian*, p. 228.

61 The second-person pronoun *jun* and the act of looking into a mirror, two factors later readers often point to as indications of a "feminine voice" in this poem, are not gender-specific in Xu Gan's time.

the Southern courts of the 5th and 6th centuries. Several of these quatrains are included in the *Yutai xinyong*. They are all modeled on the last four lines of the "Thoughts in a Chamber." The earliest extant poem of this style was written by Liu Jun 劉峻, Emperor Xiaowu 孝武 of the Liu-Song dynasty (r. 453–464):

自君之出矣	Since you left,
金翠暗無精	my gold and emerald [jewelry] are dark without glare.
思君如日月	My longing for you resembles the sun and moon:
迴環晝夜生	returning in circle, it grows day and night.[62]

Here is another by Jia Fengji 賈馮吉, a Chen 陳 dynasty (557–589) poet:

自君之出矣	Since you left,
红颜转憔悴	my lovely appearance turns weary.
思君如明烛	My longing for you resembles the bright candle:
煎心且衔泪	burned in the heart while holding back tears.[63]

To these poems' contemporary readers, the longing for an absent lover in a confined chamber, the description of jewelry, and attending to one's appearance are strong, if not definite, indicators of the feminine voice. Compared with the poems in imitation of the "Nineteen Old Poems" discussed earlier, these quatrains, rewriting a fragment of Xu Gan's poem and taking it out of the original context, are not "imitations" (*ni* 擬) of Xu Gan's "Thoughts in a Chamber." Moreover, they do not claim to be imitations. Most of them do not have titles and may have been the result of group compositions in a court setting. Yet people still read them later as imitations of Xu Gan's poem. Liu Jun's quatrain and Wang Rong's 王融 (467–493) quatrain, for example, bear the titles of "In Imitation of Xu Gan" (Ni Xu Gan 擬徐幹) and "In the Voice of Xu Gan"

62 *Yutai xinyong jianzhu* 10.475. This poem even incorporates a line (line 2) verbatim from another Xu Gan poem, "Poem on Feelings" (*Qing shi* 情詩), which has a clear feminine voice: *XianQin Han Wei Jin Nanbeichao shi* 1.376. Some of the quatrains do not have a gender marker as clear as this one, but most later readers still take them as being in the feminine voice, the emotion of longing aside, partly because many of these poems were composed by court poets at a time when so-called palace-style poetry was popular. Writing about women and composing poetry in the feminine voice are among the most prevalent characteristics of the "palace style."

63 *XianQin Han Wei Jin Nanbeichao shi* 3.2608. Both the "heart" (*xin* 心) and "tears" (*lei* 泪) are puns that describe the poetic speaker as well as the candle, her metaphor. The former in the compound "burned in the heart" (*jian xin* 煎心) is a homophone with the expression "trim the candle/lamp" (*jian xin* 剪心). The latter also refers to the wax that drips down when a candle is burning.

(Dai Xu Gan 代徐幹), respectively, in the *Yutai xinyong*, but they are untitled in all other sources.[64] The perceived feminine voice in these quatrains was retrospectively applied to Xu Gan's "Thoughts in a Chamber," so that it was read as a woman longing for her absent lover. This reading likely affected the choice of textual variants in the *Yutai xinyong* version of the poem.

By the 5th century, the so-called boudoir resentment, in which a woman was represented as being left behind in the boudoir and desperately longing for the return of her beloved man, had become a popular theme in five-syllable poetry. The expression of longing in the situation of separation came to be closely associated with a feminine voice. This association likely also contributed to the reading of a feminine voice in Xu Gan's poem. Jiang Yan's "Poems in Various Styles" provide another example. The first among the group is called "Ancient Parting" (Gu libie 古離別):

遠與君別者	At a long distance, I part from you;
乃至雁門關	[you] arrived at the Yanmen Pass.
黃雲蔽千里	Yellow clouds cover one thousand *li*;
游子何時還	when will the traveler return home?
送君如昨日	It is like yesterday that I sent you off.
檐前露已團	Dew on the eave has already formed orbs.
不惜蕙草晚	I do not pity that the *hui* grass is late;
所悲道里寒	that which I lament is the coldness on the road.
君在天一涯	You are at the other end of the world.
妾身長別離	I, your concubine, am separated from you for long.
願一見顏色	I hope I can see your face once more;
不异瓊樹枝	it will be no less [precious] than branches from the jade tree.
菟絲及水蘋	Dodder and aquatic duckweed,
所寄終不移	from the place they consign themselves, they never move.[65]

Parting is the most pervasive theme in early five-syllable poems. This "Ancient Parting" could be the imitation of any work with this theme. Although it is difficult to locate any one specific source, there are some possible sources in

64 *Yutai xinyong jianzhu* 10.475 and 487; *XianQin Han Wei Jin Nanbeichao shi* 2.1219 and 1404.

65 *XianQin Han Wei Jin Nanbeichao shi* 2.1570. Jiang Yan arranges his imitations in an order corresponding to the rough chronology of the "originals," so this is supposed to be an imitation of an earlier poem than those by Li Ling, the speaker of the second poem in this set.

early poetry. For example, the following two couplets, from the "Nineteen Old Poems" and the Li Ling poems, respectively, are close to the second and fifth couplets of the previous poem:

浮雲蔽白日	Floating clouds conceal the bright sun;
游子不顧返	the traveler does not turn back and go home.[66]

風波一失所	Once losing original places due to winds and waves,
各在天一隅	we are each at one corner of the world.[67]

Jiang Yan's imitation presents a distinctive feminine voice marked by the first-person pronoun "I, your concubine" (*qieshen* 妾身) in line 10. The voice speaks of the longing a woman feels when the man she loves travels to "the other end of the world." The speaker's gender in most old parting poems is ambiguous. For example, in the two couplets quoted previously, the speaker in Poem 1 of the "Nineteen Old Poems" could be male or female, and the poem attributed to Li Ling is intended to be read in the masculine (Li Ling's) voice. Jiang Yan's choice of the feminine voice to represent old parting poems in the five-syllable line is especially revealing and indicates a conscious association of the sentiment of parting with a female speaker. Moreover, the woman's submissive role in the relationship is accentuated in the last couplet with two metaphors (dodder and aquatic duckweed) representing emotional dependency, *ji* 寄. But in many old parting poems, the two parties share the same degree of yearning for and dependence on the other. A sentiment that is not necessarily gender-specific in early works came to be considered feminine and indicative of a power differential by readers in the 5th century.

If the reading of a masculine voice in poems such as the "Nineteen Old Poems" I is plausible, why can't we read "Thoughts in a Chamber" in Xu Gan's own voice as a lovesick man expressing his longing for a woman? The romantic longing for a beautiful woman or goddess was a tradition in the *fu* genre. Even in the genre of five-syllable poetry, Pan Yue's famous series of mourning poems are about his grief over the death of his wife and his longing for her presence.[68] Xu Gan wrote a poem in the voice of a boatman expressing sorrow over being

66 Ibid. 1.329.

67 Ibid. 1.337.

68 *XianQin Han Wei Jin Nanbeichao shi* 1.635–36. The speaker's voice in Pan Yue's three poems is unmistakably masculine, with explicit allusions to a man's mourning for a deceased wife such as Zhuangzi's singing at his wife's funeral.

separated from his new wife.[69] It is not my intention here to dispute the reading of the feminine voice in Xu Gan's poem. In a poetic world in which the speaker's gender is often indeterminate, and very generic expressions could be applied to various personae as well as situations, there is no way and no need to determine the gender of the voice in a poem. An equally plausible situation is that there was never an "original" poem of "Thoughts in a Chamber" as a fixed written text. The variants in the pronouns in different versions of this poem suggest that the same poem could have been articulated in the voice of a man on the road or a woman at home. When the poem was written down and anthologized in the 5th and 6th centuries, people felt it necessary to assign a consistent gender to the poetic voice to stabilize the poem's meaning and text.

5 Taming the Manipulative Woman

In early medieval literati's mapping of gender expressions and gendered voices, the persona of the traveler, the feeling of homesickness and weariness on the road, and the pursuit of officialdom were charted onto masculine territories. The persona of someone staying at home, emotional dependency, and the feeling of abandonment and longing became markers of the feminine voice. Little space was left in literati's writing for a type of female image that used to be popular in early texts: the mysterious woman who provokes and manipulates male desire, such as the goddess in the two *fu* on the goddess attributed to Song Yu, the mulberry-picking girl in the "*Fu* on Master Dengtu the Lecher," Luofu in "Mulberries by the Path," and the woman in a tower in the "Nineteen Old Poems" II. Since the 6th century, readers and writers have felt the need to explain or rewrite the image of the manipulative woman found in early works to fit her into established gender conventions.[70]

Zhang Heng's "Poem on Four Sorrows" (*Si chou shi* 四愁詩) describes the speaker's yearning for a "beautiful person" (*meiren* 美人) and lamentation about her inaccessibility in four stanzas. Here I translate the first stanza:

---

69 See Xu Gan, "Poem on Seeing a Boatman Bidding Farewell to His New Wife at Qinghe," *XianQin Han Wei Jin Nanbeichao shi* 1.378. The same poem is attributed to Cao Pi in the *Yutai xinyong*: *Yutai xinyong jianzhu* 2.55.

70 This is certainly not to say that the image of manipulative women has disappeared in literature. But the need to justify or explain such an image demonstrates the powerful impact of gender conventions formed in the early medieval period.

我所思兮在太山　The person I long for, alas, dwells in Mount Tai,
欲往從之梁父艱　I desire to go and follow her, yet Liangfu is treacherous.[71]
側身東望涕沾翰　I lean to gaze east, tears soaking my writing brush.
美人贈我金錯刀　The beautiful person bestowed on me a knife inlaid with gold,
何以報之英瓊瑤　How do I repay her?—with precious jade.
路遠莫致倚逍遙　The road is far away. Unable to reach her, I am lingering at ease.
何為懷憂心煩勞　For what reason is my heart filled with sorrow and vexation?[72]

The remaining three stanzas follow the same structure and plot: the speaker longs for a beautiful person in a remote place. He receives a gift from that person and hopes to send her something in return. Yet she is always beyond his reach. In the end, the speaker is overwhelmed with sorrow and regret. The inaccessible beauty, the failed gift exchange, and the obstruction of their communication resonate with the pursuit of mysterious women in early court *fu* discussed in Chapter 1. However, a preface to this poem quoted in the *Wen xuan* suggests a different take on gender:

> 張衡不樂久處機密，陽嘉中出爲河間相。時國王驕奢，不遵法度，又多豪右幷兼之家。衡下車，治威嚴，能內察屬縣。姧猾行巧劫，皆密知名，下吏收捕，盡服擒。諸豪俠游客悉惶懼逃出境，郡中大治，爭訟息，獄無繫囚。時天下漸弊，鬱鬱不得志。爲四愁詩效屈原以美人爲君子，以珍寶爲仁義，以水深雪雰爲小人。思以道術爲報，貽于時君，而懼讒邪不得以通。

> Zhang Heng was not happy with being in the pivotal office for a prolonged time. During the Yangjia reign (132–135) he was appointed Minister of Hejian, a post outside of the capital. At that time, the prince of Hejian was arrogant and extravagant, and did not abide by the law. Many powerful households annexed and seized lands. Once Zhang Heng took office, he managed the area with strict authority. He was able to investigate criminal activities in the affiliated counties. When treacherous and cunning people committed a deceitful robbery, Zhang secretly learned the names of all the perpetrators, and ordered officers to arrest them. All wandering

71 Liangfu is a small hill at the foot of Mount Tai.
72 *XianQin Han Wei Jin Nanbeichao shi* 1.180.

> knights errant and itinerant visitors fled the territory in fear, and order was restored throughout the county. Struggles and lawsuits all ceased, and no criminals were detained in jail. At that time, however, the empire was in gradual decline and Zhang was upset at not being recognized. He composed the "Poem on Four Sorrows," following Qu Yuan to use a beautiful person to refer to the prince, precious treasure to humaneness and righteousness, and deep water and heavy snow to petty men. He thought to reciprocate the current ruler by presenting the Way and skills, but was afraid that he could not get through [to the ruler] due to slanderers and villains.[73]

This "preface" is narrated from a third-person perspective and does not appear to have been written by Zhang Heng. It is not included with the poem in the *Yutai xinyong*, nor is it mentioned in any engagement with the poem before the *Wen xuan*, including Fu Xuan's imitation, which has a preface criticizing the style of the original as "narrow and vulgar" (*ti xiao er su* 體小而俗).[74] Most scholars have deemed this "preface" to be a later addition.[75] It identifies the poetic persona with Zhang Heng himself and understands the poem in the context of Zhang's own experience. The idea of "using a beautiful person to refer to the prince" is derived from Wang Yi's interpretation of "Encountering Sorrow" and other *Chuci* pieces as Qu Yuan's expressions of his own political frustration.[76] This allegorical reading reverses the gender—the "beautiful person" cannot be an inaccessible and fickle woman who takes control of the romantic relationship and must symbolize the powerful (male) ruler. Accordingly, the speaker takes the role of the subject who is in the powerless and therefore "feminine" position in the relationship.

As shown in Chapter 2, the theme of the search for a mysterious woman was still popular in Jian'an court writing. This includes the group composition on pacifying the passions written at the request of Cao Pi. Although many were written in the genre of *fu*, Po Qin's five-syllable "Poem on Pacifying the Passions" (Dingqing shi 定情詩) was most likely written on the same occasion. The poem contains all the essential components of the theme and follows the same sequence of events as extant Jian'an *fu* on pacifying the passions:

---

73 *Wen xuan* 29.1356–58; *XianQin Han Wei Jin Nanbeichao shi* 1.180.

74 *XianQin Han Wei Jin Nanbeichao shi* 1.573–74.

75 Ibid. 1.180.

76 For example, Wang explains the speaker's heavenly journey to seek a beautiful person in "Encountering Sorrow" as a metaphor for a loyal minister's search for a wise ruler. See Hong Xingzu 洪興祖 (1090–1155), ed., *Chuci buzhu* 楚辭補註 (Beijing: Zhonghua shuju, 1983) 1.1–3.

我出東門游	I go out of the eastern gate for an excursion,[77]
邂逅承清塵	By accident, I gratefully receive the clear dust [stirred by your chariot].
思君即幽房	I long for you and approach your secluded chamber,[78]
侍寢執衣巾	serve at your bedside, holding your clothes.
時無桑中契	At that time there is no "vows among the mulberry trees,"[79]
迫此路側人	I meet this person by the road.
我既媚君姿	I already admire your manner,
君亦悅我顏	You also take delight in my appearance.
何以致拳拳	How do I express my sincerity?—
綰臂雙金環	a pair of golden bracelets around the arm.
何以致殷懃	How do I express my courtesy?—
約指一雙銀	a pair of silver rings on the finger.
何以致區區	How do I express my heart?—
耳中雙明珠	a pair of bright pearls in the ears.
何以致叩叩	How do I express my earnestness?—
香囊系肘後	a fragrant sachet tied behind the elbow.
何以致契闊	How do I express my longing after parting?—
繞腕雙跳脫	a pair of bracelets circling the wrist.
何以結恩情	How do I consolidate our affection?—
佩玉綴羅纓	a jade pendant decorating the silk fringe.
何以結中心	How do I bond our hearts?—
素縷連雙針	a plain thread tying a pair of needles.
何以結相於	How do I form our companionship?—
金薄畫搔頭	a hair clasp painted with gold foil.
何以慰別離	How do I console the separation?—
耳後玳瑁釵	a hairpin made of tortoise shell behind the ear.
何以答歡欣	How do I requite happiness and joy?—
紈素三條裾	a plain silk skirt embroidered with three layers of laces.

77 This line alludes to Mao 93, "Chu qi dongmen" 出其東門 (Out of the eastern gate), in which a man declares his unmitigated affection for a girl he met out of the eastern gate. *Maoshi zhengyi* 4.370–74.

78 Depending on where one wants to place the caesura, this line could also read: "I long for you to come to my secluded chamber."

79 This refers to Mao 48, "Sangzhong" 桑中 (Among the mulberry trees), about a man's "appointments" (*qi* 期) with beautiful girls among the mulberry trees. *Maoshi zhengyi* 3.225–28.

何以結愁悲	How do I form sorrow and grief?—
白絹雙中衣	a pair of underclothing made of white silk.
與我期何所	Where do you set to meet me?—
乃期東山隅	at the corner of the eastern mountain.
日旰兮不來	Late in the day, alas, you have not come,
谷風吹我襦	the valley wind blows my jacket.[80]
遠望無所見	I gaze afar and see no one.
涕泣起踟蹰	In tears, I rise and step back and forth.
與我期何所	Where do you set to meet me?—
乃期山南陽	It is at the sunny side of the mountain.
日中兮不來	In the middle of the day, alas, you have not come,
飄風吹我裳	The sweeping wind blows my skirt.
逍遙莫誰睹	No one could see me at ease;
望君愁我腸	the longing for you brings sorrow to my inside.
與我期何所	Where do you set to meet me?—
乃期西山側	It is at the side of the western mountain.
日夕兮不來	At sunset, alas, you have not come,
躑躅長嘆息	I step back and forth and heave a long sigh.
遠望凉風至	I gaze afar, and the chilly wind arrives.
俯仰正衣服	In a hurry I adjust my clothes.
與我期何所	Where do you set to meet me?—
乃期山北岑	It is at the northern peak of the mountain.
日暮兮不來	At sunset, alas, you have not come,
凄風吹我襟	The mournful wind blows my lapel.
望君不能坐	Expecting you, I could not sit down;
悲苦愁我心	grief and bitterness bring sorrow to my heart.
愛身以何爲	For what reason do I treasure my body?
惜我華色時	I cherish the time when I had youthful looks.
中情既款款	My feeling inside was already sincere,
然後剋密期	And then we were able to make a date in secret.
褰衣躡茂草	Lifting my jacket, I walk in dense grass,
謂君不我欺	I thought you would not betray me.
廁此醜陋質	With this ugly and humble nature,
徙倚無所之	I linger in hesitation, with no place to go.

80 It is a reference to Mao 35, "Gu feng" 谷風 (Valley wind), which is often understood to be the condemnation by an abandoned wife of her husband. *Maoshi zhengyi* 2.171–80.

自傷失所欲	I take pity on myself for the loss of what I desire.
淚下如連絲	Tears fall like continuous threads.[81]

The chance meeting among the mulberry trees in lines 5–6 recalls the Qin minister's encounter with mulberry-picking girls in the "*Fu* on Master Dengtu the Lecher." The mutual appreciation between the lovers in lines 7–8, as Chapter 2 has shown, is a common element in Jian'an literati's writings about encounters with beautiful women. The character "*zi*" 姿 in line 7 echoes Chen Lin's description of the goddess's beautiful appearance (*yanzi* 豔姿) in his "*Fu* on the Goddess."[82] The extensive listing of clothing and decorative items in lines 9–30 and the speaker's anxious waiting for the loved one in different places in lines 31–52 are common elements of *fu* on pacifying the passions. Po Qin's poem starts with a description of the dazzling beauty and irresistible charm of a woman in the form of a long list of clothes and ornaments as gifts and moves on to the speaker's diligent pursuit of her and her betrayal of her promise. It ends with the speaker's tearful realization of the unattainability and untrustworthiness of the woman.

Despite the unmistakable connection to the theme of pacifying the passions, Po Qin's poem has been read in the voice of a lamenting and regretful woman following remarks by the early Tang critic Wu Jing:

> 定情詩，漢繁欽所作也。言婦人不能以禮從人，而自相悅媚。乃解衣服玩好致之，以結綢繆之志。若臂環致拳拳，指環致慇懃，耳珠致區區，香囊致扣扣，跳脫致契闊，佩玉結恩情。自以爲得志。而期于山隅山陽山西山北，終而不答，乃自悔傷焉。

> "Poem on Pacifying the Passions" was written by Po Qin of the Han dynasty. It speaks about a woman who did not serve the other person according to the rites. On the contrary, she pleased and seduced him at her own will. She then removed her clothes and beloved objects to give him, hoping to form an emotional bond. For example, arm bracelets to express sincerity; rings to express courtesy; ear pearls to express her heart; a fragrant sachet to express earnestness; bracelets to express longing after parting; a jade pendant to express affection, etc. She thought that she had won his favor, and expected to meet him at the corner, the

81 *XianQin Han Wei Jin Nanbeichao shi* 1.385–86.

82 *Yiwen leiju* 79.1351. See the discussion in Chapter 2.

> south, the west, and the north of the mountain. At the end, her lover did not reciprocate [her love]. Thereupon she felt regretful and painful.[83]

Wu Jing reads the poem to be the lamentation and confession of a woman who violated ritual propriety to pursue a man and was punished for her indiscretion. This reading makes the woman the victim of abandonment and assigns to her the passive role in the relationship. This later assigned gender role complies with the established conventions about the feminine voice, despite contradicting the theme of pacifying the passions and many explicit literary references in the poem. Wu takes the whole list of clothing items and ornaments as the woman's gift to the man, yet it is rather unusual for a woman to remove her clothes and accessories to gift them to a man. The description of the woman's clothing items in the writings on pacifying the passions often serves to express the man's wish to turn into these items in order to stay close to the woman, not the other way around. The repeated expression of the speaker's anxious and futile expectation of the arrival of a loved one echoes Mao 42 "Jing nü" 静女 (A fine girl), in which a man is waiting for a fine girl who never shows up.[84] The feelings of loss and bewilderment at the end of the poem are a common ending in Jian'an *fu* on pacifying the passions, describing the male protagonist's failed pursuit of a woman.

Wu Jing's contemporary Qiao Zhizhi 喬知之 (d. 697) wrote a "Song on Pacifying the Passions" (Dingqing pian 定情篇). It takes on an unmistakably feminine voice, marked with the first-person pronoun *qie*, to convey the speaker's chastity and longing for her husband.[85] The poem describes a relationship marked by an obvious power differential:

共君結新婚	With you I form a new marriage,
歲寒心未卜	it is the cold season of the year, [your] heart is unpredicted.
相與遊春園	Together we take a stroll in the spring garden,
各隨情所逐	each following their passions.
君愛菖蒲花	You love the flowers of sweet flag;
妾感苦寒竹	I am touched by bamboos in the bitter cold.
菖花多豔姿	Flowers of sweet flag have beautiful appearance;
寒竹有貞葉	winter bamboos have firm leaves.[86]

83 *XianQin Han Wei Jin Nanbeichao shi* 1.385; *Yuefu shiji* 76.1076.

84 *Maoshi Zhengyi* 2.204–05.

85 *Yuefu shiji* 76.1077–78; *Quan Tang shi* 26.368–69.

86 Here the character *zhen* 貞 plays on its other meaning, chastity, when applied to women.

此時妾比君	At this moment comparing me and you,
君心不如妾	Your heart cannot be compared to mine.
…	

In the following lines, the poem talks about a chance encounter between a mulberry-picking girl and an office-seeking man:

復有遊宦子	Again there was a man traveling to seek office,
結援從梁陳	making connections and seeking assistance, he followed [the rulers of] Liang and Chen.[87]
燕居崇三朝	He sojourned there for three whole years;
去來歷九春	between his departure and return there were nine springs.
誓心妾終始	Taking a vow in my heart, I am constant till the end;
蠶桑奉所親	by raising silkworms and mulberries I care for the parents.

It is hard to miss the similarity to the section about the Qin minister's encounter with a mulberry-picking girl on his way to search for a wise ruler to serve in the "*Fu* on Master Dengtu the Lecher." But the emphasis in Qiao's poem falls on her steadfast loyalty to her husband and diligent service to her in-laws.[88] The following lines clearly resonate with the several lines starting with "*heyi*" 何以 (how do I) in Po Qin's poem:

何用念芳春	For what reason one misses the fragrant spring?
芳春有流易	The fragrant spring is prone to disappearance and change.
何用重歡娛	For what reason one values pleasure and joy?
歡娛俄戚戚	Pleasure and joy are momentary [and leave one with] sorrow.

Yet Qiao's poem makes the woman the giver of many gifts to the man, which is consistent with Wu Jing's understanding of Po Qin's poem:

87 These are two fiefdoms in the early Han, both in modern Henan province.

88 In this sense the mulberry-picking girl is closer to the image of Qiu Hu's 秋胡 wife, a variation of Luofu and the mulberry-picking girl of the "*Fu* on Master Dengtu the Lecher," who is a chaste wife and filial daughter-in-law. See Allen, "From Saint to Singing Girl," pp. 341–50.

桂枝不須折	There is no need to break cinnamon branches;
碧流清且潔	the green stream is clear and pure.
贈君比芳菲	I present them to you like fragrant flowers;
愛惠常不歇	my love and favor are constant, without stop.
贈君泪潺湲	I present them to you, my tears falling slowly;
相思無斷絕	my longing is ceaseless.
妾有秦家鏡	I have a mirror of the house of Qin,
寶匣裝珠璣	in a jewel box filled with pearls and gems.
鑑來年二八	The mirror arrived when I was sixteen;
不記易陰暉	I do not remember the changes of light and shadow.
妾無光寂寂	There is no still light for me to
委照影依依	cast a slender shadow.
今日持爲贈	Today I take it to present to you;
相識莫相違	once we get to know each other, do not turn your back.

The "mirror of the house of Qin" (*Qinjia jing* 秦家鏡) among her gifts alludes to one of the three five-syllable "Poems Presented to My Wife" (Zeng fu shi 贈婦詩) attributed to Qin Jia in the *Yutai xinyong* that describes a mirror that is his gift to his wife Xu Shu.[89] Yet the genders of the presenter and receiver of gifts are reversed in Qiao's poem. Qiao Zhizhi's poem "fixes" all traits of the mulberry-picking girl in previous literature that are not in accordance with the conventional feminine image. If the woman is often unpredictable and manipulative in earlier works on pacifying the passions, she is reshaped to be faithful and submissive, completely at the mercy of her husband's fickle heart.

In the preceding cases, any possible reading of a manipulative and elusive woman was explained away through political allegory or gender reversal, because the trope no longer held a valid position in the gender attributes mapped out in the early medieval period. In a story from the 9th-century collection *Chuanqi* 傳奇 (Tales of the marvelous), the Luo goddess in Cao Zhi's celebrated *fu* is stripped of her power and becomes an abandoned wife (of Cao Pi) and devoted lover (of Cao Zhi as well as the male protagonist in the story).[90] The story is set in the Taihe 太和 era (827–836). A scholar named Xiao Kuang 蕭曠 was approached one night by a beautiful woman while staying in a lodge

89 *XianQin Han Wei Jin Nanbeichao shi* 1.187; *Yutai xinyong jianzhu* 1.31. See the discussion of poems attributed to Qin Jia and his wife Xu Shu in Chapter 3.

90 The collection was compiled by Pei Xing 裴铏 (fl. 9th century) and preserved in the early Song story collection *Taiping guangji* 太平廣記 (Extensive records of the Taiping [xingguo] reign [976–983]): Li Fang et al., eds, *Taiping guangji* (Beijing: Renmin wenxue chubanshe, 1959) 311.2459–61.

by the Luo river. She introduced herself as Empress Zhen/the Luo goddess and had an extended conversation with him while two maids served him food and ale. Unlike Cao Zhi in the "*Fu* on the Luo Goddess," Xiao Kuang consummated the relationship with the goddess, who was joined by a dragon princess. Poems were exchanged, and the two goddesses bestowed extravagant gifts on Xiao Kuang and promised to secretly assist (*yinzhu* 陰助) him to achieve immortality before departure. The story contains a conversation between Xiao Kuang and the two goddesses in which they answer, in detail, all his meticulous and technical questions about the immortal world. In the "*Fu* on the Luo Goddess," the vast difference between the ways of humans and immortals (*renshen zhi dao shu* 人神之道殊) accounts for the goddess's departure and the termination of the relationship.[91] In the *Chuanqi* story, however, by explaining everything about "the way of immortals," the goddesses willingly give away the mystery and inaccessibility in which their power and manipulation reside to please the male protagonist. Once again, the power dynamic between the two genders is reversed. The women are in a clearly subordinate position in their interaction with Xiao Kuang (both the Luo goddess and the dragon princess refer to themselves with the humble pronoun *qie*), even though they are of a higher order of beings. The contrast is even more striking if we consider that Cao Zhi was a prince and Xiao Kuang a mere scholar (*chushi* 處士).[92] Through the rewriting of the romantic encounter with the Luo goddess, this story conforms to the established gender conventions that have women serve men, with sexuality, wealth, and secrets to immortality, from an inferior position. Not accidentally, in the Xiao Kuang story it is women who give gifts to a man, including shining pearls (*mingzhu* 明珠), halcyon plumes (*cuiyu* 翠羽), and a piece of raw silk (*qingxiao* 輕綃) worth ten thousand in gold.[93]

6 Conclusion

The formation of gender conventions was a historical process that occurred in specific cultural and literary circumstances, one crucial element of which was the weakening of the performative setting and the rise of individual authorship

91 *Wen xuan* 19.900.

92 "*Chushi*" often refers to someone who is educated or talented but choose not to enter public service.

93 Both "shining pearls" and "halcyon plumes" appear in the "*Fu* on the Luo Goddess," where they are used to describe the activities of the cohort of immortals accompanying the goddess: "some gather shining pearls; / some collect halcyon plumes" 或採明珠/或拾翠羽: *Wen xuan* 19.899; Knechtges, *Wen xuan or Selections of Refined Literature*, Vol. 3, p. 363.

in early medieval literature. From the late 3rd century onward, the notion of poetic writing underwent significant changes, with one being keener attention to the individuated side of poetic expression. Poetic writing and literary writing in general came to be taken as a personal endeavor as opposed to (involuntary) expressions of general human situations or normative sentiments. This latter view is pervasive in early theories on literary writing, especially the "Great Preface" to the *Shijing*, in which poems are said to be the reflection of state governance and people's lives.[94] The reading of gender was irrelevant when the interpretation centered on what was common among a whole group of people. That explains why the Mao commentary takes poems with explicitly feminine voices about a woman's personal agony, such as Mao 35 "Gu feng" and Mao 58 "Meng" 氓, as representative of the degenerating moral situation in a state.[95] In terms of the generality and anonymity in their expressions, the "Nineteen Old Poems" and many early *yuefu* poems are much like the *Shijing* poems.

It was the gradual loss or downplaying of poetry's performativity that led to this keener attention to the individuated side of poetic expression. A new concept of authorship started to take hold in the 3rd century. Cao Pi takes notice of personal styles associated with the writer's personality in "A Discourse on Writing."[96] When Lu Ji talks about the "intention" (*yi* 意) in the "*Fu* on Writing" (Wen fu 文賦), what he means is no longer a normative thought, but something closer to the notion of "authorial intention," or the formulated ideas in the mind of an individual author. Lu Ji's *fu* begins with a keen recognition of the difficulty for the author's mind/intent to match the object of writing and for the writing to capture what is on the author's mind/intent (*yibu chengwu, wenbu daiyi* 意不稱物，文不逮意). In other words, Lu Ji views writing as an act of an individuated mind controlled by the writer, although this control is not always successful.[97] Following this new notion, a literary text could be read as the volitional expression and occasional composition of an individual author. When older poems were reread in this framework, determining the gender and role of their speakers became the necessary first step to decode the meaning. The allegorical connection made between the faithful wife and the loyal minister is an effort to explain the author's intent where an apparent conflict in gender stands in the way. It is only applicable with the assumption of individual authorship.

94 *Maoshi zhengyi*, 1.5–24.
95 See *Guofeng jishuo*, 1.323 and 564.
96 *Wen xuan* 52.2270–73.
97 Ibid. 17.761–74.

Gender conventions formulated by early medieval literati continue to shape our reading of literary texts. For example, the poem "Heaven O!" (Shangye 上邪), preserved in the "Treatise on Music" of the *Song shu*, is included in almost every modern anthology of early poetry:

上邪	Heaven O!
我欲與君相知	I wish to know you,
長命無絕衰	[our love] be everlasting and never fade.
山無陵	When the mountains have lost their ridges;
江水為竭	rivers have dried up;
冬雷震震	Thunders have rolled in winter;
夏雨雪	Snow has fallen in summer;
天地合	Heaven and earth have become one;
乃敢與君絕	until then do I dare to break off from you.[98]

The poem is a declaration of intense affection and fear of its loss by a devoted lover, whose gender is not clear from the text. Yet many readers from pre-modern to modern times assume a feminine voice based on the intense expression of love and fear.[99] The Qing scholar Zhuang Shuzu's 莊述祖 (1751–1816) suggested reading this poem and another Han *yuefu* poem entitled "I Have Someone in Mind" (You suo si 有所思) together as a dialogue between a man and a woman in love. "Heaven O!" is "the man's words to comfort the woman" (*nan wei nü zhi ci* 男慰女之辭). Yet Zhuang's reading was disputed by many, including Wen Yiduo 聞一多 (1899–1946) and Yu Guanying, two leading Chinese scholars on *yuefu* poetry. Both Wen and Yu accepted Zhuang's proposal to read the two poems together yet took both as articulated by the same girl.[100] Given the indeterminacy in gender in early performance texts, such debates are beside the point. The poem could take on a man's or a

98 *XianQin Han Wei Jin Nanbeichao shi* 1.160–61.

99 For example, Wu Ruyu 吳汝煜 asserts that the speaker "is a simple and straightforward girl from the north expressing love to a man to whom she devotes her affection" 是一位心直口快的北方姑娘向其傾心相愛的男子表述愛情. In Wu Xiaoru, ed., *Han Wei Liuchao shi jianshang cidian*, pp. 74–75.

100 See Geng Zhaolin 耿兆林, "'You suo si' yu 'Shangye' 'dangwei yipian' ma?" 《有所思》與《上邪》"當為一篇"嗎, *Tianjin shizhuan xuebao* 3 (1981): 68–69. Modern scholars almost unanimously side with Wen and Yu. The only support of Zhuang's reading I have found is based on the belief that the beginning exclamation "Heaven O!" is too strong and direct to be articulated by a girl, which confirms the stereotypical associations with women's voices. Zeng Xiangxu 曾祥旭, "Lizhi cheng xiliu, he guan zou qixiang: 'Shangye' he 'You suo si' biejie" "離之成細流，合觀奏奇響：《上邪》和《有所思》別解", *Academic Forum of Nandu* 1 (2000): 49–50.

woman's voice, depending on the gender of its performer or the context of its performance. It does not even have to be about a romantic relationship and could address a wide range of emotional bonds between two people. But since the early medieval period, ideas about the masculine and feminine in literary expression have become part of the cultural establishment and sometimes cultural intuition. They have influenced our reading and understanding of texts in many subtle and subconscious ways.

CHAPTER 5

Neglected Voices of Early Medieval Women Writers

Male writers' writings, especially their persona compositions in women's voices, played the primary role in the formation of gender conventions. But what role did women writers play in the making of conventions about the feminine voice? What is the relationship between the conventional feminine voice and women's own voices? These questions are not easy to answer due to the limited number of credible pre-Tang women's writings. As Chapter 3 has shown, most attributions of literary works to women before the Jian'an period are questionable, many resulting from the conflation of the poetic persona and the author. The absence of actual women's voices in literature is the result of many different historical and cultural factors, including the low literacy rate among women, the loss of texts due to the destruction of imperial libraries, and the lack of interest and care in circulating and preserving women's works. The few sources that preserve women's writings include official dynastic histories, which sometimes quote literary works by elite women; encyclopedias, which tend to keep only fragments of writing; and literary anthologies, which select literary works by women with varying degrees of credibility regarding the ascription of authorship.

This chapter examines women's literary writing in the early medieval period with full awareness of the limitations on materials and knowledge accessible to us. Women's voices in some less-studied texts, most of which are chance survivals in encyclopedic and historical sources, show notable differences from the feminine voice represented in popular literary sources of the time. By "popular literary sources," I refer to literary anthologies such as the *Yutai xinyong* and *Wen xuan* and works of literary criticism such as the *Shi pin* and *Wenxin diaolong*. These were compiled with contemporary readership and literary taste in mind. Their selections and discussions of literary works convey the compiler's opinions and judgements regarding what is valuable and noteworthy in literature. It should be pointed out here that these few works are themselves chance survivals among a wealth of literary scholarship that was produced in the 6th century, especially in the Liang court.[1] Their literary views, therefore, should not be taken as authoritative or even representative without critical examination. But they nonetheless offer valuable and otherwise

1 For a thorough examination of literary scholarship in the court of Liang, see Tian, *Beacon Fire and Shooting Star*, pp. 77–161.

 | DOI:10.1163/9789004546455_007

inaccessible information about contemporary views regarding women's writing and women's literary voices. Moreover, as this chapter will show, these several works share many common perceptions, including those regarding gender. The comparison between popular literary sources on the one hand and historical and encyclopedic sources on the other suggests that the former's selected representation of women's writings has reduced the diversity in the voices of women and reinforced conventions about the feminine in literature.

1 Women's Voices in the *Yutai xinyong*: A Unique "Female Perspective"?

Our primary source for early medieval women's poetic works is the 6th-century anthology of poetry *Yutai xinyong*. With a stated interest in female authorship and readership (to be discussed below), the anthology includes a range of poems, from the renowned "Poem on Resentment" attributed to Lady Ban in the Western Han to roughly contemporary pieces by elite women such as Liu Lingxian 劉令嫻 (late 5th–early 6th century) and Shen Manyuan 沈滿願 (fl. *c.*540). The authenticity of poems before the 3rd century in this anthology is often dubious, such as the poem attributed to Empress Zhen that were discussed in the Introduction and the poems attributed to Lady Ban, Xu Shu, and Wang Song that were examined in Chapter 3. These questionable attributions are all characterized by the scarcity of works (each with a single title) and their absence in other sources. This is not the case, however, for works by elite women poets from the Southern dynasties featured in this anthology, including Bao Linghui 鮑令暉 (fl. 464), Shen Manyuan, Liu Lingxian, and her younger sister Mrs. Wang, who was married to Wang Shuying 王叔英 of the prestigious Wang clan of Langye 琅琊. Seven poems by Bao Linghui, ten poems by Shen Manyuan, eight by Liu Lingxian, and three by Liu Lingxian's sister are included in the anthology.[2] These women were contemporaneous or nearly so to the compilation of the anthology and their poems are quoted or discussed elsewhere, including in historical records, anecdotal accounts, and works of literary criticism. Therefore, we can be confident in accepting the authorship.

2 What complicates the issue is the complex textual history of the *Yutai xinyong* and its multiple editions. My calculation is based on the 1633 edition compiled by Zhao Jun 趙均. It contains 656 poems and is based on a no-longer-extant 1215 edition. The numbers here are therefore only of relative value. For studies on the textual history of the anthology, see Liu Yuejin, *Yutai xinyong yanjiu*; and Anne Birrell, *Games Poets Play: Readings in Medieval Chinese Poetry* (Cambridge: McGuinness China Monographs, 2004), pp. 304–25.

Poems attributed to women before the 3rd century in the *Yutai xinyong* largely conform to the established conventions of the feminine voice. Most of them are written from the perspective of a lonely, abandoned woman expressing her loyalty to her husband and her hope for the return of his love and favor. This is not surprising given that they were most likely persona compositions by male writers. But the majority of poems in the same anthology by actual women writers follow these conventions too. All seven poems by Bao Linghui are about parting and longing; five among Liu Lingxian's eight poems are about longing and separation, while the rest are about adorning oneself and the exchange of gifts (flowers and embroideries respectively) with female friends; and all three poems by Mrs. Wang concern resentment, loneliness, or longing for the absent husband. Shen Manyuan's poems show the widest range of topics (probably because she is represented by the largest number of poems). Among her ten poems, five are about romantic longing, two are "poems on things" (*yongwu* 詠物) describing boudoir objects, one mocks another woman's romantic relationship, and two is about adorning oneself. In sum, all the poems touch on boudoir themes, while over 70 percent of them specifically concern romantic longing and/or abandonment. One of Bao Linghui's poems is an imitation of the "Nineteen Old Poems" 11 (Ni Qingqing hepan cao 擬青青河畔草):

裹裹臨窗竹	Svelte, svelte are bamboo by the window,
藹藹垂門桐	thick, thick are catalpa leaning over the gate.
灼灼青軒女	Glowing is a girl by the green window,
泠泠高臺中	in the chilly, tall terrace.
明志逸秋霜	Her bright intent is loftier than autumn frost;
玉顏豔春紅	her jade face is lovelier than spring flowers.
人生誰不別	In life who does not part?
恨君早從戎	I regret that you went to the army early.
鳴弦慚夜月	My chiming strings put the night moon to shame;
紺黛羞春風	my indigo kohl makes the spring wind bashful.[3]

Like Lu Ji's imitation of the "old poems," Bao Linghui rewrites the original poem line by line and corrects its problematic morality. The poem transforms the image of a seductive wanderer's wife (*dangzi fu* 蕩子婦) into one of a chaste

3 *Yutai xinyong jianzhu* 4.152; *XianQin Han Wei Jin Nanbeichao shi* 2.1313. I consulted Birrell's translation in Anne Birrell, trans., *New Songs from a Jade Terrace: An Anthology of Early Chinese Love Poetry* (London: Allen & Unwin, 1982), p. 122.

wife longing and waiting for her absent husband.[4] The woman's theatrical display of her beauty and the presence of the sensualizing gaze in the original poem are completely removed from the scene. The lush grass and willows symbolizing sensual desire in the original poem are replaced with bamboo and catalpa trees, symbols of integrity, sublimity, and transcendence. The vegetation in the original directs the beholder's eyes up to the charming woman in a tower, whereas the bamboo and catalpa trees in Bao's poem conceal her from the sensualizing gaze. A feeling of coldness and loftiness is present throughout Bao Linghui's imitation and significantly downplays the provocative spring scenery in the original. The woman's intent is compared to autumn frost, another symbol of virtue and chastity, and her appearance to jade, a token of integrity, coldness, and composure.[5] Like Lu Ji's imitation, Bao's poem turns the perspective of the description inward. It assumes the woman's voice in the fourth couplet to directly address her husband. She is alone and lonely, utterly absorbed in pining for him. The only witnesses of her beauty and talent are the moon and the wind. This imitation contains all the essential features of the conventional feminine voice—five-syllable form, sentiments of longing, resentment of the lover's absence, and a pledge of chastity. Bao Linghui's other poems in the *Yutai xinyong* are similar articulations of romantic longing in this type of voice, including two poems she wrote on behalf of another woman addressing to the woman's husband.[6]

Some scholars see a unique female viewpoint or a female sensibility in women's poems in the *Yutai xinyong* that is distinct from the feminine voice in male authors' persona writing. Some also applaud the anthology for representing the authentic voices of women.[7] It is true that some of these poems present interesting twists on familiar literary tropes, such as Liu Lingxian's "Poem in Reply to My Husband" II (Da wai shi 答外詩):

4 Xiaofei Tian sees Bao Linghui's poem, along with Lu Ji's and Liu Shuo's imitations of the "Nineteen Old Poems" II, as a general trend of "a remedial rewriting of the image of 'the wanderer's wife' in the Han poem." The configuration of female desire in the image of a faithful wife in Bao's poem, she points out, distinguishes it from the works of her male predecessors. Tian, "Configuring the Feminine," pp. 113–17.

5 Line 6 in the *Gushiji* version of this poem has "to conceal" (*yan* 掩) instead of *yan* 艷. *XianQin Han Wei Jin Nanbeichao shi* 2.1313.

6 *Yutai xinyong jianzhu* 4.154–55.

7 An example is Birrell's discussion of the works of Bao Linghui, Shen Manyuan, and Liu Lingxian in the anthology: Birrell, *Games Poets Play*, pp. 176–208.

東家挺奇麗	"Of eastern neighbor the most beautiful!"[8]
南國擅榮輝	"Of southern lands by far the brightest face!"[9]
夜月方神女	"Just like a goddess on a moonlit night!"[10]
朝霞喻洛妃	"Or like the goddess of the Luo in the morning mist!"[11]
還看鏡中色	But then I see my own face in the mirror,
比艷似知非	I know I am not the equal of those stunners.
摛詞徒妙好	Your choice of words is wonderful and nice of no avail,
連類頓乖違	since your comparisons are always off the mark.
智夫雖已麗	My wise husband, you may think me pretty—
傾城未敢希	"City-toppling" I would not dare hope to be.[12]

In this poem Liu quotes, likely from her husband's now lost poem, stock similes and allusions in praise of female beauty, only to reject them all on the ground that her own appearance is far inferior. One may want to read the poem as Liu's refusal to be categorized according to literary clichés and empty allusions, and as her firm refusal to accept the mode of femininity imposed on her by men.[13] But the speaker's modest rather than subversive tone throughout the poem contradicts this reading. The woman does find fault with her husband's choice of words, which she makes sure to extol as "wonderful and nice." What she feels is "off the mark" is not his descriptions of female beauty, but his application of these descriptions to her. Instead of an expression of discontent and defiance, this poem is a wife's humble and polite declining of her husband's praise. One should also not overlook the fact that this poem is one of two pieces entitled "Poem in Reply to My Husband" by Liu Lingxian. The other poem speaks of the ennui and sorrow the female speaker feels in her chamber while waiting for her husband's return. The final couplet reads:

8 This alludes to the beautiful daughter of the eastern neighbor who tried in vain to seduce Song Yu in the "*Fu* on Master Dengtu the Lecher."

9 This probably refers to the fair lady in Cao Zhi's "Miscellaneous Poem" IV that begins with the line "In the southland there is a fair lady" (*nanguo you jiaren* 南國有佳人): *XianQin Han WeiJin Nanbeichao shi* 1.457.

10 This is an allusion to the "*Fu* on the Goddess" attributed to Song Yu.

11 "The Luo goddess" is the subject of Cao Zhi's famous "*Fu* on the Luo Goddess."

12 "City toppling" (*qingcheng* 傾城) is the phrase Li Yannian uses to describe the beauty of his sister in his "Song on a Fair Lady." This poem is discussed in Chapter 3. *Yutai xinyong jianzhu* 6.255. I use Grant and Idema's translation in Beata Grant and Wilt Idema, eds. and trans., *The Red Brush: Writing Women of Imperial China* (Cambridge, MA: Harvard University Asia Center, 2004), p. 150, with modifications. The notes are mine.

13 For example, see Tian's reading of this poem in "Configuring the Feminine," pp. 220–22.

欲知幽怨多	If you want to know how much my hidden resentment is—
春閨深且暮	in the spring boudoir, deep and dark.[14]

The mention of "resentment" (*yuan* 怨) and "boudoir" (*gui* 閨), along with an alternative title, "Resentment in the Spring Boudoir" (Chungui yuan 春閨怨), identifies explicitly with the conventional trope of "boudoir resentment." Even if we do not assume that the two poems were composed on the same occasion, both share the humble tone of a faithful wife longing for her husband.

Another poem by Liu Lingxian included in the anthology is often taken by modern scholars to showcase its female (sometimes even labeled "feminist") perspective. It is "Matching Lady Ban's Resentment" (He Jieyu yuan 和婕妤怨):

日落應門閉	The sun has set, the gate is surely closed;
愁思百端生	and sorrowful thoughts rise in a hundred ways.
況復昭陽近	The more so as the Zhaoyang palace is so near;[15]
風傳歌吹聲	The breeze carries the sounds of song and music!
寵移終不恨	I do not regret for the change of favor,
讒枉太無情	but that false slander was simply too cruel.[16]
只言爭分理	I only care about principles and reasons—
非妬舞腰輕	I am not jealous of her waist, however slim![17]

By Liu Lingxian's time, an abandoned woman grieving a loss of favor had become a recurrent trope in poems in the feminine voice. The "Poem on Resentment" attributed to Lady Ban anticipates abandonment when the favor is still present. Liu Lingxian's matching poem, in Lady Ban' voice, moves the time of composition forward to when she has already lost imperial favor. This temporal change fits the theme of "resentment" even better than the original. Among the *Yutai xinyong*'s selections are poems on the same topic by Liu Lingxian's male contemporaries, including her brother Liu Xiaochuo 劉孝綽 (d. 539) and He Sicheng 何思澄 (*c*.481–534). Liu Lingxian's last two couplets

14 *Yutai xinyong jianzhu* 6.255.

15 Zhaoyang is the name of the palace where the Zhao sisters live.

16 Lady Ban was accused of practicing witchcraft (*meidao* 媚道) by the Zhao sisters: *Han shu* 97b.3984.

17 *Yutai xinyong jianzhu* 8.359. The poem is attributed to Mrs. Wang in the (much later) *Yuefu shiji*. I use Grant and Idema's translation in *The Red Brush*, p. 149, with modifications. The Zhao sisters are famous for their dancing skills and slim figures. Legend has it that Zhao Feiyan was good at "dancing in a palm" (*zhangshang wu* 掌上舞) for the slenderness of her figure.

deny her feelings of jealousy and attribute her anger to the insistence on "principles and reasons." Some scholars read them as reflecting a female viewpoint in contrast to the focus on the loss of favor in Liu Xiaochuo's and He Sicheng's poems.[18] The concept of "female viewpoint" is a questionable one to begin with.[19] Moreover, while it is true that Liu Lingxian's poem offers an alternative reasoning to the rivalry, it certainly cannot be explained simply by her gender. Concerns about the violation of principles are in fact not uncommon in poems about abandonment. Lu Ji's "Ballad on a Pond" in the voice of Empress Zhen, another abandoned palace lady, ends with the following lines:

天道有遷易	The Way of Heaven involves change and alteration;
人理無常全	human principles lack eternal perfection.
男歡智傾愚	When a man is in love, his intelligence collapses;
女愛衰避妍	when a woman loses favor, she avoids other beauties.
不惜微軀退	I do not grudge the withdrawal of my humble body,
但懼蒼蠅前	but only fear the advance of flies.
願君廣末光	I wish the lingering light of you would extend,
照妾薄暮年	to shine on your concubine's twilight years.[20]

The second to last couplet makes essentially the same argument as Liu Lingxian's last couplet. The only difference is the logical sequence—the structure "I do not ... I only ..." (不 … 但) in Lu's poem reverses the order of the "I only ... I do not" (只 … 非) in Liu's. Both deem the violation of principles more significant than personal loss. Liu Lingxian denies Lady Ban's jealousy to show her womanly virtue in opposition to the Zhao sisters, who are known for their extreme jealousy. The contrast between the "principles" and "dancing waists" is the same as that between "serving [the emperor] with beauty" and "serving with virtue," a distinction Ban Gu made through Lady Li's voice in her *Han shu* biography.[21] Liu Lingxian's poem still follows conventions of the

18 Birrell believes that Liu Lingxian's poem "brings a female viewpoint to the theme and expresses a lively emotional response to the situation": Birrell, *Games Poets Play*, p. 195. Grant and Idema agree with her view in *The Red Brush*, p. 149. Tian observes that Liu Lingxian "enacts a voice that differentiates significantly and strikingly from that of the female persona as presented by the renowned court poet Liu Xiaochuo" and that her portrait of Lady Ban "reflects to a certain degree the personality of the poet herself." Tian, "Configuring the Feminine," p. 214 and p. 217.

19 See the discussion in the Introduction.

20 *XianQin Han Wei Jin Nanbeichao shi* 1.658–59. The poem is discussed in the Introduction.

21 "As for those who serve people with physical beauty, when the beauty withers, the love disappears; when the love disappears, the favor terminates" 夫以色事人者，色衰而愛馳，愛馳則恩絕: *Han shu* 97b.3952.

feminine voice and depicts Lady Ban as a lonely woman lamenting the loss of favor yet staying loyal to her husband.

Besides resentment and longing, poems on adorning oneself, poems on things (mostly boudoir objects), and poems exchanged with other women are also common among women's poems in the *Yutai xinyong*. All of them concern experience, objects, and sentiments in the inner chamber. The depiction of boudoir objects and adorning oneself often invokes romantic longing. Shen Manyuan's poem "Teasing Lady Xiao" (Xi Xiaoniang 戲蕭娘) treats a topic with the potential to explore female friendship and subjectivity, yet it still chooses to focus on a romantic relationship:

明珠翠羽帳	Bright pearl, kingfisher plum bed drapes,
金蒲綠綃帷	Gold leaf, sheer green silk door tapestries.
因風時暫舉	As they lift now and then with the wind,
想像見芳姿	I imagine I see your charming figure.
清晨插步搖	At dawn you put on your hairpin,
向晚解羅衣	Approaching dust you slip off your silk dress.
托意風流子	You entrust your emotion to Mr. Libertine!
佳情詎可私	How could you keep your joyful passions a secret?[22]

With no explicitly gendered pronoun, the poem could have been taken as the author's appreciation of the friend's beauty, until the revelation of the last couplet—she is adorning herself and her bedchamber for a secret lover, the "Mr. Libertine." Instead of taking a female perspective, Shen Manyuan feigns a male viewpoint (though not his voice) and expresses *his* desire toward her lady friend. The title confirms this reading: the poet is teasing her girlfriend about a love affair that the friend tries (in vain) to hide. Posing as a bystander, Shen Manyuan writes her friend into the conventional image of a lonely woman awaiting an absent lover.

It is fair to say that women writers' poems in the *Yutai xinyong* mostly comply with, rather than challenge or subvert, the male-established conventions about the feminine image and voice. Disputing the long-existing view of the anthology as a collection of poems of decadent taste and sensual pleasure, Xiaofei Tian observes that "the *Yutai xinyong* poems are in fact extremely diverse. A single-minded focus on the image of the languishing palace lady or a lonely woman pining for her absent beloved cannot do justice to the complex portrayal of women or gender relationships in this rich anthology of

22 *Yutai xinyong jianzhu* 5.209. I use Birrell's translation in *New Songs from a Jade Terrace*, p. 151, with modifications.

over 600 poems." The reason for the prejudice against the anthology, Tian believes, lies partly in its "resistance to allegorical interpretation."[23] Many poems depict, in meticulous detail, the woman's body, clothing, and ornaments, which makes it difficult to find any political connotation. The diversity in topics and resistance to allegory, however, do not apply to women's poems in the anthology, including both early works with dubious authorship and contemporary poems with more credibility. Women represent themselves—either their own image or that of other women—mostly as the resentful and lonely wife waiting for her lover in the boudoir. Does this mean that the feminine voice is not a male construct but matches the voices and self-images of actual women writers? To answer this question, we must take into consideration the active role of the anthology in selecting women's poems and representing "women's voices."

2 Xu Ling's Preface: What, How, and Why Do Women Read and Write?

As discussed in the Introduction, an anthology's selection of literary works is determined by its own agenda and influenced by the popular literary taste of its time. The *Yutai xinyong* is no exception. Since the early Tang it has been viewed as an anthology of "palace-style poetry" with the goal to "expand the style" (*yi da qi ti* 以大其體) and criticized for its moral corruption and decadence.[24] The preface by the compiler Xu Ling claims that the anthology was created for the leisure reading of palace ladies.[25] In the preface, Xu Ling portrays a "beautiful lady" (*liren* 麗人) as a writer and reader of poetry. Her image reflects those of

23 Tian, *Beacon Fire and Shooting Star*, pp. 193–94.

24 This is Liu Su's 劉肅 (fl. 742–755) statement about the agenda of the *Yutai xinyong*, which quotes the early Tang minister Yu Shinan's 虞世南 (558–638) remonstrance to Tang Taizong (r. 626–649) about his hobby of writing "romantic poems" (*yanshi* 豔詩). According to Yu Shinan, Emperor Jianwen was also fond of such poems and went so far as to order the compilation of the *Yutai xinyong* to promote and glorify them. See Liu Su, *Datang xinyu* 大唐新語 (New accounts of the great Tang) (Guilin: Guangxi shifan daxue chubanshe, 1998) 3.106.

25 Xu Ling's claim for female readership has long been questioned. Some scholars believe there are hidden (political) agendas behind this claim. Rouzer states that "the readership would very obviously have been mostly male" despite the opposite suggestion made by the preface: Rouzer, *Articulated Ladies*, p. 132. Tian, on the other hand, disputes this view and argues that many anthologies from the time that did not survive were explicitly made for women readers. Tian also reviews the debates about the agenda of the anthology and concludes that it indeed targeted female audiences: Tian, *Beacon Fire and Shooting Star*, pp. 190–91.

the four women writers best represented in the anthology—Bao Linghui, Shen Manyuan, and the Liu Lingxian sisters, who were either from prestigious literary families or related to prominent literary and/or political figures of their times.[26] It should be noted here that even if the anthology's targeted readers may indeed be elite women, we cannot not rule out its voyeuristic appeal to contemporary male readers. In that case, its construction as a work addressed to women could well have been a literary conceit on the part of the editor.

Xu Ling's preface also comments on the nature, content, and function of women's reading and writing. Following a description of the lady's stunning beauty and literary talents, he turns to the occasions that inspire her to compose poetry:

> 既而椒宮宛轉，柘館陰岑，絳鶴晨嚴，銅蠡晝靜。三星未夕，不事懷衾；五日猶賒，誰能理曲。優游少託，寂寞多閑。厭長樂之疎鐘，勞中宮之緩箭。纖腰無力，怯南陽之搗衣；生長深宮，笑扶風之織錦。雖復投壺玉女，為觀盡於百驍；爭博齊姬，心賞窮於六箸。無怡神於暇景，惟屬意於新詩。庶得代彼皋蘇，微蠲愁疾。
>
> Afterward, in the winding corridors of Pepper Hall, in the remote corners of Persimmon Lodge (where crimson hall-keys stay solemn at dawn, and bronze door knockers are silent at noon), since it is not yet the night for an imperial summons, she will not come and serve, quilt held to her chest. Since her day of service is still distant, who will help her do her hair? She has little to occupy her mind in her strolls and too much leisure in her loneliness. She grows tired of the intermittent bells of Longjoy Palace, and she wearies of the slow waterclock in the central hall. Her slender waist so weak, she is afraid of pounding clothes in Nanyang; growing up in the secluded palace, she would laugh at the woven brocade of Fufeng. Though she could act the Jade Maid and play arrow-toss, her attention would go after a hundred rounds; if she were the Qi lady competing at *liubo*, her delight would end with six tallies. Since she has no pleasure in her leisure, she turns to new verse; such works can replace those herbs that mysteriously relieve melancholy and grief.[27]

26 Bao Linghui's brother Bao Zhao was a prominent literary figure of the time; Shen Manyuan was the granddaughter of Shen Yue, a powerful official and leading literary figure; the Liu sisters came from a prestigious family that produced major literary and political characters such as Liu Hui 劉繪 (458–502) and Liu Xiaochuo 劉孝綽.

27 *Yutai xinyong jianzhu* 1.12–13. I use Rouzer's translation in *Articulated Ladies*, p. 135. For an alternative translation of the preface, see Birrell, *New Songs from a Jade Terrace*, pp. 339–43.

The lady's life revolves around serving (*shi* 事) the lord or husband and, even when she is not with him, her mind is completely occupied with longing for him. She is the embodiment of the lonely and resentful (abandoned) wife in poems in the feminine voice. Since writing and reading poetry do not require physical strength or stepping out of her boudoir, they are perfect means to cure the loneliness and boredom she feels when she is alone. Not accidently, this beautiful lady's "melancholy and grief" (*chouji* 愁疾) are the dominant sentiments in poems by women writers in the anthology. Xu Ling describes in this preface the "typical" compositional situation of women writers, the "typical" topics and sentiments in their poems, as well as their "typical" life, as he sees it. This view of women's reading and writing guided his selection of women's works in the anthology and, as we will see shortly, was quite common among writers and literary critics of his time.

The preface then claims that the anthology's selection of "romantic poems" (*yanshi* 艷詩) suits the interests and needs of women writers in their leisure time. It carefully defines the nature of these poems:

> 曾無忝於雅頌，亦靡濫於風人，涇渭之間，若斯而已。
>
> Although they cannot be placed next to the "Odes" and "Hymns," they do not go beyond the bounds of the poets of the "Airs."[28] Just as the waters of the Jing and Wei rivers stay apart even though they flow through the same channel, so do I make the same distinction here.[29]

Xu Ling makes two observations about *yanshi*: (1) they derived from the same origin as the poems in the "Airs" and are therefore suitable reading materials for proper ladies; and (2) they are different from poems of political and social significance, such as those in the "Odes" and "Hymns" sections. Scholars often emphasize the first point, that is, Xu Ling's attempt to find a legitimate position for *yanshi* in literary history. Knechtges, for example, uses this passage to show a new emphasis on the entertainment value of poetry that emerged around this period, in contrast to the old, Confucian literary ideas about poetry's didactic and moral functions that are best demonstrated by Xiao Tong's *Wen xuan*. According to Knechtges, "one implication of this statement might be

28 Among the three sections of the *Shijing*, "Airs" are usually associated with the lives of common people and local customs of various states. This section also contains the largest number of poems about romantic relationships in the whole collection. Poems in the "Odes" (*ya* 雅) and "Hymns" (*song* 頌) are those used in court banquets, ancestor rituals, and state affairs.

29 *Yutai xinyong jianzhu* 1.13; Rouzer, *Articulated Ladies*, p. 135, with modifications.

that the erotic poetic tradition is respectable enough to exist alongside the classical tradition. Poems from the amatory tradition may not have the high status of the canonical works, but Xu Ling acknowledged that poetry need not always be sober and serious and that it could be used to provide pleasure and entertainment during idle moments."[30] What is equally remarkable, however, is Xu Ling's recognition of certain topics—such as politics—as not suitable for women's reading and writing.[31] This view certainly accounts for the limitation and homogeneity in the subject matter of women's poems represented in the anthology.

The following passage expands on his ideas about female readers and writers of poetry:

> 至如青牛帳裏，餘曲既終；朱鳥窓前，新妝已竟，方當開茲縹帙，散此縚繩，永對翫於書幃，長循環於纖手。豈如鄧學春秋，儒者之功難習；竇專黃老，金丹之術不成。因勝西蜀豪家，託情窮於魯殿；東儲甲觀，流詠止於洞簫。孌彼諸姬，聊同棄日，猗歟彤管，無或譏焉。

> Just when she draws aside her black-ox curtains, and that final serenade is still unplayed; just when she stands before her redbird window while her fresh toilette is still incomplete—*only then* she will unroll these emerald scrolls, undo these scroll ties, peruse the poems for a while by the library curtains, ever turning them with her slender hands. Of course, her labors are hardly like those of Empress Deng, who studied the *Spring and Autumn Annals* (a scholar's achievement, so difficult to emulate!); or those of Empress Dou, who gave herself over to Daoist techniques (the art of gold and cinnabar is still unperfected!). Nonetheless, they are far superior to that rich man of Western Shu, who exhausted all emotion in "Lu Palace," or the heir-apparent in his quarters, where fluid chanting ended with "The Flute." "Charming those maids of Qi"—I hope they will use this to cast away their days. "Lovely that red writing brush"—let there be none who malign it![32]

30 Knechtges, "Culling the Weeds and Selecting Prime Blossoms," p. 234.

31 Although not explicitly stated, the difference he makes between the romantic ("Airs") and the political ("Odes" and "Hymns") may also indicate gender difference, with the former deemed feminine and the latter masculine.

32 *Yutai xinyong jianzhu* 1.13; Rouzer, *Articulated Ladies*, pp. 136–37, with modifications. Italics added by me.

The adverb "*fang*" 方 (only then) suggests that the lady is supposed to pass her time with the anthology *only* after completing her primary undertaking—the performance of music and application of makeup to please her lord/husband. Then Xu alludes to two famous palace ladies from the past. Empress Deng (81–121) was the empress of Emperor He of the Eastern Han. According to her *Hou Han shu* biography, she started learning Confucian classics at an early age and was jokingly called "the scholar" (*zhusheng* 諸生) by her relatives for her diligent study and lack of interest in housework (*jujia zhishi* 居家之事). Later she studied with Ban Zhao 班昭 (*c.*45–*c.*117), the famous woman scholar and sister of the historian Ban Gu.[33] Empress Dou (d. 135 BCE) was the empress of Emperor Wen of the Western Han. After the emperor died, she managed state affairs in the role of empress dowager for a number of years. An avid advocate of the Huang–Lao 黃老 school of philosophy, she promoted officials sympathetic to Daoism rather than Confucianism.[34] These two empresses are presented here as "negative models," for their pursuits are too difficult to achieve (*nanxi* 難習 and *bucheng* 不成) for women. Since the beautiful lady in the preface only has time for casual reading between her more important duties as wife or concubine, she cannot devote herself to scholarly and political endeavors. Literary education serves very different ends for her than for the empresses Dou and Deng. It does not give her political power or scholarly authority but helps her win the lord's favor and console herself in her loneliness in his absence. The phrase "casting away the days" (*qiri* 棄日) is borrowed from Sima Xiangru's "*Fu* on the Imperial Park" (Shanglin fu 上林賦), in which it is posited in opposition to "attending to state affairs" (*lanting* 覽聽).[35] The same contrast is implied in Xu Ling's preface: women's learning, reading, and writing serve no political or public purpose. Their significance lies solely in their entertaining value.

Xu Ling's preface reveals his ideas about what, how, and why women read and write, or more precisely, what, how, and why they *are supposed to* read and write. His selection of women's literary works dutifully reflects these ideas. Xu Ling was not alone in his time in associating sentiments of loneliness (*jimo* 寂寞) and melancholy and grief (*chouji* 愁疾) with women's poetic voices. One of the two works by women that made their way into the *Wen xuan* is Lady Ban's

33 *Hou Han shu* 10a.418 and 424.

34 See her biographies in the *Shi ji* 49.1972–75 and *Han shu* 97a.3945.

35 *Wen xuan* 8.376. The passage is discussed in Chapter 1.

"Poem on Resentment," which by the 6th century had become the classical piece on the theme of boudoir resentment.[36]

Zhong Rong's comments on women's writing convey similar opinions. Only four women poets are discussed in his *Shi pin*: Lady Ban in the upper gradation, Xu Shu in the middle gradation (*zhongpin* 中品), and Bao Linghui and Han Lanying 韓蘭英 in the lower gradation (*xiapin* 下品). His comments on Lady Ban are about her "Poem on Resentment":

> 團扇短章，辭旨清捷，怨深文綺，得匹婦之致。
>
> The short poem on a round fan. The gist of her writing is clear and swift. The profound resentment and elegant writing capture the demeanor of a woman.[37]

Here the "resentment" (*yuan* 怨) is viewed as a crucial component of "the demeanor of a woman." Zhong Rong's remarks on Xu Shu highlight the same emotional factor in her writing:

> 夫妻事既可傷，文亦悽怨。
>
> The events between the husband and wife are already pitiable, and the writing is indeed miserable and resentful.[38]

Zhong Rong's comments on individual poets typically trace the person's poetic style to ancient works such as the *Shijing*, *Chuci*, "Nineteen Old Poems," or at least to a poet in the upper gradation such as Cao Zhi. Thus the poets in his highest gradation almost always have poetic "descendants" in the lower gradations. Yet Lady Ban is an exception. While her poetry is said to "originate in Li Ling" (*yuan chuyu Li Ling* 源出於李陵), not a single poet's style is traced to her. The irony is hard to miss—as the only woman poet in the upper gradation, she is left with no offspring. All later women poets discussed in the book are compared with her, yet the word "origin/originate" (*yuan* 源) is never used. Zhong Rong appears to draw an exclusive lineage of women's poetic tradition that, although derived from the male tradition traced back to Li Ling and then up to *Chuci*, does not exert any influence on the development of the male tradition.

36 This can be attested by many imitations in which the poet speaks in the voice of Lady Ban, including those by Liu Lingxian, Liu Xiaochuo, and He Sicheng.

37 *Shi pin jizhu*, p. 113.

38 Ibid., p. 249.

This idea of men's poetry being the origin and inspiration of women's poetry (and not vice versa) explains why far more men's poems than women's poems were selected for the *Yutai xinyong*, an anthology claiming to offer reading pleasure and writing models for women. It cannot simply be explained by the shortage of women's writing. The *Sui shu* bibliography lists many literary collections by elite women and several anthologies or collections of women's writing compiled in the 6th century.[39]

Zhong Rong's comments on Bao Linghui and Han Lanying treat women's poetic writing as a separate and self-contained tradition:

> 令暉歌詩，往往斷絕清巧，擬古尤勝，唯百願淫矣。照嘗答孝武云："臣妹才自亞於左芬，臣才不及太沖爾。"蘭英綺密，甚有名篇。又善談笑，齊武謂韓云："藉使二媛生於上葉，則玉階之賦，紈素之辭，未詎多也。"
>
> Bao Linghui's songs and poems are often extremely lucid and skillful. Her imitations of old poems are especially outstanding. Only the "A Hundred Wishes" is excessive. Bao Zhao once replied to Emperor Xiaowu, "The talent of my sister is certainly inferior to Zuo Fen and my talent also cannot reach Taichong (Zuo Si)." [The style of] Han Lanying is elegant and dense. She has many famous pieces and is also good at conversation. Emperor Wu of Qi said to her, "If you two ladies were born in the last century, the *fu* on jade steps and poem on plain silk would not have been superior."[40]

The *fu* on jade steps refers to Lady Ban's "*Fu* on Self Lamentation" (Zidao fu 自悼賦) cited in her *Han shu* biography. It contains the line "The splendid palace is full of dust, alas, the jade steps covered by mosses" 華殿塵兮玉階落.[41] "The poem on plain silk" is the "Poem on Resentment" attributed to her, the first line of which is "Newly cut, fine plain silk from Qi" 新裂齊紈素.[42] Zhong Rong places the two women writers exclusively in the lineage of women poets such as Lady Ban and Zuo Fen, even though he does not include Zuo Fen in his ranking. Bao Zhao's response to Emperor Xiaowu is also gender specific. While he compares himself with Zuo Si 左思 (*c.*250–305), a male poet in Zhong Rong's upper gradation, his sister's poetic talent has to be pitted against Zuo Fen's. Emperor Wu of Qi similarly praises the poetic skills of Bao Linghui and

39 See *Sui shu* 35.1070–71 and 1082.

40 *Shi pin jizhu*, p. 592.

41 *Han shu* 97b.3987.

42 *XianQin Han Wei Jin Nanbeichao shi* 1.116–17.

Han Lanying within the tradition of women's writing, the exemplary works of which he gives treat the theme of boudoir resentment. It is hardly surprising that all remarks and judgements on women's writing are made by men.

A certain consensus regarding women's writing existed in popular literary discourse of the 6th century. There was a preference for women's poetic voices that speak of romantic longing and domestic life. Women's writing was perceived as a separate tradition from men's, with different topics and sentiments. These views are consistent with the male-constructed conventions of the feminine voice, which center around the image of an abandoned woman and her longing and resentment. Women's poems in the *Yutai xinyong* were selected for their conformity to these perceptions, which explains the homogeneity of their voices. It must be noted, however, that what is shown here is a common tendency in representing women's writings and perceiving women's literary voices in the 6th century, as demonstrated by available sources. Exceptions exist, including the other piece of women's writing selected for the *Wen xuan*: Ban Zhao's "*Fu* on the Journey to the East" (Dong zheng fu 東征賦).[43] It describes Ban's journey to the capital city Luoyang, accompanying her son to his new official post, and reflects on her motherly duties and moral principles. The speaker's voice and tone have nothing in common with the abandoned wife trope. This may be explained by the generic difference—after all, as demonstrated in earlier chapters, five-syllable poetry is the primary medium for the conventional feminine voice. But different voices of women did exist and sometimes they found their way into the popular literary discourse. This serves as a reminder of the inevitably partial understanding we will ever be able to attain of the early medieval literary world, due to the immense loss of primary materials.

3 Women's Other Lifestyles

Women's poems in 6th-century literary anthologies give the impression that women writers spent most of their time in the inner chamber and had little interest or experience beyond the family compound. Kang-i Sun Chang makes the following observation about "traditional women poets":

> 一般說來，傳統女詩人作品大都局限於閨怨的狹隘內容，因爲她們大都缺乏自覺的歷史意識和政治關懷，故很少寫詩見證政治與社會的興亡盛衰。

43 *Wen xuan* 9.432–37.

> Generally speaking, works of traditional women poets are mostly limited in the narrow content of boudoir resentment. Because most of them lacked historical consciousness and political concerns, they seldom wrote poems bearing witness of the rise and fall of state and society.[44]

Chang's argument could be well supported by women's writings as seen in the 6th-century anthologies. Records from the early medieval period, however, suggest there were other aspects to women's lives than what may be inferred from these writings. Ge Hong, an Eastern Jin scholar, condemns contemporary women for violating established social and ritual codes in his *Baopu zi* 抱樸子 (The master who embraces simplicity):

> 今俗婦女, 休其蠶織之業, 廢其玄紞之務, 不績其麻, 市也婆娑。舍中饋之事，修周施之好，更相從詣，之適親戚，承星舉火，不已於行。多將侍從，暐曄盈路，婢使吏卒，錯雜如市；尋道褻謔，可憎可惡。或宿於他門，或冒夜而返；游戲佛寺，觀視漁畋；登高臨水，出境慶吊；開車褰幃，周章城邑；盃觴路酌，弦歌行奏。轉相高尚，習非成俗。… 願諸君子, 少可禁絕。婦無外事, 所以防微矣。

> As for the custom of the current time, women neglect sericulture and weaving and abandon their work on ceremonial garments. Instead of spinning the linen, they go out dancing in the marketplace. They cast aside the work in the kitchen and cultivate the merits of giving alms. Moreover, they follow each other and visit relatives. Day and night they won't stop. Accompanied by many servants, they dazzlingly fill in all streets. Their maids, messengers, clerks, and servants make up a mixed crowd like in a marketplace. Along the road they are on intimate terms with others and act frivolously. It is indeed loathsome and detestable! Some (women) lodge in others' house and some return home late at night. They take pleasure excursions in Buddhist temples, watch fishing and hunting; they climb mountains and go to the riverbanks, they leave their family compounds to attend celebration and mourning; they go around cities with the curtains of their carriages lifted; they drink by the road with cups and wine vessels, singing and playing music along the way. They admire and respect such behavior and make these wrong conducts custom. I hope you gentlemen will prohibit and put a stop to it.

44 Kang-i Sun Chang, "Modai cainü de luanli shi" 末代才女的亂離詩, in *Gudai nü shiren yanjiu* 古代女詩人研究, ed. Zhang Hongsheng 張宏聲 and Zhang Yan 張燕 (Wuhan: Hubei jiaoyu chubanshe, 2002), pp. 224–46.

> Women should not have engagement outside their households, by which we can prevent bad things from happening in the first place.[45]

In Ge Hong's time, group excursions to mountains and riverbanks (*dengshan linshui* 登高臨水), drinking by the roadside (*beishang luzhuo* 杯觴路酌), and singing and playing music on the road (*xiange xingzou* 弦歌行奏) often inspired male literati to write poetry. Famous examples include the literary gathering in Shi Chong's private garden in the Golden Valley (*jingu* 金谷) in 296 and the poetic outing in the Orchid Pavilion (*lanting* 蘭亭) in 353. It is entirely possible that women also wrote poems during the excursions described in the previous passage, but if they did, none of their poems survived. Ge Hong may have exaggerated the actual situation for the sake of critique and warning, but women at the time certainly must have ventured out of their chambers and taken an active part in public events to trigger this kind of critique.[46] Historical records also show that early medieval women enjoyed a certain degree of freedom both within and outside their family compounds. Slightly earlier than Ge Hong, Yang Xiu 羊琇 (246–282), a Western Jin minister, hosted outings and parties in which his female relatives actively participated:

> (琇) 性奢侈… 又喜遊讌，以夜續晝，中外五親無男女之別。
>
> Yang Xiu's nature was extravagant. He also liked to take pleasure excursions and hold banquets all day and all night. There was no distinction between men and women in and out of his household and relatives.[47]

Yan Zhitui 顏之推 (531–591), a southerner staying in the north after the defeat of Emperor Yuan of Liang 梁元帝 (r. 552–554) by the Western Wei 西魏 troops, was shocked by the "subversive" behavior of northern women:

> 鄴下風俗，專以婦持門戶。爭訟曲直，造請逢迎，車乘填街衢，綺羅盈府寺。代子求官，為夫訴屈。此乃桓、代之遺風乎？
>
> It is the custom of Ye that women have the exclusive privilege to manage households. They make lawsuits, argue for right and wrong, pay visits and

45 Yang Mingzhao 楊明照, ed., *Baopi zi waipian jiaojian* 抱樸子外篇校箋 (Beijing: Zhonghua shuju, 1991) 25.616–19.

46 Gan Bao made similar remarks on what he saw as improper behaviors of women in the "General Discussion" (Zonglun 總論) of his *Jinji* 晉紀 (Records of Jin): *Wen xuan* 49.2187–88.

47 *Jin shu* 93.2411.

> receive guests. Their carriages fill streets and intersections and their silk clothes crowd bureaus and temples. They seek government positions on behalf of their sons and appeal against wrongful cases for their husbands. Isn't this the legacy of Huan and Dai?[48]

Yan Zhitui laid the blame on the "barbarian" legacy in the north, implying that no such transgressions ever existed among the women of his native south (*Jiangdong* 江東). But Ge Hong's account suggests otherwise. Xie Daoyun 謝道韞 (second half of the 4th century), an elite woman from the illustrious Xie family in the south, did "appeal against a wrongful case" (*suqu* 訴屈) for her family members. After her husband and sons lost their lives in the chaos of Sun En's 孫恩 (d. 402) rebellion in 399, she led her household servants to resist the rebels. When she was captured with the rest of her family members, she bravely defended her grandson in front of Sun En, who spared their lives.[49] Alarmed by his observations, Yan Zhitui, like Ge Hong, suggests confining women's activities to household chores and forbidding them from participating in public affairs. Otherwise, he warns, the disaster of "hens crowing in the morning" (*pin ji chen ming* 牝雞晨鳴)—gender subversion—will surely befall them. The use of the word "crowing" (*ming* 鳴) is interesting: it is dangerous if women behave in an independent way, and even more so when they gain voices of their own.

Early medieval male literati's remarks on contemporary women's behavior displayed an anxiety about women's violation of their culturally sanctioned gender role. This anxiety was behind the selection and promotion of women's writings that abide by the idea that "women should not have engagement outside their households" (*fuwu waishi* 婦無外事) in popular literary sources.

4 Women's Other Poetic Voices

Many early medieval women writers left literary collections. The *Sui shu* bibliography lists literary collections by Wang Shaozhi 王劭之, Zuo Fen 左芬, Li Wan 李婉, Xin Xiao 辛蕭, Sun Qiong 孫瓊, and Xie Daoyun in the Jin Dynasty; Han Lanying and Mrs. Qian 牽氏 in the Liu-Song Dynasty; Shen Manyuan, Princess Lin'an 臨安公主, and the Liu Lingxian sisters in the Liang Dynasty;

48 Zhuang Huiming 莊輝明 and Zhang Yihe 章義和, eds., *Yanshi jiaxun yizhu* 顏氏家訓譯註 (Shanghai: Shanghai guji chubanshe, 1999) 1.39. "Huan" and "Dai" are names of ancient kingdoms founded by non-Han peoples in the north.

49 *Jin shu* 96.2517.

Empress Shen 沈皇后 in the Chen Dynasty; and others.[50] Most of them were celebrated authors in their own times, but with few exceptions their names and literary works had sunk into oblivion by the Song dynasty. Although some were still well-known names in later generations, seldom were their literary talents and accomplishments discussed seriously beyond their general reputation as "talented women" (*cainü* 才女). Only a handful of poems by early medieval women writers are preserved in the *Wen xuan* and *Yutai xinyong*. The sharp contrast with the list of women writers and their collections in the *Sui shu* bibliography shows the extremely limited access we have to the world of early medieval women's writing. Fortunately, a very small number of poems by women survived (though mostly in fragmentation) accidentally through citations in encyclopedic, anecdotal, and historical sources. Almost all these chance survivals contain women's voices and images quite different from those represented in popular literary anthologies.

4.1 *Emotional and Philosophical Transcendence*

Popular literary discourse of the 6th century associates the feminine voice with feelings of melancholy and resentment, as amply conveyed in the ending couplet of the poem attributed to Xu Shu:

長吟兮永歎	I chant long, alas, and give drawn-out sighs,
淚下兮沾衣	tears fall, alas, and soak my clothes.[51]

The characters "*chang*" 長 (long) and "*yong*" 永 (lasting) emphasize the intensity and perpetuity of such feelings. No wonder Birrell describes women's attitude toward love in the Southern dynasty poems as "obsessive."[52] But is it true that women lack the capacity for self-consolation, emotional detachment or transcendence? The one literary work that can be attributed to Lady Ban with certainty is the "*Fu* on Self Lamentation" quoted in her *Han shu* biography. This *fu* was composed after she lost imperial favor to the Zhao sisters and moved to the Eastern Palace to take care of the empress dowager. It describes her

50 *Sui shu* 35. 1070–71, 1075, 1079 and 1080. This list is far from complete. Many women's writings may have been lost even before the composition of the *Sui shu* bibliography. For a list of early medieval women writers and brief introductions to their lives and works, see Hu Wenkai 胡文楷, *Lidai funü zhuzuokao* 歷代婦女著作考 (Shanghai: Shangwu yinshuguan, 1957), pp. 1–13. For a discussion of women writers of the Liang dynasty, see Tian, *Beacon Fire and Shooting Star*, pp. 109–10. On women's education in this period, see Beatrice Spade, "The Education of Women in China during the Southern Dynasties," *Journal of Asian History* 13, no. 1 (1979): 15–41.

51 *XianQin Han Wei Jin Nanbeichao shi* 1.188.

52 Birrell, *Games Poets Play*, p. 14.

prestigious family lineage, her moral and scholarly cultivation, and her reception and loss of imperial favor. Although most of the *fu* is dominated by sorrowful feelings, there is a change of tone toward the end:

俯視兮丹墀	Looking downwards at the red stairs,
思君兮履綦	I long for your footsteps, my lord.
仰視兮雲屋	Looking up at the palace hidden in the clouds,
雙涕兮橫流	my tears run down turbulently.
顧左右兮和顏	I look at my attendants with composure,
酌羽觴兮銷憂	fill a feathered goblet with wine to dispel my grief.
惟人生兮一世	A person's life only lasts one life span,
忽一過兮若浮	Swiftly, it passes by like floating.
已獨享兮高明	Already I have solitarily enjoyed sublimity and brilliance,
處生民兮極休	and experienced the utmost blessing of human beings.
勉虞精兮極樂	Having exerted my spirit to extreme joy,
與福祿兮無期	I do not expect good fortune and wealth.
綠衣兮白華	"Green Coat" and "White Flower,"[53]
自古兮有之	things like these have existed since ancient times.[54]

This final twist sets this *fu* apart from writings in the conventional feminine voice. Instead of becoming engulfed by sorrow and desperation, the speaker sought moral and spiritual transcendence through philosophical and historical reflection. The *fu* follows the tradition of "consolation through philosophy," that is, to dispel grief and frustration through philosophical or religious meditation. Representative works in this tradition include the "Fisherman" (Yufu 漁父), attributed to Qu Yuan, and Jia Yi's 賈誼 (200–168 BCE) "*Fu* on the Houlet" (Funiao fu 鵩鳥賦).[55] But aside from Lady Ban's *fu*, "consolation through philosophy" is very rarely seen in writings in women's voices. While the escape from grief and frustration is a willful choice for male writers, for women the same emotion is almost always presented as overwhelming and everlasting.

53 These are allusions to the Mao interpretations of *Shijing* poems. Mao 27 "Lü yi" 綠衣 is taken to be a critique of the concubine's assumption of the role of the principal wife, and Mao 229 "Bai hua" 白華 as the Zhou people's critique of King You's 幽王 deposition of his empress in favor of the femme fatale Baosi 褒姒. *Maoshi zhengyi* 2.138 and 9.711.

54 *Han shu* 97b.3987. The *fu* is translated in its entirely in Knechtges's "The Poetry of an Imperial Concubine," pp. 137–43. This translation is mine.

55 *Wen xuan* 33.1532–33, 13.604–11. Rouzer also notes this similarity between Lady Ban's *fu* and Jia Yi's in *Articulated Ladies*, p. 120.

Self-condolence or emotional transcendence is completely absent in the five-syllable "Poem on Resentment" attributed to Lady Ban, the entire concern of which is the loss of favor and its emotional consequences.[56] It is telling that, compared with the more credible "*Fu* on Self Lamentation," the five-syllable poem was much better known in the tradition as Lady Ban's work. The most memorable image of her is as an abandoned wife, not a solemn thinker.

A highly esteemed poet in her own time, Xie Daoyun's work is not represented in the *Yutai xinyong*. Her "Chant on Mount Tai" (Taishan yin 泰山吟) is preserved in the encyclopedia *Yiwen leiju*:

峨峨東岳高	How majestic! The Eastern Peak is high.
秀極沖青天	Extremely graceful, it soars into the blue sky.
巖中間虛宇	Inside its rocks there is an empty space;
寂寞幽以玄	lonely, obscure, and mysterious.
非工復非匠	It was not built by workers or crafters,
雲構發自然	The cloudy structure rose from What Is Naturally So.
器象爾何物	The phenomenal world, what are you?—
遂令我屢遷	you made me change frequently.
逝將宅斯宇	Gone forever, I am about to dwell in that space,
可以盡天年	by which I can exhaust my natural life span.[57]

In this poem, Xie Daoyun is most likely describing a spiritual or imaginary journey to Mount Tai, for she probably never set foot in the region due to the division of north and south.[58] Like Sun Chuo's 孫綽 (320–377) famous "*Fu* on a Journey to Mount Tiantai" (You Tiantai shan fu 游天台山賦), the poet's imaginary roaming in the mountain results in spiritual transcendence.[59] Despite its imaginative nature, the scope of this topic goes far beyond the inner chamber and domestic life. "Mystery" (*xuan* 玄) and "What Is Naturally So" (*ziran* 自然) are central concepts in the "poetry on the discourse of the Mystery" (*xuanyan shi* 玄言詩) that was popular among elite literati in Xie Daoyun's time, yet they are rare topics in extant women's writings. In the poem, Xie Daoyun's philosophical reflection on nature's sublimity and constancy leads to a decision to abandon the mundane, everyday life. This transcendence is achieved

56 The difference in emotion also has to do with the different genres. As argued in Chapter 3, a strong connection is established between five-syllable poetry, the feminine voice, and the sentiments of abandonment and resentment in early medieval literature.

57 *Yiwen leiju* 7.123; *XianQin Han WeiJin Nanbeichao shi* 2.912.

58 The mountain fell under the Eastern Jin rule for only a few years during Xie's lifetime, thanks to her own brother Xie Xuan's 謝玄 (343–388) military victory.

59 *Wen xuan* 11.493–502.

not through physical departure from the world, but by obtaining a higher level of understanding in this world. The *Yiwen leiju* quotes another poem by Xie Daoyun entitled "Imitation of the Poem on a Pine Tree by the Court Gentleman Xi" (Ni Xi Zhongsan yong song shi 擬嵇中散詠松詩), in which she expresses skepticism about the very idea of achieving physical immortality through the encounter with immortals:

遙望山上松 I gaze at that pine tree yonder on the hill from afar;
隆冬不能雕 The coldest winter cannot make it wither.
願想游下憩 I long to go there, roam and rest beneath it,
瞻彼萬仞條 where I can watch its branches rising for ten thousand *ren*.
騰躍未能升 I jump up, but cannot soar in flight;
頓足俟王喬 Stamping my feet I wait for Prince Qiao.[60]
時哉不我與 But time, alas, has never been on my side,
大運所飄颻 And I am swept along with the Grand Transformation.[61]

The pine tree is a symbol of immortality. The poem by Xi Kang 嵇康 (223–262) that Xie Daoyun imitates is "Poem on Roaming Immortals" (Youxian shi 游仙詩), which describes the speaker meeting with the immortals, receiving the elixir and knowledge of the Way, and eventually departing this world.[62] Xi's is a standard rendition of the theme of "roaming immortals" that can be traced back to the depictions of heavenly journeys in the *Chuci*. Xie Daoyun's imitation begins by expressing a similar wish to transcend the mundane world and achieve immortality but gives an interesting twist to the familiar plot. The failure to meet the immortals prompts her to cultivate another form of transcendence by following Nature. Not unlike her poem on Mount Tai, the speaker forgoes the "unnatural" methods for attaining immortality to seek an epistemological transcendence. Xie Daoyun's two poems convey similar ideas to those found in Tao Qian's "Body, Shadow and Spirit" (Xing ying shen 形影神). Taking on the voice of the spirit, Tao elucidates his understanding of life and death:

60 Prince Qiao is an immortal often featured in poems on roaming immortals (*youxian shi* 遊仙詩) as the provider of elixirs and instructions on methods of attaining immortality.

61 "The Grand Transformation" (*dayun* 大運) in the last line refers to the movement of Nature. *XianQin Han Wei Jin Nanbeichao shi* 2.912; *Yiwen leiju* 88.1513. I use Grant and Idema's translation in *The Red Brush*, p. 141, with modifications.

62 *XianQin Han Wei Jin Nanbeichao shi* 1.484.

甚念傷吾生	Too much thinking harms my life,
正宜委運去	It is appropriate to follow the Transformation.
縱浪大化中	Roaming freely in the Grand Transformation,
不喜亦不懼	I have neither joy nor fear.[63]

Like Xie Daoyun, Tao Qian decides to entrust himself to the Transformation of Nature (*wei yun* 委運) in response to the body's sorrowful recognition of its lack of means to attain physical transcendence (*wo wu teng hua shu* 我無騰化朮).[64] The absence of immortals that Xie Daoyun's poems describe became a prevalent theme in the works of her clansman Xie Lingyun decades later. In Xie Lingyun's landscape poems, the speaker sets out to confirm his knowledge about immortals in received texts in the actual landscape but is always disappointed by the absence of their traces. His expeditions, however, lead to fresh discovery and a deeper understanding of Nature's own beauty.[65]A similar pattern of expectation, pursuit, disappointment, and realization was already present in Xie Daoyun's poems a generation before Xie Lingyun was active. As in Lingyun's poems, her expectation of an encounter with the immortals came from received texts, including Xi Kang's poem. The decision to follow the Grand Transformation was the result of both the disenchantment with immortality and the affirmation of Nature's innate charm. This new angle of appreciating Nature as is, rather than as the embodiment of religious or philosophical truth, was later regarded as a pivotal turn in Chinese landscape aesthetics.[66] While the poems by Xie Lingyun and Tao Qian are commonly viewed as its earliest manifestations, Xie Daoyun's poems about transcendence are rarely mentioned.

Xie Daoyun's admirable knowledge of the "Learning of the Mystery" (*xuanxue* 玄學) and unsurpassed skills at "Pure Conversation" (*qingtan* 清談) are celebrated in many anecdotal and historical sources, including the following passage from the *Jin shu*:

63 Ibid. 2.990. Xie Daoyun was a contemporary of Tao Qian. They may have known each other's poems given the fame both enjoyed in their lifetimes. A more plausible explanation, however, is that the skepticism about immortality and the alternative solution to achieve transcendence in this world were general tendency among contemporary elite intellectuals.

64 Ibid. 2.989.

65 Stephen Owen, "The Librarian in Exile: Xie Lingyun's Bookish Landscapes," *Early Medieval China* 10–11, no. 1 (2004): 203–26.

66 For example, Liu Xie points out that, at the beginning of the Liu-Song dynasty, the Daoist elements in poetry started to be replaced by the description of natural scenery 宋初文詠，體有因革，莊老告退，而山水方滋. See *Wenxin diaolong zhu* 2.67.

> 凝之弟獻之嘗與賓客談議，詞理將屈，道韞遣婢白獻之曰:"欲為小郎解圍。"乃施青綾步鄣自蔽，申献獻之前議，客不能屈。
>
> Once, Ningzhi's younger brother Xianzhi was engaged in a philosophical discussion with some guests. Just as he was about to concede defeat, Daoyun sent a servant girl to tell him: "Let me lift the siege for my little brother-in-law!" Then, shielding herself from their gaze behind a movable screen of green silk, she defended Xianzhi's earlier argument so skillfully that the guests were unable to defeat her.[67]

Similar stories are found in the *Shishuo xinyu*. Its 19th chapter, "Worthy Ladies" (Xianyuan 賢媛), contains anecdotes about women with superior intelligence, perception, virtue, and judgement.[68] Put in the context of such stories, Xie Daoyun's writing on the topic of transcendence is not surprising. These stories also suggest that women participated in philosophical and intellectual activities along with men, just as they did in outings, banquets, and other public affairs. No doubt other women had written on philosophical and religious subjects, yet most of their works did not survive.[69] According to the *Jin shu*, Xie Daoyun's "poems and poetic expositions, elegies and hymns all circulated in the world" 道韞所著詩賦誄頌並傳於世.[70] But the *Sui shu* bibliography lists her works in a mere two *juan*, suggesting a considerable loss of her works already by that point. What is left of her works today is only a short fragment from her "Encomium on the *Analects*" (*Lun yu* zan 論語贊)[71] and the two poems quoted earlier, all preserved in the *Yiwen leiju*.

In contrast to her absence from popular literary sources, Xie Daoyun features prominently in historical and anecdotal sources from the early medieval period. For example, the following passage appears in both the *Jin shu* and *Shishuo xinyu*:

> 謝遏絕重其姊，張玄常稱其妹， 欲以敵之。有濟尼者，並游張、謝二家，人問其優劣，答曰: "王夫人神情散朗，故有林下風氣；顧家婦清心玉映，自是閨房之秀。"

67 *Jin shu* 96.2517. I use Grant and Idema's translation in *The Red Brush*, p. 139.

68 *Shishuo xinyu jianshu* 19.663–701.

69 Grant and Idema, *The Red Brush*, pp. 153–63, devotes a whole section to Buddhist nuns and Daoist mystics in the medieval period. According to accounts of their lives in hagiographies such as *Biographies of Bhiksunis* (Biqiuni zhuan 比丘尼傳), some were prolific authors, yet most of their works did not survive.

70 *Jin shu* 96.2517.

71 *Yiwen leiju* 55.985.

> Xie E extremely valued his elder sister and Zhang Xuan always praised his younger sister. They wanted a competition between the two sisters. There was a nun by the name Ji who frequented both the Zhang and the Xie households. People asked her for a comparison, and she responded, "The spirit and disposition of Lady Wang are carefree and sanguine, which resembles manners of 'those under the Grove.'[72] Lady Gu is pure-minded and shines like jade, naturally she stands out in the boudoir."[73]

The nun cleverly phrases her comments on each person as an evaluation in opposite gender terms to avoid taking sides. Xie Daoyun is ranked along with the "Seven Worthies of the Bamboo Grove," whereas Lady Gu is praised for her feminine qualities. No one in the anecdote took issue with the comparison across the gender boundary or the association of masculine characteristics with a woman. The following conversation with her uncle Xie An in her *Jin shu* biography could be a demonstration of Xie Daoyun's "manners of those under the Grove" (*linxia fengqi* 林下風氣):

> 叔父安嘗問：「毛詩何句最佳？」道蘊稱：「吉甫作頌，穆如清風。仲山甫永懷，以慰其心。」安謂有雅人深致。

> Her uncle Xie An once asked: "What are the finest lines in the Mao edition of the *Shijing*?" Daoyun declared: "Jifu made the hymn, / solemn like clear wind. / Zhongshan Fu sang his cares, / to console his heart." An said [Daoyun] has the profound sentiments of a refined person.[74]

The lines Xie Daoyun quotes in her response are from Mao 260 "Zhengmin" 烝民 (Multitudes of people) in the "Odes" section. According to the Mao interpretation, the poem was written by Yin Jifu 尹吉甫, a minister, to praise King Xuan of Zhou's 周宣王 recruitment of capable men to restore the house of Zhou.[75] Xie Daoyun's appraisal of a poem concerning political and military matters debunks the perceived limitations on the subject matter of women's reading and writing. In particular, it challenges Xu Ling's view of the "Odes" as not suitable for women's reading in the preface to the *Yutai xinyong*. It is also worth noting Xie An's reaction. As a leading literary figure of the time, he

72 "Those under the Grove" (*linxia* 林下) refers to the famous "Seven Worthies of the Bamboo Grove" (*zhulin qi xian* 竹林七賢), whose members include Xi Kang and Ruan Ji.

73 *Shishuo xinyu jianshu* 19.30.698; *Jin shu* 96.2517.

74 *Jin shu* 96.2517.

75 *Maoshi zhengyi* 18.1432.

approved of his niece's taste in literature. Xie An's remark on Daoyun as "having the profound sentiments of a refined person" blurs gender divisions in the same way as the nun's comment. Interestingly, another version of this anecdote included in the *Shishuo xinyu* does not feature Xie Daoyun at all:

> 謝公因子弟集聚，問毛詩何句最佳？遏稱曰：「昔我往矣，楊柳依依；今我來思，雨雪霏霏。」公曰：「訏謨定命，遠猷辰告。」謂此句偏有雅人深致。
>
> On the occasion of a gathering of the young men of his family, Xie An once asked, "What are the finest lines in the Mao edition of the *Shijing*?" An's nephew, Xuan, answered, "Then, when we departed, / poplars and willows were waving; / now, as we're returning, / sleet and snow are flying." An said, "With mighty counsels he determines the Mandate; / with farsighted plans he makes timely announcements." He went on to say, "These lines uniquely have the profound sentiments of a refined person."[76]

The lines that receive Xie An's ultimate praise are from Mao 256 "Yi" 抑 (Repressed), which Mao takes to be Duke Wu of Wei's remonstration against King Li of Zhou (*Wei Wugong ci Liwang* 衛武公刺厲王).[77] In this version the remark "the profound sentiments of a refined person" (*yaren shenzhi* 雅人深致) is made on the heavily politically charged lines about a proper (male) ruler.

But the most well-known and frequently quoted anecdote concerning Xie Daoyun's literary taste and talents in the later tradition is the following:

> 謝太傅寒雪日內集，與兒女講論文義。俄而雪驟，公欣然曰："白雪紛紛為何所似？"兄子胡兒曰："撒鹽空中差可擬。"兄女曰："未若柳絮因風起。"公大笑樂。即公大兄無奕女，左將軍王凝之妻也。
>
> On a cold snowy day the Grand Guardian Xie An gathered young members of his family indoors and was discussing literature and philosophy with them, when suddenly there was a violent flurry of snow. Delighted, Xie began, "The white snow flies and flurries—what does it resemble?" His nephew, Lang, came back with, "Scattered salt in midair—may perhaps

76 *Shishuo xinyu jianshu* 4.52.235; Richard Mather, trans., *Shi-Shuo Hsin-Yü: A New Account of Tales of the World* (Ann Arbor: University of Michigan Press, 2002), p. 125, with modifications.

77 *Maoshi zhengyi* 18.1365–66.

> be likened." His niece, Daoyun, chimed in, "Even more the willow catkins on the wind uplifted." Xie laughed aloud with delight. She was the daughter of his eldest brother, Xie I, and the wife of Wang Ningzhi, General on the Left.[78]

This anecdote was often discussed in the late imperial period, when there was an increased interest in female talent, as an early model for women's poetic talent. The contrast with young male members of the Xie family offered an especially strong argument for women's erudition.[79] Because of her experience later in life, Xie's analogy of willow catkins drifting in the wind in this youthful composition was often taken as self-referential or prophetic, a symbol of the unfortunate fate of talented women. An example is the female protagonist of the *Dream of the Red Chamber* (Honglou meng 紅樓夢), the talented yet tragic poet Lin Daiyu 林黛玉. The prophetic verse foretelling her fate in chapter 5 contains the line "pitiable is her talent of chanting the willow catkins" (*kanlian yongxu cai* 堪憐詠絮才).[80] In the epitaph of the young poet Ye Xiaoluan 葉小鸞 (1616–1632), her mother Shen Yixiu 沈宜修 (1590–1635) recalls, with profound love and grief, Ye's extraordinary talent for poetry in her early years: "At that time I adored her for her cleverness and talent of 'willow catkins on the wind uplifted.' How sad that it turned out to be a sign of untimely death!" 爾時喜其敏捷，有'柳絮因風' 之思，悲夫！豈竟為不壽之徵乎![81] This association of women's poetic talent with misfortune is heavily influenced by the male-constructed feminine sensibility that is characterized by abandonment and resentment. Yet the association is certainly not present in the *Shishuo xinyu* anecdote. The image of Xie Daoyun as a talented young girl and as a vulnerable beauty living in a troubled time nonetheless prevailed in later generations' reception of her story. Her philosophical and scholarly reputations have largely been eclipsed.

The makeover of Xie Daoyun's cultural image from a woman scholar to an ill-fated talented girl went hand in hand with the neglect and loss of her works on philosophical reflection and transcendent experience in popular literary sources. It is a powerful demonstration of the great impact the established mode of the feminine voice had on the reception of women's writings.

---

78 *Shishuo xinyu jianshu* 2.71.130–31 and *Jin shu* 96.2516; Mather, *Shi-Shuo Hsin-Yü*, p. 67, with modifications.

79 See Mann, *Precious Records*, pp. 81–83.

80 Cao Xueqin 曹雪芹 (*c.*1715–*c.*1763), *Hong lou meng* 紅樓夢 (Beijing: Renmin wenxue chubanshe, 2000), p. 53.

81 Ye Shaoyuan 葉紹袁, *Wumeng tang ji* 午夢堂集 (Beijing: Zhonghua shuju, 1998), pp. 201–02.

Xie Daoyun was most likely not the only woman poet writing on the "Learning of the Mystery" or other philosophical topics. Yet further poems by her as well as those by other women poets have been lost in textual transmission without a trace.

4.2 *Women in Charge*

In contrast to the docile and submissive feminine voice, a quite different kind of women's voice is found in a few poems preserved in the *Yiwen leiju*. They depict women stepping out of the boudoir to participate and take the lead on public occasions such as banquets and ritual celebrations. The "Poem on the Winter Solstice" (Dongzhi shi 冬至詩) by Mrs. Li 李氏 of the Jin dynasty describes a banquet where people gather to celebrate the change of season:

靈象尋數回	The heavenly omens return in cycle;
四氣平運散	The four [seasonal] atmospheres operate and dissipate with even division.
陰律鼓微陽	The pitch pipes of *Yin* vibrate the slight *Yang*;[82]
大明啓修旦	The Great Brightness initiates a fine day.[83]
感興時來多	My feelings are stirred many times;
心隨逝化嘆	My heart sighs with the passing [of time] and transformation.
式宴集中堂	Ceremony and banquet are both held in the central hall;
賓客盈朝館	Guests fill up the visitors' lodge.[84]

Mrs. Li presides over events in the "central hall" (*zhongtang* 中堂) and welcomes guests in the "visitors' lodge" (*chaoguan* 朝館). Her image as a capable woman cannot be further removed from the lonely and helpless woman in the secluded chamber. The able housewife reminds readers of the woman receiving guests in her husband's absence in the Han *yuefu* "Ballad on Longxi" (Longxi xing 隴西行):

健婦持門戶	A strong woman takes charge of a household;
亦勝一丈夫	Indeed she is better than a grown man![85]

82 As the result of the change of season, the warm atmosphere, *yang*, is weakened and replaced by the cold atmosphere, *yin*.

83 "The Great Brightness" refers to the sun.

84 *XianQin Han Wei Jin Nanbeichao shi* 2.955.

85 Ibid. 1.267–68.

This stalwart woman puzzled later readers so much that they came up with intriguing explanations for this "strange" occurrence. Some scholars claim, based on the word "Longxi" in the title, that it describes a distinct local custom that is not seen in other places.[86] Yet the titles of *yuefu* poems do not necessarily have a direct connection to the content. Some scholars take the ballad to be a satire on the corrupt political and social situation that prevailed toward the end of the Han dynasty, in particular the usurpation of imperial power by empress dowagers and other imperial in-laws.[87] Yet there is no tangible evidence to support this interpretation. The perception of this woman's behavior as unusual and suspicious echoes Yan Zhitui's association of unacceptable women's behaviors with non-Han customs in the North. The idea that there is something "abnormal" about women in charge implies that the opposite, that is, women confined to the inner chamber and assuming a subservient role, is perceived as the norm. If the "Ballad on Longxi" was accepted into the literary canon as an early *yuefu* piece about an exotic custom, it was harder for the "Poem on the Winter Solstice" to find a place in the mainstream literary discourse that did not favor the voice of a strong and powerful elite woman in the Jin dynasty.

Two other women from the Jin dynasty, Xi Xiao 辛蕭 and Mrs. Wang 王氏, wrote poems on the celebration of New Year's Day, known variably as *Yuanhui* 元會, *Yuanzheng* 元正, or *Zhengzhao* 正朝. The significance of these poems lies in the political weight of the occasion. The celebration originated in the Han imperial court as a ritualized display of the emperor's absolute sovereignty. At a banquet presided over by the emperor himself, officials and foreign ambassadors paid homage and presented tributes; court musicians performed ritual music; and the emperor made symbolic inquiries on state affairs to show his concern for his people and territory. As one of the ritual and political reforms implemented at the beginning of the new regime, Emperor Wu of the Jin dynasty (r. 265–290) had the "Rites of New Year's Day Ceremony" (Yuanhui yi

86 Longxi is on the northwestern frontier of the Qin and Han empires, in modern-day Gansu and Ningxia provinces. Hu Shi 胡適 (1891–1962) suggests this possibility in his *Baihua wenxueshi* 白話文學史 (Taipei: Dongfang chubanshe, 1996), p. 37. It has since been widely accepted among scholars from mainland China.

87 Birrell views this poem as a satire on the inappropriate behavior of what she calls "modern Han wives": "The song is a sly joke at the expense of 'modern' Han wives who have become liberated from the social mores of their sterner Chou forbears. The singer is amused rather than outraged by contemporary mores": Anne Birrell, ed. and trans., *Popular Songs and Ballads of Han China* (Honolulu: University of Hawai'i Press, 1993), p. 166.

元會儀) revised.[88] The two poems by Mrs. Wang and Xin Xiao describe the celebration of New Year's Day in the family, which appears to follow the same rites and procedures as those at the imperial court on a smaller scale. Xin Xiao's poem reads:

元正啟令節	The ceremony of New Year's Day initiates a festive season,
嘉慶肇自茲	Auspicious celebration starts from now.
咸奏萬年觴	All offer wishes for longevity over wine goblet,
小大同悅熙	Young and old share the same joy and prosperity.[89]

The New Year's Day celebration brings all the members of the family together and symbolizes the unifying power of family, the miniature embodiment of the empire. Women's writing in commemoration of such important ceremonies demonstrates their crucial role in the management of domestic affairs and their ability to take on duties of political and social significance.[90]

Throughout China's long imperial history there was no shortage of palace ladies who wielded considerable political power and influence, especially in the role of empress dowager. But sometimes even a relatively low-ranked palace lady had the chance to participate in politics and decision-making. One of the four women poets ranked in the *Shi pin*, Han Lanying, was known for her competence in managing the imperial household and drafting official documents. She presented a "*Fu* on Restoration" (Zhongxing fu 中興賦) to Emperor Xiaowu 孝武 of Liu-Song (r. 453–464) and was appointed as a tutor to the palace ladies. She was also said to be the ghostwriter for Prince Yulin 鬱林 of Qi (473–494) and wrote his edict to depose Emperor Ming 明帝 (r. 494–498). For her erudition and ability, she was known in the imperial palace as "Master Han" 韩公, a title that deliberately blurs gender boundaries.[91] A collection of her work in four *juan* is listed in the *Sui shu* bibliography but has since been lost. Zhong Rong's comment does not mention her scholarly or

88 *Jin shu* 21.649. For an extensive discussion of the origin and evolution of the *yuanhui* rites, see Zhang Yu 張瑜, "Shilun Handai 'yuanhui yi' suo tixian de yinyue zhengzhilun sixiang" 試論漢代'元會儀' 所體現的音樂政治論思想, *Xi'an yinyue xueyuan xuebao* 27, no. 4 (2008): 87–94.

89 *XianQin Han Wei Jin Nanbeichao shi* 2.954.

90 The most famous piece of literary writing on this ceremony is Cao Zhi's "Poem on the New Year's Day Ceremony" (Yuanhui/Yuanzheng shi 元會詩/正會詩) in the four-syllable line, a poetic form suitable for stately occasions. Ibid. 1.449.

91 Xiao Yi, *Jinlou zi jiaojian* 金樓子校箋, ed. Xu Yimin 許逸民 (Beijing: Zhonghua shuju, 2011) 1 2.340; *Nan Qi shu* 20.392.

political accomplishments but compares her poems with Lady Ban's "Poem on Resentment." Such an impression of Han Lanying's works is consistent with the only extant piece of her works preserved in Xiao Yi's 蕭繹 (508–555) *Jinlou zi* 金樓子 (Master of the golden tower). According to the book, Han wrote the poem on behalf of a palace lady who had entered the palace against her will:

絲竹猶在御	Strings and pipes are still being played,
愁人獨向隅	the sorrowful person is weeping alone in the corner.[92]
棄置將已矣	Drop it, and it will be over,
誰憐微薄軀	who pities my humble body?[93]

The poem portrays an abandoned and resentful palace lady in much the same way as the "Poem on Resentment." As the story goes, the emperor was deeply moved by this poem and granted the girl permission to return home. It is interesting that both the *Jinlou zi* and *Shi pin* chose Han Lanying's writings on abandonment and resentment to represent her literary talents. Her reputation as "Master Han" and her composition of the "*Fu* on Restoration" suggest that her literary style was more diverse and her scope of topics much broader than the inner chamber. Yet the popular literary discourse of the 6th century only recorded and discussed her works that speak in the conventional feminine voice. In Han Lanying and in Xie Daoyun, the image of the woman writer that was later constructed and traditionally sanctioned does not match their contemporary reputations but rather aligns with established notions of femininity.

4.3 *Women's "Improper" Desire*

Conventions about the feminine voice leave little or no room for the direct expression of desire, especially sexual/physical desire by women.[94] Chapter 1 showed how a woman's bold articulation of sexual desire in the "Nineteen Old Poems" II has been "corrected" as the longing for her husband in male literati's imitations since the 3rd century. Bao Linghui's imitation of that poem follows the same trend of eliminating sexual tension. The same moral correction was also evident in the transformation of the Luofu narrative. Toward the end of the

92 The expression "facing the corner" (*xiang yu* 向隅) comes from an anecdote recorded in *Shuo yuan*, in which a person facing the corner and weeping at a banquet triggers sorrow among everyone present.

93 *Jinlou zi jiaojian* 1.2.347–48; *XianQin Han Wei Jin Nanbeichao shi* 2.1479.

94 This is to be distinguished from the expression of longing for the husband, which is not only morally legitimate but also tends to remain on an emotional level and seldom reaches the physical or sensual level.

Han *yuefu* ballad "Mulberries by the Path," Luofu expresses her desire for a good-looking and well-mannered man whom she claims to be her husband. Yet her role as desiring agent largely disappears in the later renditions of the story.

Zhong Rong's comments on Bao Linghui and her works are mostly positive except for her poem(s) on "A Hundred Wishes" (Bai yuan 百願), which he deems "excessive" (*yin* 淫).[95] The poem(s) no longer exists and we can only wonder why it is called "excessive" or even "lascivious," which are very harsh critiques of the writing of an elite woman.[96] The title is reminiscent of the ten "wishes" listed in Tao Qian's "*Fu* on Stilling the Passions," in which the speaker, consumed by his extreme desire for a woman, wishes (*yuan* 願) to transform into objects close to her body. The first two "wishes" read:

願在衣而為領	I would like to be the collar of your dress,
承華首之餘芳	and breathe the lingering fragrance of your flower-adorned hair.
悲羅襟之宵離	But at night you take your silken dress off—
怨秋夜之未央	How hateful autumn nights that never end.
願在裳而為帶	I would like to be the girdle of your skirt,
束窈窕之纖身	and bind the modest slender body.
嗟溫涼之異氣	But as weather changes, cool or warm
或脫故而服新	The old is cast aside, the new put on.[97]

Tao Qian's *fu* was criticized by Xiao Tong, *Wen xuan*'s editor and an avid admirer of Tao, for being the "tiny blemish on a white jade" (*baibi weixia* 白璧微瑕) and making the mistake of "giving a hundred encouragements followed by a single remonstrance."[98] Although the exact reason for Xiao Tong's disproval

95 Some Ming dynasty editions of the *Shi pin* have "*baiyun*" 百韻 (a hundred rhymes) instead of "*baiyuan*." See *Shi pin jizhu*, pp. 592–94. But there is no sufficient evidence to dispute the title *baiyuan* and no evidence of poems with a hundred rhymes before or during Bao Linghui's time. For a discussion of the variant, see Huang Yanli 黃嫣梨, "*Shi pin* Qi Bao Linghui Qi Han Lanying jianzheng" 詩品齊鮑令暉齊韓蘭英籤證, *Shehui kexue zhanxian* 4 (1997): 115–19. Huang concludes that "*baiyuan*" is the correct wording.

96 The character, even in the sense of "excess," is often associated with moral decadence. It is especially the case when used in relation to women. For example, it is one of the seven reasons for a husband to divorce his wife (*qi chu* 七出 or *qi qu* 七去) in the *Li ji* 禮記 (Records of rites).

97 Lu Qinli, ed., *Tao Yuanming ji* 陶淵明集 (Beijing: Zhonghua shuju, 1997), pp. 152–59. I use Hightower's translation in "The *Fu* of T'ao Ch'ien," p. 183.

98 Xiao Tong, "Preface to the Collected Works of Tao Yuanming" (Tao Yuanming ji xu 陶淵明集序), in *Tao Yuanming ji*, p. 10. For a study of Xiao Tong's views on Tao Yuanming and a translation of his preface, see Wang, *The Age of Courtly Writing*, pp. 261–77.

is unknown, Hightower is probably right that it is a "moralizing judgment."[99] Other than the apparent disjunction between the romantic feelings expressed in this *fu* and the culturally constructed image of Tao as an upright recluse living in poverty and simplicity, the "excessive" display of romantic and sexual yearning may also have been the cause of Xiao Tong's unfavorable opinion. We cannot be sure that Bao Linghui's "A Hundred Wishes" treats the same topic, but such a direct expression of extensive wishes to find intimacy with the lover's body could have earned the remark of being excessive and/or lascivious (*yin* 淫). There is much in common in the 6th-century reception of "A Hundred Wishes" and Tao Qian's "*Fu* on Stilling the Passions." Zhong Rong's declaration that this poem is the *sole exception* (*wei* 唯) among Bao's poems echoes Xiao Tong's view of the *fu* as the "*tiny* (*wei* 微) blemish" in Tao Qian's oeuvre. In the same way that the lovesick persona in the *fu* offers a sharp contrast to Tao Qian's stern cultural image, the idea of "excessive" or "erotic" contradicts the voice of a submissive and modest woman in Bao's other poems. As Xiao Tong excluded the *fu* from his *Wen xuan*, *Yutai xinyong* did not select Bao's poem on "A Hundred Wishes." The fact that Bao Linghui's "A Hundred Wishes" disappeared from textual transmission whereas her poems of longing and resentment survived shows the power of the popular literary discourse of the 6th century in controlling the later reception and understanding of women's literary voices.

5 Conclusion

Our notion of the literary past is affected by many factors, including the availability of texts, the nature of primary sources, changing literary values and tastes, and others. In a way, we will never be able to obtain an unclouded or unmediated view of the world of pre-Tang literature. Moreover, texts that survived from that time are just the tiny tip of a giant iceberg. The majority of anthologies, individual and general collections, encyclopedias, and works of literary criticism have long been lost. The materials we have access to are extremely limited and, in many cases, heavily edited. The situation is worse when it comes to women's writing. Lists of collected works of women writers, anthologies of women's works, and books composed for female readership such as *Furen ji chao* 婦人集鈔 (Copies of women's collections) and *Furen ji* 婦人集 (Collections of women writers) in the bibliography of official histories are empty reminders of a lost world of women's writing in the early medieval

99 Hightower, "The *Fu* of T'ao Ch'ien," pp. 191–92.

period.[100] Although it is impossible to reconstruct a comprehensive picture, through careful examination of extant materials and comparison between texts surviving through different sources we can find traces of formerly overlooked aspects of women's life and writing. We can also catch a glimpse of the richness and complexity of women's writing, which went far beyond the topics of romantic longing and the resentment of abandoned women. The very fact that the handful of literary anthologies and works of literary criticism surviving from the 6th century display very similar views on women's voices and women's writing suggests the presence of a certain consensus about the feminine voice by that time. With full awareness of the inevitable partiality in any conclusion that may be deduced from available sources, we can conclude that the feminine voice that entails a melancholic and lonely woman pining for an absent lover had been widely accepted, in many genres but particularly in five-syllable poetry, by the 6th century.

100 *Sui shu* 35.1082.

Epilogue: Creating the Voice of an Other

A quick perusal of the titles of extant 6th-century poems is sufficient to show the popularity of the theme of boudoir resentment by an abandoned woman in literati's compositions in the voice of a woman. "Poem of Resentment on behalf of Someone's Concubine" (Wei ren qie yuanshi 為人妾怨詩), "Resentment at the Long Gate" (Changmen yuan 長門怨), "Resentment of Zhaojun" (Zhaojun yuan 昭君怨), "Poem on Master He's Concubine Harboring Resentment" (Hesheng jiren youyuan shi 何生姬人有怨詩), "Poem on Thoughts in the Spring Chamber" (Chungui si shi 春閨思詩), and "Poem on Boudoir Resentment" (Guiyuan shi 閨怨詩) are just a few examples. This is even more remarkable given that the title "Boudoir Resentment" and its many variants did not appear in poems until the 6th century. Even outside popular literary anthologies such as the *Yutai xinyong* or *Wen xuan*, one finds the following "Boudoir Resentment" by Wu Jun 吳均 (469–520), preserved in the *Yiwen leiju*:

胡笳屢凄斷	The barbarian flute repeats profound misery and grief;
征蓬未肯還	the drifting weeds have yet to return home.[1]
妾坐江之介	I, your concubine, sit by the Yangzi River;
君戍小長安	You, my lord, are stationed in Chang'an.
相去三千里	Separated by three thousand *li*;
參商書信難	it is hard for us, like the Orion and Antares, to send letters.
四時無人見	All four seasons no one sets eyes on me—
誰復重羅紈	Who would again value silk and gauze?[2]

The writing about a wife's longing for her husband in the army combines boudoir resentment with the frontier motif, which gained popularity among the early medieval poets. In her discussion of the "birth of frontier poetry" at the Liang court, Tian argues that the integration of boudoir lament into the frontier theme is a way to "accentuate a distant, exotic space 'out there' that belongs exclusively to men."[3] The two tropes—the frontier and boudoir lament—were perceived in the 6th century as the ultimate embodiments of

1 *Peng* (weeds) are rootless and tend to float along with the wind. It is a common metaphor for a person traveling far away from home.

2 *XianQin Han Wei Jin Nanbeichao shi* 2.1746; *Yiwen leiju* 32.566–67.

3 Tian, *Beacon Fire and Shooting Star*, p. 330.

 | DOI:10.1163/9789004546455_008

masculinity and femininity. The balanced display of masculinity and femininity, or the martial/exotic and the domestic, made the combined theme one of the staple tropes in Tang and later poetry. Gender conventions that had been constructed by early medieval literati were to exert a long-lasting influence on literary imaginations of the feminine as well as the masculine for centuries to come.

Nothing speaks more clearly about the wide acceptance of a convention than the presence of its antithesis, or "other." While formulating the conventional feminine voice in their own writing, early medieval literati discovered, or rather created, its other in the voice of unrefined and unsophisticated local women, in the corpus of the "sounds of Wu" (*Wusheng*) or "Wu Songs" (*Wuge*) (hereafter Wu songs).[4] These are mostly short verses in the five-syllable line about the lives and emotions of commoners. They often deliver a distinct "local flavor" marked by straightforward expression, lack of literary ornament, and colloquiality.[5] Originating in the area around Jiankang 建康 (in modern-day Nanjing, Jiangsu province),[6] they were collected by elite literati and performed at the southern courts, and they were passed down to later generations through their inclusion in court musical repertoires.[7] Although the corpus contains poems in both male and female voices, a large number of them are in the voice of local women. In fact, the Wu songs are by far the largest pre-Tang corpus of poetry in women's voices.

Elite literati's interest in local songs, as Owen has argued, lay primarily in the world of a naive and inferior other that they represent.[8] Voices of local women constitute a major part of the otherness as the antithesis to the

4 Another group of local songs from the southern area, known as the "western tunes" (*xiqu*), have much in common with Wu songs in their origins and later collection and adaptation by elite literati. Most of the characteristics of women's voices in Wu songs discussed here apply to the western tunes as well. I choose to focus on the Wu songs because there are relatively more historical records available, especially regarding elite literati's involvement in their transmission and preservation.

5 For a systematic study of the poetic style of these songs, see Marilyn Jane Coutant Evans, "Popular Songs of the Southern Dynasties: A Study in Poetic Style" (PhD diss., Yale University, 1966).

6 Since the fall of the Western Jin dynasty and the migration of the Jin royal house to the south of the Yangzi River in 317, Jiankang had been the capital of five consecutive dynasties, namely the Eastern Jin, Song, Qi, Liang, and Chen.

7 Extant sources are either unclear or offer conflicting accounts regarding their origins, but most state that they were songs of the local people in the Jin, Song, and Qi eras. *Song Shu* 19.549; *Jin shu* 23.716; *Yuefu shiji* 44.639–40.

8 Stephen Owen, "Xia Jiangnan: Guanyu Dong Jin pingmin de huanxiang" 下江南：關於東晉平民的幻想, in *Xia Jiangnan: Suzhou daxue haiwai Hanxue yanjianglu* 下江南：蘇州大學海外漢學演講錄, ed. Wang Yao 王堯 and Ji Jin 季進 (Shanghai: Fudan daxue chubanshe,

established notion of femininity in elite writing. If the portrayal of women in literati writings took an internal turn from the 3rd century, the opposite is the case in extant Wu songs. Many are characterized by a considerable degree of theatricality and focus their portrayals of women on the external. Even when a song seems to reveal the woman's inner thoughts, the attention is drawn to her appearance and sexual appeal. The following Ziye song (*Ziye ge* 子夜歌) is a case in point:

宿昔不梳頭	At night I do not comb my hair,
絲發披兩肩	Silky hair spreads on my shoulders.
婉伸郎膝上	It stretches gracefully on your knees,
何處不可憐	What is not lovely [about my body]?[9]

The poem is entirely about the girl's appearance and its effect on her viewers, including her lover, the *lang* 郎 in the third line, and the elite audience of the song's performance. The whimsical question in the last line takes on the beholders' point of view to draw full attention to her body. The display of female beauty is bold and unapologetic. Chapter 1 demonstrated the emergence of the sympathetic beholder and the contemplative object in 3rd-century poetry as the precondition for the rise of the feminine voice. This song, and many Wu songs, feature a very different type of beholder and object, as well as a distinct dynamic between them.

If speaking in the feminine voice allowed literati to remove the sensualizing male gaze from the scene, many Wu songs place the gaze front and center. The girl in the following Ziye song is clearly aware of her exposure to the male gaze:

攣裙未結帶	I put on my skirt leaving the sash untied;
約眉出前窗	paint my eyebrows and come out to the front window.
羅裳易飄颺	My silk skirt is easy to be tossed about,
小開罵春風	It opens a little; and I curse the spring wind.[10]

Besides the apparent eroticism of her open skirt, the girl's charm also resides in her presumed naivety and ignorance of social and moral decorum,

2009), pp. 27–41. Recently I have attributed émigré elite's fascination with Wu songs to their attempts to domesticate local culture and integrate it into their own: Qiulei Hu, "From Singing Ghosts to Docile Concubines: Elite Domestication of the Local in the Wu Songs," *Journal of the American Oriental Society* 139, no. 4 (2019): 843–58.

9 *Yuefu shiji* 44.641. "Ziye songs" is a major sub-group of the Wu songs, the original of which was traced to a girl named Ziye who lived in the Jin era.

10 Ibid. 44.643.

characteristics expected in an unsophisticated local girl. On the surface, the poem depicts the girl as being alone and visible to no one. But one wonders why she "paints the eyebrows" (*yuemei* 約眉) if she is all by herself. The curse in the last line only makes sense if she is aware of the male gaze. She also draws attention to her uncovered body and its exposure to beholders. The poem resembles the "Nineteen Old Poems" II in its strong theatricality. Like the wanderer's wife in a tower, the girl shows a stage consciousness in her gesture of standing behind an open window with makeup on and sash loose. If the wanderer's wife displays her sexual availability and expectation, the girl in this Ziye song exhibits her innocence and naivety, with a not-so-naive intention to seduce her elite audience.

To avoid theatricality in the image of women, early medieval literati often place her in a state of deep contemplation and total absorption in her thoughts. The beautiful lady in Cao Zhi's "Song on a Beauty," for instance, gets up at night and laments her lack of a worthy match. The world of representation is self-contained, with the perspective internalized as the lady's own.[11] The following Ziye song begins with a similar scene of sleeplessness at night:

夜長不得眠	The night is long; I cannot sleep;
明月何灼灼	How shining the bright moon is!
想聞散喚聲	In my imagination I heard a fragmented calling voice:
虛應空中喏	To no avail I answered "yes" to the air.[12]

An imagined conversation with the absent lover appears in Cao Zhi's "Poem on Resentment," where it internalizes the perspective and turns the poem into a monologue about the woman's inner thoughts and feelings.[13] In the above Ziye song, however, the girl's longing for her lover becomes a chance to theatricalize the moment, with her answering the imagined call of her lover. The women in both Cao Zhi's "Song on a Beauty" and "Poem on Resentment" are completely absorbed in their thoughts and pay no attention to any possible beholders. The girl in the Ziye song, in contrast, acts out her thoughts in a dramatic way. Her naivety and the spontaneity of her actions cater to an elite audience.

The sentiments of women in Wu songs, despite them being overwhelmingly associated with romantic relationships, display much more diversity than the longing, resentment, and despair that dominate elite writing. The lover's absence, for example, could provoke blunt complaints about unfulfilled desire:

---

11 *XianQin Han WeiJin Nanbeichao shi* 1.431–32. See the discussion in Chapter 1.

12 *Yuefu shiji* 44.642.

13 *XianQin Han WeiJin Nanbeichao shi* 1.458–59. See the discussion in Chapter 1.

開門白水	Right outside of the door there is a clear river;
側近橋樑	nearby there is a bridge.
小姑所居	The place where the maiden dwells,
獨處無郎	she is alone without a lover.[14]

The poem is attached to a story about a young scholar traveling in the Wu area at night. His singing attracted a beautiful woman, who spent the night with him. The next day he visited a local temple, and only then did he realize the girl was none other than the presiding deity, "the Maiden of Blue Creek" (*qingxi xiaogu* 青溪小姑). He died on the spot.[15] In both the poem and the frame story, the lonely woman yearns for sexual fulfillment rather than worthy companionship or an absent husband, as her counterparts in elite poetry usually do. Such a bold expression of desire by a woman in a powerful position discourages any attempts at allegorical reading.

The male lover's betrayal or abandonment could trigger anger and firm resolution to terminate the relationship:

郎為旁人取	You were taken by some other girl,
負儂非一事	and betrayed me on more matter than one.
攤門不安橫	leaving the door open without a middle bar—
無復相關意	I no longer want to close it / I no longer want to have anything to do with you.[16]

Such emotional independence is rarely seen in women's voices in literati's writings of the time. Like the expression of desire, there is little room for the application of political allegory. The stark contrast between women's voices in Wu songs and the conventional feminine voice found in literati poetry is not a coincidence, nor should it be explained as a difference between folk and literati compositions. It is the result of a deliberate construction at the hands of elite literati, who were responsible for the collection, organization, and preservation of the received corpus of Wu songs. The creation of several song titles

14 *Yuefu shiji* 47.684–85. Note the song is in the four-syllable line, a less common (but not unique) form in Wu songs, but the image and voice it represents are consistent with the rest of the corpus.

15 The story is from Wu Jun's *Xu Qi xie ji* 續齊諧記. The *Yuefu shiji* quotes the story yet leaves out the ending of the story—the death of the scholar named Zhao Wenshao 趙文韶. See *Hanwei liuchao biji xiaoshuo daguan* 漢魏六朝筆記小說大觀 (Shanghai: Shanghai guji chubanshe, 1999), p. 1009.

16 *Yuefu shiji* 44.642. The last line puns on the character "*guan*," which means both "to close" and "to care."

is explicitly credited to members of the elite.[17] Scholars have used stylistic and linguistic evidence to demonstrate that several extant Wu songs, including most of the "four seasons of Ziye song" (Ziye sishi ge 子夜四時歌), were written or at least heavily edited by elite literati.[18] The corpus of Wu songs, therefore, reflects not the unfiltered local voices as they were heard in the southern local areas, but what elite literati chose and in some cases created to enjoy as such. The voices of women in the corpus are as much a cultural and literary construct by early medieval literati as the conventional feminine voice is in their own writings. These two types of "women's voices" were shaped to form a perfect foil for each other. The theatrical display of sensuality, unapologetic expression of desire, emotional independence, and resistance to allegorical association in the voices of "local" women are all traits opposite to the resentful abandoned woman in the writings of the elite. They testify, from a negative point of view, to the wide recognition of the latter as the standard for the feminine voice in literati writing.

The construction of the feminine voice in literature occurred when the general literary context shifted away from anonymous performativity toward individualized expression. The differences between the two returned in the Southern dynasties era in the class and regional dynamics of anonymous local women versus elite women. While elite literati greatly enjoyed the staged voices of local women, they showed little tolerance toward elite women's voices with similar qualities, as shown in the discussion in Chapter 5. The significance of performativity and theatricality in shaping women's voices is also evident in the rise of the genre of *ci*, which started as performance texts and was marked by the prevalence of women's voices at its early stage. How the nature of performance and role-play affect the construction and development of the feminine voice in *ci* and its relations with the established conventions in *shi* poetry

17 For example, the "Treatise on Music" in the *Song shu* lists Shen Chong 沈充, an Eastern Jin general, as the creator of the "Song of the Front Creek" (Qianxi ge 前溪歌): *Song shu* 19.549. The *Gujin yuelu* has Wang Xianzhi 王獻之 (344–386) as the creator of the "Song of Peach Leaf" (Tiaoye ge 桃葉歌): *Yuefu shiji* 44. 664. Sun Chuo is listed as the author of two "Songs of Green Jade" (Biyu ge 碧玉歌) in the *Yutai xinyong*: 10.470–71. There are also Wu songs attributed to elite members of the Liu–Song dynasty, including Emperor Shao 宋少帝 (406–424) and Liu Yiqing 劉義慶 (403–444): *Yuefu shiji* 44.667 and 690.

18 Evidence of elite intervention includes references to elite poetry or Confucian classics, as well as of expressions, topics, and imagery commonly found in elite poetry. See Wang Yunxi 王運熙, "Lun Wusheng yu xiqu" 論吳聲與西曲, in *Yuefu shi shulun* 樂府詩述論 (Shanghai: Shanghai guji chubanshe, 2006), pp. 452–86; Cao Daoheng 曹道衡, "Tan Nanchao yuefu minge" 談南朝樂府民歌, *Wenshi zhishi* 4 (1986): 11–16; and Weng Qibin 翁其斌, "Wuge Xiqu wenren nizuo kao" 吳歌西曲文人擬作考, *Shanghai shifan daxue xuebao* 3 (1996): 23–27.

are interesting topics for future study.[19] This would offer new insights into the literary community of a different historical period—the Tang–Song transition, one that underwent no less drastic social and cultural changes than the early medieval period.[20]

Largely the male literati's construct, ideas about femininity in literature were always defined in relation to masculinity and were used to establish and reinforce male literati's self-identity. Over time there have emerged certain common stereotypes for the masculine in literature, such as the "men/husbands in the army or in pursuit of officialdom," "frustrated scholars," and "loyal ministers." They are male counterparts to the abandoned yet faithful woman. The construction of the feminine also informs important changes in the view and representation of masculinity in the early medieval period, an in-depth study of which will be a fascinating project in the future.[21]

---

19 Owen's recent book on *ci* proposes that some well-known works of *ci* attributed to famous literati lyricists in the Northern Song may have been heavily revised or even composed by professional singers, many of whom were women. The attribution to male lyricists was, among other things, a way to ensure a work's circulation and preservation. This theory challenges the commonly accepted perception of the genre's origin as male literati's persona composition set in the voice of the female singer. Owen also calls for reconsideration of the common association of the world of *ci* with the discourse of femininity. He argues that the appeal of the genre comes from "a larger discourse of sensibility, defined against the male *public* world" it provides for its audience to enter and leave at will: Stephen Owen, *Just a Song: Chinese Lyrics from the Eleventh and Early Twelfth Centuries* (Cambridge, MA: Harvard University Asia Center, 2019), pp. 31–33, 103.

20 For a study of the intellectual history of the Tang–Song transition, see Peter Bol, *"This Culture of Ours": Intellectual Transitions in T'ang and Sung China* (Stanford, CA: Stanford University Press, 1992). Manling Luo's *Literati Story Telling in Late Medieval China* (Seattle: University of Washington Press, 2015) explores the social and cultural changes experienced by the scholar-literati in the second part of Tang dynasty by looking at classical short stories they created and circulated.

21 Martin Huang has done an excellent study of the discourse of masculinity in Ming and Qing literature, which makes brief references to earlier times, especially the literary trope of "loyal ministers." One of Huang's central concerns is "the complicated and often opposite roles assigned to the feminine 'other' in a man's negotiation of his identity in late imperial China." See Martin Huang, *Negotiating Masculinities in Late Imperial China* (Honolulu: University of Hawai'i Press, 2006), p. 2.

Bibliography

Allen, Joseph Roe. "Chih Yü's Discussions of Different Types of Literature: A Translation and Brief Comment." In Joseph Roe Allen, *Parerga 3: Two Studies in Chinese Literary Criticism*, pp. 3–36. Seattle: Institute for Comparative and Foreign Area Studies, University of Washington, 1976.

Allen, Joseph Roe. "From Saint to Singing Girl: The Rewriting of the Lo-fu Narrative in Chinese Literati Poetry." *Harvard Journal of Asiatic Studies* 48, no. 2 (1988): 321–61.

Allen, Joseph Roe. *In the Voice of Others: Chinese Music Bureau Poetry*. Ann Arbor: University of Michigan Center for Chinese Studies, 1992.

Barlow, Tani E. "Theorizing Women: *Funü, guojia, jiating*." In *Body, Subject, and Power in China*, edited by Angela Zito and Tani E. Barlow, pp. 253–89. Oxford: Oxford University Press, 1994.

Birrell, Anne. *Games Poets Play: Readings in Medieval Chinese Poetry*. Cambridge: McGuinness China Monographs, 2004.

Birrell, Anne, trans. *New Songs from a Jade Terrace: An Anthology of Early Chinese Love Poetry*. London: Allen & Unwin, 1982.

Birrell, Anne, ed. and trans. *Popular Songs and Ballads of Han China*. Honolulu: University of Hawai'i Press, 1993.

Bol, Peter. *"This Culture of Ours": Intellectual Transitions in T'ang and Sung China*. Stanford, CA: Stanford University Press, 1992.

Butler, Judith. *Gender Trouble: Feminism and the Subversion of Identity*. London: Routledge, 1990.

Cai Zong-qi. "A New Exploration of Early Pentasyllabic Poetry: Rhythms, Syntax, Structures, and Visions." *Bulletin of the Institute of Chinese Literature and Philosophy* 44 (2014): 1–56.

Cao Daoheng 曹道衡. "Tan Nanchao yuefu minge" 談南朝樂府民歌. *Wenshi zhishi* 4 (1986): 11–16.

Cao Xu 曹旭, ed. *Shi pin jizhu* 詩品集註. Shanghai: Shanghai guji chubanshe, 1994.

Cao Xueqin 曹雪芹. *Hong lou meng* 紅樓夢. Beijing: Renmin wenxue chubanshe, 2000.

Cao Zhi 曹植. *Cao Zhi ji jiaozhu* 曹植集校註, edited by Zhao Youwen 趙幼文. Beijing: Renmin wenxue chubanshe, 1984.

Chang, Sun Kang-i. "Modai cainü de luanli shi" 末代才女的亂離詩. In *Gudai nü shiren yanjiu* 古代女詩人研究, edited by Zhang Hongsheng 張宏聲 and Zhang Yan 張燕, pp. 224–46. Wuhan: Hubei jiaoyu chubanshe, 2002.

Cheng Liang-shu 鄭良樹. "Chu ti feng zuo—Cao Wei jituan de fuzuo huodong" 出題奉作——曹魏集團的賦作活動. In *Wei Jin Nanbeichao wenxue lunji* 魏晉南北朝文學論集, edited by Xianggang zhongwen daxue zhongguo yuyan wenxue xi, pp. 181–290. Taipei: Wenshizhe chubanshe, 1994.

Cheng Shude 程樹德, ed. *Lun yu ji shi* 論語集釋. Beijing: Zhonghua shuju, 1990.

Cheng Yu-yu 鄭毓瑜. *Liuchao qingjing meixue zonglun* 六朝情境美學綜論. Taipei: Xuesheng shuju, 1996.

Cheng Yu-yu 鄭毓瑜. *Xingbie yu jia guo: Han Jin cifu de Chu sao lunshu* 性別與家國:漢晉辭賦的楚騷論述. Shanghai: Sanlian shudian, 2006.

Choo, Jessey J. C. "*Yiwen leiju*." In *Early Medieval Chinese Texts*, edited by Chennault, Cynthia Li, Keith N. Knapp, Alan J. Berkowitz, and Albert E. Dien, pp. 454–64. Berkeley: Institute of East Asian Studies, University of California Press, 2015.

Chu Hsiao-hai 朱曉海. "Liang Han Liuchao shi wen zhong de Li Ling xianxiang" 兩漢六朝詩文中的李陵現象. *Gudian wenxian yanjiu* 14 (2011): 1–60.

Connery, Christopher. *The Empire of the Text: Writing and Authority in Early Imperial China*. Lanham, MD: Rowman & Littlefield, 1998.

Cutter, Robert Joe. "Cao Zhi's Symposium Poems." *Chinese Literature: Essays, Articles, Reviews* 6, no. 1/2 (1984): 1–32.

Cutter, Robert Joe. "The Incident at the Gate: Cao Zhi, the Succession, and Literary Fame." *T'oung Pao* 71 (1985): 228–62.

Cutter, Robert Joe. "The Death of Empress Zhen: Fiction and Historiography in Early Medieval China." *Journal of the American Oriental Society* 112, no. 4 (1992): 577–83.

Cutter, Robert Joe. "To Make Her Mine: Women and the Rhetoric of Property in Early and Early Medieval *Fu*." *Early Medieval China* 19 (2013): 39–57.

Cutter, Robert Joe. "Gastropoetics in the Jian'an Period: Food and Memory in Early Medieval China." *Early Medieval China* 24 (2018): 1–23.

Diény, Jean-Pierre. "*Les Dix-neuf poèmes anciens* 古詩十九首." *Bulletin de la Maison Franco-Japonaise, Nouvelle Série* 7, no. 4 (1963): 1–194.

Diény, Jean-Pierre. *Aux origines de la poésie classique en Chine: Étude sur la poésie lyrique à l'époque des Han*. Leiden: Brill, 1968.

Diény, Jean-Pierre. *Pastourelles et magnanarelles: essai sur un thème littéraire chinoise*. Geneva and Paris: Librairie Droz, 1977. (Translated into Chinese in Qian Linsen 錢林森, trans., *Munü yu canniang* 牧女與蠶娘 (Shanghai: Shanghai guji chubanshe, 1990), pp. 154–206).

Dong Zhongshu 董仲舒. *Chunqiu fanlu* 春秋繁露, *Sibu beiyao* edition.

Doran, Rebecca. *Transgressive Typologies: Constructions of Gender and Power in Early Tang China*. Cambridge, MA: Harvard University Asia Center, 2017.

Du You 杜佑. *Tong Dian* 通典. Beijing: Zhonghua shuju, 1988.

Ebrey, Patricia. *The Inner Quarters: Marriage and the Lives of Chinese Women in the Sung Period*. Berkeley: University of California Press, 1993.

Egan, Charles H. "Reconsidering the Role of Folk Songs in Pre-T'ang 'Yüeh-Fu' Development." *T'oung Pao* 86 (2000): 47–99.

Evans, Marilyn Jane Coutant. "Popular Songs of the Southern Dynasties: A Study in Poetic Style." PhD diss., Yale University, 1966.

Fong, Grace. *Herself an Author: Gender, Agency and Writing in Late Imperial China.* Honolulu: University of Hawai'i Press, 2008.

Frankel, Hans H. "The 'I' in Chinese Lyric Poetry." *Oriens* 10, no. 1 (1957): 128–30.

Frankel, Hans H. "Fifteen Poems by Ts'ao Chih: An Attempt at a New Approach." *Journal of the American Oriental Society* 84 (1964): 1–14.

Frankel, Hans H. "Yüeh-fu Poetry." In *Studies in Chinese Literary Genres*, edited by Cyril Birch, pp. 69–107. Berkeley: University of California Press, 1977.

Frankel, Hans H. "Cai Yan and the Poems Attributed to Her." *Chinese Literature: Essays, Articles and Reviews* 5 (1983): 133–56.

Fried, Michael. *Absorption and Theatricality: Painting and Beholder in the Age of Diderot.* Chicago, IL: University of Chicago Press, 1980.

Ge Xiaoyin 葛曉音. "Zaoqi wuyanshi de shengcheng tujing jiqi dui hanshi yishu de yingxiang" 早期五言詩的生成途徑及其對漢詩藝術的影響. *Wenxue yichan* 6 (2006): 15–27.

Geng Zhaolin 耿兆林. "'You suo si' yu 'Shangye' 'dangwei yipian' ma?" 《有所思》與《上邪》"當為一篇"嗎? *Tianjin shizhuan xuebao* 3 (1981): 68–69.

Grant, Beata and Idema, Wilt, eds. and trans. *The Red Brush: Writing Women of Imperial China.* Cambridge, MA: Harvard University Asia Center, 2004.

Guo Maoqian 郭茂倩, ed. *Yuefu shiji* 樂府詩集. Beijing: Zhonghua shuju, 1979.

Guo Qingfan 郭慶藩, ed. *Zhuangzi jishi* 莊子集釋. Beijing: Zhonghua shuju, 1961.

Han shu 漢書. Beijing: Zhonghua shuju, 1962.

Han Wei Liuchao biji xiaoshuo daguan 漢魏六朝筆記小說大觀. Shanghai: Shanghai guji chubanshe, 1999.

Hawkes, David. "The Quest of the Goddess." In *Studies in Chinese Literary Genres*, edited by Cyril Birch, pp. 42–68. Berkeley: University of California Press, 1974.

Hightower, James. "The *Fu* of T'ao Ch'ien." *Harvard Journal of Asiatic Studies* 17, no. 1/2 (1954): 169–230.

Holzman, Donald. "Les premiers vers pentasyllabuques datés dans la poésie chinoise." In *Mélanges de sinologies offerts à Monsieur Paul Demiéville, II*, pp. 77–116. Paris: Presses universitaires de France, 1974.

Holzman, Donald. "Immortality-Seeking in Early Chinese Poetry." In *The Power of Culture: Studies in Chinese Cultural History*, edited by Willard J. Peterson, Andrew H. Plaks, and Ying-Shih Yü, pp. 103–18. Hong Kong: The Chinese University Press, 1994.

Hong Xingzu 洪興祖, ed. *Chuci buzhu* 楚辭補註. Beijing: Zhonghua shuju, 1983.

Hou Han shu 後漢書. Beijing: Zhonghua shuju, 1965.

Hsieh, Daniel. "The Origin and Nature of the 'Nineteen Old Poems.'" *Sino-Platonic Papers* 77 (1998): 1–49.

Hu Daojing 胡道靜, Jin Liangnian 金良年, and Hu Xiaojing 胡小靜, trans. *Mengxi bitan quanyi* 夢溪筆談全譯. Guiyang: Guizhou renmin chubanshe, 1998.

Hu Ming 胡明. "Guanyu zhongguo gudai de funü wenxue" 關於中國古代的婦女文學. *Wenxue pinglun* 3 (1995): 95–108.

Hu Qiulei. "Reading the Conflicting Voices: An Examination of the Interpretative Traditions about 'Han Guang'." *Chinese Literature: Essays, Articles and Reviews* 34 (2012): 1–13.

Hu Qiulei. "Mapping Gender and Poetic Role in Early Medieval Poetry." *Early Medieval China* 21 (2015): 38–62.

Hu Qiulei. "From Singing Ghosts to Docile Concubines: Elite Domestication of the Local in the Wu Songs." *Journal of the American Oriental Society* 139, no. 4 (2019): 843–58.

Hu Qiulei. "In Search of a Perfect Match: Jian'an (196–220) Writing about Women and the Formation of a Literati Community." *Nan Nü: Men, Women and Gender in China* 21 (2019): 194–223.

Hu Qiulei. "Following the Troops, Carrying Along our Brushes: Jian'an (196–220 AD) *Fu* and *Shi* Written for Military Campaigns." *Asia Major* (2020) *3d ser.* Vol. 33.2: 61–91.

Hu Shi 胡適. *Baihua wenxueshi* 白話文學史, 1928; rpt. Taipei: Dongfang chubanshe, 1996.

Hu Wenkai 胡文楷. *Lidai funü zhuzuokao* 歷代婦女著作考. Shanghai: Shangwu yinshuguan, 1957.

Hu Zhiji 胡之驥, ed. *Jiang Wentong ji huizhu* 江文通集彙註. Beijing: Zhonghua shuju, 1984.

Huang, Martin. *Negotiating Masculinities in Late Imperial China.* Honolulu: University of Hawai'i Press, 2006.

Huang Yanli 黃嫣梨. "*Shi pin* Qi Bao Linghui Qi Han Lanying jianzheng" 詩品齊鮑令暉齊韓蘭英鑒證. *Shehui kexue zhanxian* 4 (1997): 115–19.

Hucker, Charles O. *A Dictionary of Official Titles in Imperial China.* Stanford, CA: Stanford University Press, 1985.

Jia Jinhua. *Gender, Power and Talent: The Journey of Daoist Priestesses in Tang China.* New York: Columbia University Press, 2018.

Jin shu 晉書. Beijing: Zhonghua shuju, 1974.

Jingyin Song ben Wuchen jizhu Wen xuan 景印宋本五臣集注文選. Taipei: Guoli Zhongyang tushuguan, 1981.

Kern, Martin. "Western Han Aesthetics and the Genesis of the *Fu*." *Harvard Journal of Asiatic Studies* 63, no. 2 (2003): 383–437.

Kern, Martin. "Poetry of Han Historiography." *Early Medieval China* 10–11, no. 1 (2004): 23–65.

Knapp, Keith. *Selfless Offspring: Filial Children and Social Order in Medieval China.* Honolulu: University of Hawai'i Press, 2005.

Knechtges, David R. "To Praise the Han: The Eastern Capital *Fu* of Pan Ku and His Contemporaries." In *Thought and Law in Qin and Han China*, edited by W. L. Idema and E. Zürcher, pp. 118–39. Leiden: Brill, 1990.

Knechtges, David R. "The Poetry of an Imperial Concubine: The Favorite Beauty Ban." *Oriens Extremus* 36, no. 2 (1993): 127–44.

Knechtges, David R. "Culling the Weeds and Selecting Prime Blossoms: The Anthology in Early Medieval China." In *Culture and Power in the Reconstitution of the Chinese Realm, 200–600*, edited by Scott Pearce, Audrey Shapiro, and Patricia Ebrey, pp. 200–14. Cambridge, MA: Harvard University Asia Center, 2001.

Knechtges, David R. *Court Culture and Literature in Early China*. Variorum Collected Studies Series. Aldershot: Ashgate, 2002.

Knechtges, David R. "Sweet-peel Orange or Southern Gold? Regional Identity in Western Jin Literature." In *Studies in Early Medieval Chinese Literature and Cultural History: In Honor of Richard B. Mather and Donald Holzman*, edited by Paul W. Kroll and David R. Knechtges, pp. 21–79. Provo, UT: T'ang Studies Society, 2003.

Knechtges, David R., trans. *Wen Xuan or Selections of Refined Literature*, Vol. 2: *Rhapsodies on Sacrifices, Hunting, Travels, Sightseeing, Palaces and Halls, Rivers and Seas*. Princeton, NJ: Princeton University Press, 1987.

Knechtges, David R., trans. *Wen xuan or Selections of Refined Literature*, Vol. 3: *Rhapsodies on Natural Phenomena, Birds and Animals, Aspirations and Feelings, Sorrowful Laments, Literature, Music, and Passions*. Princeton, NJ: Princeton University Press, 1996.

Knechtges, David R. and Chang Taiping, eds. *Ancient and Early Medieval Chinese Literature: A Reference Guide, Part Two*. Leiden: Brill, 2013.

Knechtges, David R. "Group Literary Composition in the Court of Ye in the Later Eastern Han." Unpublished paper.

Ko, Dorothy. *Teachers of the Inner Chambers: Women and Culture in Seventeenth-Century China*. Stanford, CA: Stanford University Press, 1994.

Kong Yingda 孔穎達, ed. *Maoshi Zhengyi* 毛詩正義. *Shisanjing zhushu zhengyi* edition. Beijing: Beijing daxue chubanshe, 1999.

Lai, C. M. "The Craft of Original Imitation: Lu Ji's Imitations of Han Old Poems." In *Studies in Early Medieval Chinese Literature and Cultural History in Honor of Richard B. Mather and Donald Holzman*, edited by Paul W. Kroll and David R. Knechtges, pp. 117–48. Provo, UT: T'ang Studies Society, 2003.

Li Fang 李昉 et al., eds. *Taiping guangji* 太平廣記. Beijing: Renmin wenxue chubanshe, 1959.

Li Fang et al., eds. *Taiping yulan* 太平御覽. Beijing: Zhonghua shuju, 1960.

Li, Wai-yee. *Enchantment and Disenchantment: Love and Illusion in Chinese Literature*. Princeton, NJ: Princeton University Press, 1993.

Li Xiaorong. *Women's Poetry of Late Imperial China: Transforming the Inner Chambers.* Stanford, CA: Stanford University Press, 2012.

Liao Guodong 廖國棟. *Jian'an cifu zhi chuancheng yu tuoxin: yi ticai ji zhuti wei fanwei* 建安辭賦之傳承與拓新：以題材及主題為範圍. Taipei: Wenjin chubanshe, 2000.

Lin Wenyue 林文月. "Penglai wenzhang Jian'an gu—shilun zhongshiji shitan fenggu zhi shiwei yu fuxing" 蓬萊文章建安骨——試論中世紀詩壇風骨之式微與復興. In *Zhonggu wenxue luncong* 中古文學論叢, pp. 1–54. Taipei: Da'an chubanshe, 1989.

Lin Xiaoguang 林曉光. "Lun *Yiwen leiju* cunlu fangshi zaocheng de Liuchao wenxue bianmao" 論《藝文類聚》存錄方式造成的六朝文學變貌. *Wenxue yichan* 3 (2014): 34–44.

Lin Xiaoguang 林曉光. "'Xianqing fu' puxi de wenxian huanyuan—jiyu zhongshi wenxian gouzao yu wentixing de zonghe yanjiu" 《閒情賦》譜系的文獻還原——基於中世文獻構造與文體性的綜合研究. *Wenxue pinglun* 3 (2014): 204–14.

Liu Jingyun 劉景雲. "Hou Han Qin Jia Xu Shu shiwen kao" 後漢秦嘉徐淑詩文考. *Dunhuang yanjiu* 2 (2003): 88–92.

Liu Su 劉肅. *Datang xinyu* 大唐新語. Guilin: Guangxi shifan daxue chubanshe, 1998.

Liu Xie 劉勰. *Wenxin diaolong zhu* 文心雕龍註, edited by Fan Wenlan 范文瀾. Beijing: Renmin wenxue chubanshe, 2000.

Liu Yiqing 劉義慶. *Shishuo xinyu jianshu* 世說新語箋疏, edited by Yu Jiaxi 余嘉錫. Shanghai: Shanghai guji chubanshe, 1993.

Liu Yuejin 劉躍進. *Zhonggu wenxue wenxianxue* 中古文学文獻學. Nanjing: Jiangsu guji chubanshe, 1997.

Liu Yuejin 劉躍進. *Yutai xinyong yanjiu* 玉臺新詠研究. Beijing: Zhonghua shuju, 2000.

Liu Zhiji 劉知幾. *Shi tong* 史通. *Sibucongkan* edition.

Lü Buwei 呂不韋. *Lüshi chuqiu* 呂氏春秋. Beijing: Zhonghua shuju, 1954.

Lu Qinli 逯欽立, ed. *Tao Yuanming ji* 陶淵明集. Beijing: Zhonghua shuju, 1997.

Lu Qinli 逯欽立, ed. *XianQin Han Wei Jin Nanbeichao shi* 先秦漢魏晉南北朝詩. Beijing: Zhonghua shuju, 1983.

Luo Guowei 羅國威, ed. *Ricang Hongren ben Wenguan cilin jiaozheng* 日藏弘仁本文館詞林校證. Beijing: Zhonghua shuju, 2001.

Luo Manling. *Literati Story Telling in Late Medieval China.* Seattle: University of Washington Press, 2015.

Mann, Susan. *Precious Records: Women in China's Long Eighteenth Century.* Stanford, CA: Stanford University Press, 1997.

Mather, Richard B., trans. *A New Account of Tales of the World.* Minneapolis: University of Minnesota Press, 1976.

Mei Chia-Ling 梅家玲. *Han Wei Liuchao wenxue xinlun: nidai yu zengda pian* 漢魏六朝文學新論：擬代與贈答篇. Taipei: Liren shuju, 1997.

Mu Zhai 木齋. "Lun Jian'an nüxing ticai de xingqi—Jianlun 'Yuan shi' de zuozhe" 論建安五言詩女性題材的興起一兼論《怨詩》的作者. *Shanxi daxue xuebao* 29, no. 2 (2009): 36–41.

Mulvey, Laura. "Visual Pleasure and Narrative Cinema." In *Visual and Other Pleasures*, pp. 14–26. London: Palgrave, 1989.

Nan Qi shu 南齊書. Beijing: Zhonghua shuju, 1972.

Nienhauser, William H. "Once Again, the Authorship of the *Hsi-ching tsa-chi*." *Journal of the American Oriental Society* 98, no. 3 (1978): 219–36.

Ouyang Xun 歐陽詢 et al., eds. *Yiwen leiju* 藝文類聚. Shanghai: Shanghaiguji chubanshe, 1965.

Owen, Stephen. *Traditional Chinese Poetry and Poetics: Omen of the World*. Madison: University of Wisconsin Press, 1985.

Owen, Stephen. *Mi-lou: Poetry and the Labyrinth of Desire*. Cambridge, MA: Harvard University Press, 1989.

Owen, Stephen. "Liu Xie and the Discourse Machine." In *A Chinese Literary Mind: Culture, Creativity and Rhetoric in Wenxin Diaolong*, edited by Cai Zong-qi, pp. 175–91. Stanford, CA: Stanford University Press, 2001.

Owen, Stephen. "The Librarian in Exile: Xie Lingyun's Bookish Landscapes." *Early Medieval China* 10–11, no. 1 (2004): 203–26.

Owen, Stephen. "One Sight: The *Han shu* Biography of Lady Li." In *Rhetoric and the Discourses of Power in Court Culture: China, Europe and Japan*, edited by David Knechtges and Eugene Vance, pp. 239–59. Seattle and London: University of Washington Press, 2004.

Owen, Stephen. *The Making of Early Chinese Classical Poetry*. Cambridge, MA: Harvard University Asia Center, 2006.

Owen, Stephen. "Xia Jiangnan: Guanyu Dong Jin pingmin de huanxiang" 下江南：關於東晉平民的幻想. In *Xia Jiangnan: Suzhou daxue haiwai Hanxue yanjianglu* 下江南：蘇州大學海外漢學演講錄, edited by Wang Yao 王堯 and Ji Jin 季進, pp. 27–41. Shanghai: Fudan daxue chubanshe, 2009.

Owen, Stephen. *Just a Song: Chinese Lyrics from the Eleventh and Early Twelfth Centuries*. Cambridge, MA: Harvard University Asia Center, 2019.

Owen, Stephen, ed. and trans. *Readings in Chinese Literary Thought*. Cambridge, MA: Harvard University Asia Center, 1992.

Owen, Stephen, ed. and trans. *An Anthology of Chinese Literature: Beginning to 1911*. New York: W. W. Norton, 1996.

Qian Zhixi 錢志熙. "Shidafu wenhua shijiao zhongde zhongguo gudai nüxing shige fazhan shi" 士大夫文化視角中的中國古代女性詩歌發展史. *Zhongguo gaoxiao shehui kexue* 5 (2019): 95–107.

Quan Tang shi 全唐詩. Beijing: Zhonghua shuju, 1960.

Raft, Zeb. "Four-Syllable Poetry in Early Medieval China." PhD diss., Harvard University, 2007.

Raphals, Lisa. *Sharing the Light: Representations of Women and Virtue in Early China*. Albany: State University of New York Press, 1998.

Robertson, Maureen. "Voicing the Feminine: Constructions of the Gendered Subject in Lyric Poetry by Women of Medieval and Late Imperial China." *Late Imperial China* 13, no. 1 (June 1992): 63–110.

Rouzer, Paul. *Articulated Ladies: Gender and the Male Community in Early Chinese Texts*. Cambridge, MA: Harvard University Asia Center, 2001.

Roy, David T. "The Theme of the Neglected Wife in the Poetry of Ts'ao Chih." *The Journal of Asian Studies* 19, no. 1 (1959): 25–31.

Samei, Maija Bell. *Gendered Persona and Poetic Voice: The Abandoned Woman in Early Chinese Song Lyrics*. Lanham, MD: Lexington Books, 2004.

San Cao ziliao huibian 三曹資料彙編. Beijing: Zhonghua shuju, 1980.

Sanguo zhi 三國志. Beijing: Zhonghua shuju, 1959.

Schaberg, David. "Song and the Historical Imagination in Early China." *Harvard Journal of Asiatic Studies* 59, no. 2 (1999): 305–61.

Shen Deqian 沈德潛, ed. *Gushi yuan* 古詩源. Beijing: Zhonghua shuju, 1963.

Shields, Anna M. *One Who Knows Me: Friendship and Literary Culture in Mid-Tang China*. Cambridge, MA: Harvard University Asia Center, 2015.

Shih Hsiang-Lin. "Jian'an Literature Revisited: Poetic Dialogues in the Last Three Decades of the Han Dynasty." PhD diss., University of Washington, 2013.

Shi ji 史記. Beijing: Zhonghua shuju, 1959.

Song shu 宋書. Beijing: Zhonghua shuju, 1974.

Spade, Beatrice. "The Education of Women in China during the Southern Dynasties." *Journal of Asian History* 13, no. 1 (1979): 15–41.

Spring, Madeline. "The Presentation of Love Tokens in the *Shih Ching* and *Ch'u Tz'u*." *Tamkang Review* 9, no. 1 (1978): 1–31.

Su Shi wenji 蘇軾文集. Beijing: Zhonghua shuju, 1986.

Sui Shusen 隋樹森, ed. *Gushi shijiushou jishi* 古詩十九首集釋. Beijing: Zhonghua shuju, 1955.

Suzuki Shūji 鈴木修次. *Kan Gi shi no kenkyū* 漢魏詩の研究. Tokyo: Taishūkan shoten, 1967.

Swartz, Wendy. "Intertextuality and Cultural Memory in Early Medieval China: Jiang Yan's Imitations of Nearly Lost and Lost Writers." In *Memory in Medieval China: Text, Ritual and Community*, edited by Wendy Swartz and Robert Campany, pp. 36–62. Leiden: Brill, 2018.

Tan Qixiang 譚其驤. "Cai Wenji de shengping jiqi zuopin" 蔡文姬的生平及其作品. In *Hujia shiba pai taolunji* 胡笳十八拍討論集, edited by *Wenxue yichan* bianjibu, pp. 238–54. Beijing: Zhonghua shuju, 1959.

Tian Xiaofei. "Configuring the Feminine: Gender and Literary Transvestitism in the Southern Dynasties Poetry." PhD diss., Harvard University, 1998.

Tian Xiaofei. *Beacon Fire and Shooting Star: The Literary Culture of the Liang (502–557)*. Cambridge, MA: Harvard University Asia Center, 2007.

Tian Xiaofei. "Woman in the Tower: 'Nineteen Old Poems' and the Poetics of Un/concealment." *Early Medieval China* 15 (2009): 3–21.

Tian Xiaofei. "*Yutai xinyong* yu zhonggu wenxue de lishi zhuyi jiedu" 玉臺新詠與中古文學的歷史主義解讀. *Huadong shifan daxue xuebao* 48 (2016): 10–17.

Tian Xiaofei. "Literary Learning: Encyclopedias and Epitomes." In *The Oxford Handbook of Classical Chinese Literature*, edited by Wiebke Denecke, Wai-yee Li, and Xiaofei Tian, pp. 132–46. Cambridge: Oxford University Press, 2017.

Tian Xiaofei. *The Halberd at Red Cliff: Jian'an and the Three Kingdoms*. Cambridge, MA: Harvard University Asia Center, 2018.

Wang Ping. *The Age of Courtly Writing: Wen xuan Compiler Xiao Tong (501–531)*. Leiden: Brill, 2012.

Wang Ping. "Plaint, Lyricism and the South." In *Southern Identity and Southern Estrangement in Medieval Chinese Poetry*, edited by Wang Ping and Nicholas Morrow Williams, pp. 79–108. Hong Kong: Hong Kong University Press, 2015.

Wang Rongbao 汪榮寶, ed. *Fa yan yishu* 法言義疏. Taipei: Yiwen yinshuguan, 1968.

Wang Xianqian 王先謙, ed. *Shi sanjia yi jishu* 詩三家義集疏. Shanghai: Shanghai guji chubanshe, 1995.

Wang Yunxi 王運熙. *Yuefu shi shulun* 樂府詩述論. Shanghai: Shanghai guji chubanshe, 1996.

Whitaker, K. P. K. "Tsaur Jyr's Song of the Ill-fated Lady." *Bulletin of the School of Oriental and African Studies, University of London* 17, no. 3 (1955): 526–34.

Williams, Nicholas Morrow. *Imitations of the Self: Jiang Yan and Chinese Poetics*. Leiden: Brill, 2014.

Williams, Nicholas Morrow. "Irony and Death in the Writings of Liu Zhen." *The Bulletin of Jao Tsung-I Academy of Sinology* 4 (2014): 325–52.

Weng Qibin 翁其斌. "Wuge Xiqu wenren nizuo kao" 吳歌西曲文人擬作考. *Shanghai shifan daxue xuebao* 3 (1996): 23–27.

Wu Congxiang 吴从祥. "Lun Jian'an shiqi nüxing wenxue xingsheng de yuanyin" 論建安時期女性文學興盛的原因. *Zhongnan minzu daxue xuebao* 26, no. 2 (2006): 147–50.

Wu Shichang 吳世昌. "Lun wuyan shi qiyuan yu funü wenxue" 論五言詩起源於婦女文學. *Wenshi zhishi* 11 (1985): 35.

Wu Xiaoru 吳小如, ed. *Han Wei Liuchao shi jianshang cidian* 漢魏六朝詩鑒賞辭典. Shanghai: Shanghai cishu cubanshe, 1992.

Xiang Xinyang 向新陽 and Liu Keren 劉克任, ed. *Xijing zaji jiaozhu* 西京雜記校註. Shanghai: Shanghai guji chubanshe, 1991.

Xiao Tong 蕭統, ed. *Wen xuan* 文選. Shanghai: Shanghai guji chubanshe, 1980.

Xiao Yi 蕭繹. *Jinlou zi jiaojian* 金樓子校箋, edited by Xu Yimin 許逸民. Beijing: Zhonghua shuju, 2011.

Xu Jian 徐堅, ed. *Chuxue ji* 初學記. Beijing: Zhonghua shuju, 1962.

Xu Ling 徐陵, ed. *Yutai xinyong jianzhu* 玉臺新詠箋注. Beijing: Zhonghua shuju, 1985.

Yan Kejun 嚴可均, ed. *Quan Shanggu Sandai Qin Han Sanguo Liuchao wen* 全上古三代秦漢三國六朝文. Shanghai: Shanghai guji chubanshe, 2009.

Yang Bojun 楊伯峻, ed. *Mengzi yizhu* 孟子譯註. Beijing: Zhonghua shuju, 1960.

Yang Bojun 楊伯峻, ed. *Chunqiu Zuo zhuan zhu* 春秋左傳註. Beijing: Zhonghua shuju, 1981.

Yang Ming 楊明. "Shishui mengjian le wushan shennü—guanyu Song Yu 'Shennü fu' de yiwen" 是誰夢見了巫山神女——關於宋玉《神女賦》的異文. *Zhangzhou shifan xueyuan xuebao* 20, no. 2 (2006): 48–53.

Yang Mingzhao 楊明照, ed. *Baopi zi waipian jiaojian* 抱樸子外篇校箋. Beijing: Zhonghua shuju, 1991.

Yao Ping. "Changing Views on Sexuality in Early and Medieval China." *Journal of Daoist Studies* 8 (2015): 52–68.

Ye Shaoyuan 葉紹袁. *Wumeng tang ji* 午夢堂集. Beijing: Zhonghua shuju, 1998.

Yeh Chia-ying 葉嘉瑩. *Jialing lunshi conggao* 嘉陵論詩叢稿. Shijiazhuang: Hebei jiaoyu chubanshe, 1997.

Yu Guanying 余冠英. *Han Wei Liuchao shi luncong* 漢魏六朝詩論叢. Beijing: Shangwu yinshuguan, 2010.

Yu, Pauline. *The Reading of Imagery in the Chinese Poetic Tradition*. Princeton, NJ: Princeton University Press, 1987.

Yu Shaochu 俞紹初, ed. *Jian'an qizi ji* 建安七子集. Beijing: Zhonghua shuju, 2005.

Yuan Guangxue 袁廣雪 and Zhang Shichang 張士昌. "Cong wenxue zuopin kan zhongguo gudai nüxing diwei de bianhua" 從文學作品看中國古代女性地位的變化. *Jinzhong xueyuan xuebao* 29, no. 4 (2012): 70–74.

Zeng Xiangxu 曾祥旭. "Lizhi cheng xiliu, he guan zou qixiang: 'Shangye' he 'You suo si' biejie" 離之成細流，合觀奏奇響：《上邪》和《有所思》別解. *Academic Forum of Nandu* 1 (2000): 49–50.

Zhang Shubo 張樹波, ed. *Guofeng jishuo* 國風集說. Shijiazhuang: Hebeirenmin chubanshe, 1993.

Zhang Yu 張瑜. "Shilun Handai 'yuanhui yi' suo tixian de yinyue zhengzhilun sixiang" 試論漢代 '元會儀' 所體現的音樂政治論思想. *Xi'an yinyue xueyuan xuebao* 27, no. 4 (2008): 87–94.

Zhao Minli 趙敏俐. "Lun Handai wenren wuyanshi de yishu tezheng" 論漢代文人五言詩的藝術特徵. *Wenxue yichan* 2 (1995): 14–22.

Zheng Shanshan 鄭珊珊. "Zhongguo gudai nüxing wenxue yu nüxing yishi" 中國古代女性文學與女性意識. *Fujian luntan* 2 (2016): 117–22.

Zhuang Huiming 莊輝明 and Zhang Yihe 章義和, eds. *Yanshi jiaxun yizhu* 顏氏家訓譯註. Shanghai: Shanghai guji chubanshe, 1999.

Zhuang Xinxia 莊新霞. "Ding Yi qi 'Guafu fu' zuozhe ji xiangguan wenti kaolun" 丁儀妻《寡婦賦》作者及相關問題考論. *Zhongguo dianji yu wenhua* 2 (2001): 6–12.

Index

www.ingramcontent.com/pod-product-compliance
Lightning Source LLC
Chambersburg PA
CBHW071226230926
51849CB00001B/39
* 9 7 8 9 0 0 4 5 4 1 0 0 9 *